The New York Times
book of money

The New York Times
book of money
By Richard E. Blodgett

Quadrangle/The New York Times Book Co.

We wish to thank the following individuals and organizations for their help in the preparation of this book: First National City Bank, New York; Lester L. Nielson, Chase Manhattan Bank; Charles Culpepper and Robert B. Keane, The Hartford Insurance Group; Raymond Taylor, Shepherd-Taylor Associates, New York; Alfred J. Law, Esq.; Russell R. Jalbert, Assistant Commissioner for Public Affairs, Social Security Administration; American Bankers Association; Richard E. Pokriefke, National Association of Mutual Savings Banks; Life Insurance Agency Management Association; James O. Richards, Financial Programs Incorporated; Irving L. Straus, No-Load Mutual Fund Association; John V. Marinelli, Esq.; Arthur W. Samansky, Federal Reserve Bank of New York; Motivational Systems, Inc.; U.S. Internal Revenue Service.

Library of Congress Catalog Card Number: 72-88117

International Standard Book Number: 0-8129-0273-4

Third printing January 1975

Contents

of whole life plus term — ways to save on costs — switching policies — combination plans.

The high price of medical care — how to get good care at a reasonable cost — finding a family doctor — general practitioners, internists, group practices — prepayment plans — when to use a hospital — drug costs — health insurance — four types: hospitalization, other basic medical expenses, major medical, comprehensive — disability insurance — points to check in your policies — Medicare — Medicaid — some warnings on mail-order health insurance and "first-dollar" insurance.

The high cost of a college education — plan early — how to budget for your child's education — loans: National Defense Student Loans, Government-guaranteed loans, Bank Loans, other loans — effect on your tax bill — scholarships — how to apply — the College Work-Study Program — Educational Opportunity Grants — other federal aid programs.

When to invest — what is investment? — dividends — capital gains — the risks of investing — the need for sound advice — finding a stockbroker — the Securities Investor Protection Corporation — other important considerations — sources of advice — different kinds of investments — how to read a stock table — common stocks — preferred stock — bonds and debentures — convertible securities — warrants — buying on margin — municipal bonds — U.S. Government securities — commissions — the "odd-lot differential" — payroll deduction plans.

What a mutual fund is — advantages and disadvantages — how a fund works — "per-share net asset value" — high cost of sales fees — bid price and asked price — "no-load" versus "load" funds — investment objectives — "open-end" and "closed-end" funds — other types of investment funds — bond funds.

The difficulties women encounter — some specific examples — a woman's credit rating and her husband's financial status — husbands responsible for wives' debts — greatest areas of lending discrimination — what you can do — working wives — managing the family finances: joint accounts, half and half, separate accounts — property ownership — the effects of a divorce — how women view money.

Introduction

Welcome to *The New York Times Book of Money*. As you read through the pages that follow, there is one particularly important message that we hope will come through clearly. The message is this: you do not have to be an expert to manage your personal financial affairs wisely. What it takes is care and common sense, together with an understanding of your limitations so that you know when to seek professional advice. To this end, we have gone out of our way to point out, wherever appropriate, those specific areas of finance where we believe that professional guidance is essential.

This book is designed to serve as a basic reference work covering all major areas of personal finance in sufficient detail to get you started in the right direction. Other, more technical books are available if you wish to explore any particular area in depth. Our objective is simply to help you organize your financial affairs in an efficient and rewarding way and to help you avoid costly blunders. You will find that the text has been written in straightforward, everyday language. In those few cases where a technical term has been unavoidable, we have explained it.

One warning: interest rates, tax rules, mortgage arrangements, legal requirements, etc. are subject to constant change. Before you act on anything you read in this book, be sure to check the latest facts and figures. The information contained herein is that which applied to the best of our knowledge at the time of printing.

Chapter 1

Putting your money to work

King Solomon, so the Bible tells us, was a great believer in the power of wealth. If money was important way back then — nearly 3,000 years ago — just think how crucial it has become to a happy, healthy, worry-free life today.

Some Americans complain, in fact, that we have become *too* beholden to the power of the dollar. But this complaint, whether justified or not, in no way diminishes the fact that money is an extremely important and fascinating subject.

Three factors have directly influenced our use of money in recent years:

Three factors to consider: affluence, debt and inflation

● Most Americans no longer live at mere survival level. They earn enough to afford modern-day luxuries, to save and invest, to educate their children, and hopefully to top it all off by retiring comfortably at age 60 or 65.

● Borrowing has suddenly become an accepted way of life. Every year, tens of millions of Americans routinely take out loans — something that was unheard of in their grandparents' time.

● Inflation has begun to eat sharply into the "real" value of our dollars, forcing us to search for ways to catch up.

For most Americans, the major source of money is their salary. In the pages that follow we make no attempt to tell you how to earn more from your job. Our sole purpose is to describe how you can make *better use* of the money you already get, and how you can avoid common pitfalls.

The purpose of this book

We want to start off, however, by issuing a warning. Americans, in our opinion, are in the enviable position of being able to choose from an array of financial vehicles unmatched anywhere else in the world — numerous different ways to save and invest, numerous ways to borrow, numerous ways to insure against financial loss, etc. It is important, though, that you either:

An important warning

1) know how to go about selecting wisely from these vehicles on your own,

   or

2) have access to unbiased, professional advice.

The problem is in the area of advice. Many people of moderate means ask where they can go for good, independent financial counseling at reasonable cost. Unfortunately, in most instances

Putting your money to work

there simply is no place to go. This is a glaring weakness in our nation's economic structure. The little guy tends to lose out when it comes to finance.

Of course, stock brokers, insurance agents, real estate brokers and the like will be happy to give you guidance. But therein lies our warning. Nearly every one of these individuals is actually a salesman out to make a buck for himself by convincing you to buy the specific products or services he sells, in some cases regardless of whether they are really good for you.

Knowledge and care are important in finance

Our point is two-fold:

• In many cases you may find that you are your own best adviser. This means, however, that you must take the time and effort to be well informed before making major financial decisions.

• You should always be careful when dealing with brokers, agents and other financial salesmen. You doubtless will have the pleasure of dealing with many competent, reputable people in the world of finance. Their help can be invaluable. But a certain degree of cynicism is always in order, particularly until you have worked with an agent or broker long enough to know whether you can actually trust his word.

WISEGUIDE

Remember that a broker is a salesman, not an unbiased financial counselor. When one tries to sell you a deal that sounds too good to be true, chances are it is neither good nor true.

The uses of money

In broad terms, using money involves:

• Budgeting

• Saving and investing

• Borrowing

• Spending

Why a budget is important

With the exception of budgeting, each of these four areas is discussed in various succeeding chapters of this book. As for budgeting, we'll tackle that one right now, since the creation of a family budget is the logical starting point in any attempt to make better use of your money.

What is a budget?

Just what is budgeting? In its simplest terms, it is nothing more than a system for breaking down your anticipated expenditures into various categories — food, housing, medical care, transportation, etc. The objective is to bring these expenditures under control so

that you can keep them within the limits of your income and, if all works out according to plan, even have a little left over to put into a savings account each month.

Many people who overspend have a good idea of where they should cut back, but they lack the self-discipline to do so. Budgeting, by forcing them to take a hard look at their spending habits, can help provide the needed incentive.

WISEGUIDE

There is one question in particular that often comes up about budgeting: just how much money, many people ask, must a typical family earn to be able to live reasonably well in America today? In truth, the question isn't very meaningful. Chances are that, for the near future at least, you are stuck with what you already make. The immediate problem — and one that a budget is designed to deal with — is to fit your expenses into your income, not to build your income to match your expenses.

Expenses must be brought in line with your income, not vice versa

Budgeting, then, enables you to plan what you will do with your limited resources. But that's the easy part.

Some surveys have shown that fewer than half of all budgeters actually end up spending within the limits of their plan. This, then, becomes the real challenge of budgeting.

WISEGUIDE

A budget is by no means essential. Some people seem to have a knack for handling their day-to-day expenditures with ease. They always have a good approximate sense of where their money is going, and seldom if ever, find themselves unexpectedly short of cash. For them a formal budget may be more fuss than it is worth.

Budgeting isn't for everybody

Others, by budgeting, learn to control their expenses. Eventually they outgrow their need for this type of disciplinary mechanism.

But what about the rest of us? We're the people who never are fully in control of our financial affairs, and for whom dollars seem to disappear right out of our pockets through a mysterious process that, in our view, only a certified public accountant could understand. Sound familiar? Then some sort of simple budget is called for.

Who does need a budget?

Notice that we said "simple" budget. A common mistake is to make the family budget into such a big and complex deal that there is no way it will ever work. Figuring each category down to the exact penny or shifting cash from envelope to envelope usually is self-defeating.

Putting your money to work

What you should be after is a budget that is effective, yet easy to operate — one that doesn't become more of a burden than it is worth. For simplicity's sake, all figures should be rounded off to the nearest dollar.

How to get started

Start off by listing your "fixed" expenses on a sheet of paper — that is, expenses over which you have relatively little control. These include such items as mortgage payments or rent, insurance premiums, transportation, utilities, installment payments and taxes. You may be amazed to discover how large a portion of your expenditures, perhaps well over half, fits into this category.

It may be tougher, on the other hand, to find out just how much you are spending for other, more flexible items — food, luxuries, repairs, personal care, entertainment, etc. One approach is to keep track for two or three months in order to come up with average monthly figures.

Once you know where and how much you already are spending, you are in a position to draw up a realistic budget.

Hard choices may have to be made

You may find that you are consistently spending more than you earn. In that case you are just going to have to make some hard choices in terms of where to cut back.

WISEGUIDE

Choosing where to cut back is never easy, but it cannot be avoided if you are going to live within your means and avoid eventual financial disaster.

Cuts in personal luxuries

Perhaps deep cuts can be made in personal luxuries. Some examples: an evening cocktail hour may be costing you $500 a year; a $2.50 businessman's lunch each working day adds up to more than $700 annually; two packs of cigarettes a day come to more than $400 a year.

Savings at the supermarket

Do you shop around for the best prices as diligently as possible? Food purchases, in particular, are an area where careful shopping and selection can result in real savings. The nutritional quality of what we eat, experts point out, has little to do with the price we pay.

A few hints: always check the displays for special prices; buy food in season, when it tends to be plentiful and less expensive; always look at unit prices when they are shown on the shelf strip; buy the most economical size for your needs; avoid prepackaged "convenience" foods, which usually are expensive.

Avoiding excessive use of credit

Do you avoid unnecessary use of credit? The widespread availability of consumer loans has made the "easy" purchase of luxury items

too tempting for many Americans to resist. Much to their sorrow, they discover later that they have saddled themselves with large interest costs and installment payments that throw their expenditures way out of line when compared with their income. Don't let that happen to you. *(More on this important subject in Chapter 3.)*

WISEGUIDE

One of the worst possible moves of all is to take out a loan to meet current expenditures. The result is that you simply end up even deeper in the hole.

If you are in particularly bad financial shape, you might consider selling some of your assets. An expensive car or home may not be essential; you may even find that the large commitments such an item entails are actually at the heart of your financial problems.

Should assets be sold off?

In the final analysis, however, you may decide that you just cannot cut back and that the only answer is to take an extra job. That's fine, if you think it is the best course and are willing to put in the additional hours.

An extra job?

Although there is no "typical" way in which you should spend your money, the U.S. Bureau of Labor Statistics does keep track of the broad spending patterns of families throughout the country. A look at these patterns may give you some insights into how you should allot your own hard-earned cash.

How the average American family spends

For instance, the table on page 17 shows how the average urban family of four, with an "intermediate" level of income, spends its money. The theoretical family cited by the Bureau in this example consists of a husband aged 38, a wife not employed outside the home, a 13-year-old boy and an 8-year-old girl. Figures are based on estimated spending levels in late 1971. You will note that no provision is made for savings—a category you certainly will want to add to your own budget.

These figures, as we mentioned, should not be followed rigidly. Your own particular circumstances and needs should be taken into full account. This includes an awareness of your life-style and its financial implications. Some people choose to entertain frequently and lavishly, and to skimp on savings. Others choose to save, and to forgo entertaining. One individual isn't right and the other wrong. Both are right so long as they are satisfied with their life-style and can make ends meet.

Tailoring your budget to your own needs

In terms of the mechanics of maintaining a budget, there are a number of systems. One is to make entries on some sort of ledger sheet, just as a businessman would do to keep track of his firm's income and expenditures.
    A better approach might be to keep your budget in a standard ring-bound notebook, with a separate page devoted to each spending

The mechanics of budgeting

Putting your money to work

category. At the top of each page you can list the total amount you have budgeted for that category. Then, as the month goes by, you can keep running track of actual expenditures by listing them on the page.

If you find you are consistently overspending in a particular category, you should seriously consider the possibility of increasing your allocation there. In that case, of course, you will have to take away from another, less important category to keep the overall budget in balance.

WISEGUIDE

A budget must be a living document that changes as your spending needs and your income change.

A second kind of record-keeping

If you are the kind of person who is intrigued by the intricacies of finance, you might get some fun out of a second type of financial record-keeping — an annual computation of your "net worth."

WISEGUIDE

Net worth is the total value of all your possessions, less the amount of your liabilities.

If Howard Hughes knows, why shouldn't you?

When people say that Howard Hughes is worth several billion dollars or whatever, that's his "net worth" — or what might be described in more ordinary terms as his personal fortune. If Howard Hughes knows how much he has stashed away in various nooks and crannies, why shouldn't you know how much you are worth?

Some advantages

Actually, keeping track of this figure on a yearly basis is more than fun and games. There are some very real benefits:

How prices have risen during the past decade

1963	91.7
1964	92.9
1965	94.5
1966	97.2
1967	100.0
1968	104.2
1969	109.8
1970	116.3
1971	121.3
1972	125.3

Department of Labor consumer price index; based on 1967 prices equaling 100.

● An annual net worth calculation gives you a clear picture of your financial situation. Without this information, it is hard to decide just where you stand.

● It helps you in estate planning. Do you have enough life insurance to protect your family adequately in case you die? How can you really decide, unless you know the net value of all the other assets your wife and children stand to inherit from you. Perhaps your financial picture has changed and you should rewrite your will. Again, you don't know the answer unless you review your specific financial status.

● Are you saving as much as you should? Some financial planners suggest that an individual's net worth should increase roughly 10 per cent a year, lumping the good years together with the bad. If you aren't meeting that goal, perhaps you should earmark more of your income for savings and investments.

16

"Intermediate" budget for a family of four

	Annual cost	Percent of total budget
Food *(including meals out)*	$ 2,532	23.1%
Housing *(including heat, utilities, operating expenses, furnishings)*	2,638	24.0
Transportation	964	8.8
Clothing and personal care	1,196	10.9
Medical care *(including health insurance)*	612	5.6
Other consumption *(recreation, education, reading, etc.)*	684	6.2
Income taxes	1,366	12.5
Social security and disability insurance	419	3.8
Miscellaneous	560	5.1
Total "intermediate" budget	$ 10,971	100.0%

Where you live does make a big difference

The "intermediate" budget of $10,971 a year for a family of four is the national urban average. Living expenses actually vary quite widely from region to region and city to city.

To cite an extreme example, the cost of living in Anchorage, Alaska, is about 60 per cent higher than in some sections of the South. On a more realistic level, New York City is about 25 per cent more expensive than Dallas, Texas.

To give you an idea of how your particular region or city stacks up against the national average, here is a sampling of figures from the U.S. Bureau of Labor Statistics.

Annual 'intermediate' budget for a family of four		Relative cost in relation to the U.S. average
Urban U.S. average	$10,971	100.0%
NORTHEAST		
Boston	$12,819	116.8
Buffalo	11,666	106.3
Hartford, Conn.	12,029	109.6
Lancaster, Pa.	10,786	98.3
New York	12,585	114.7
Philadelphia	11,404	103.9
Pittsburgh	10,686	97.4
Portland, Maine	11,169	101.8
Nonmetropolitan areas	10,773	98.2
NORTH CENTRAL		
Cedar Rapids, Iowa	$11,029	100.5
Champaign-Urbana, Ill.	11,214	102.2
Chicago	11,460	104.5
Cincinnati	10,493	95.6
Cleveland	11,330	103.3
Dayton, Ohio	10,218	93.1
Detroit	10,754	98.0
Green Bay, Wis.	10,935	99.7
Indianapolis	11,093	101.1
Kansas City	10,981	100.1
Milwaukee	11,685	106.5
Minneapolis-St. Paul	11,183	101.9
St. Louis	10,944	99.8
Wichita, Kansas	10,217	93.1
Nonmetropolitan areas	10,078	91.9
SOUTH		
Atlanta	$ 9,813	89.4
Austin, Texas	9,408	85.8
Baltimore	11,013	100.4
Baton Rouge, La.	9,885	90.1
Dallas	10,056	91.7
Durham, N.C.	10,489	95.6
Houston	9,894	90.2
Nashville, Tenn.	9,976	90.9
Orlando, Fla.	9,695	88.4
Washington, D.C.	11,252	102.6
Nonmetropolitan areas	9,180	83.7
WEST		
Anchorage, Alaska	$14,867	135.5
Bakersfield, Calif.	10,236	93.3
Denver	10,639	97.0
Honolulu	13,108	119.5
Los Angeles	10,985	100.1
San Diego	10,670	97.3
San Francisco	11,683	106.5
Seattle	11,124	101.4

Putting your money to work

• Exactly what assets do you own? A yearly inventory—marking down serial numbers and other identifying data, where appropriate—is a highly valuable exercise. It gives you detailed information to back up insurance claims in case of fire or theft. And it provides the executor of your estate with a basic list of assets in case you die.

• Finally, some people who compute their net worth each year report that, while they have a natural tendency to overspend, the net worth computation makes them discipline themselves against doing so.

How to calculate your net worth

On the plus side of your net worth table are such items as cash (including money in your checking account), savings, value of your house and furnishings, value of your car, investments, cash value of your life insurance and value of your pension-plan holdings at work. On the negative side are such items as your home mortgage, other debts, future installment payments and unpaid bills.

A typical annual report on your personal net worth might look something like the table at left.

Where to get the information

As you can see, this is a relatively simple process. The only hard part is getting some of the individual pieces of information.

Cash and savings are easy to ascertain. Investments should be listed at current market value. You can make your own rough estimates of the value of your home, car and furnishings; it's best to be on the conservative side when estimating the value of these items, however, since you are trying to figure out what you could get if you tried to sell them rather than what it would cost you to buy new ones.

You will have to ask at work about the value of your pension benefits, unless your employer automatically gives you the figure each year. Likewise, you probably will have to ask your insurance agent about the cash value of your life insurance policies.

You may be surprised by how much you actually are worth. There are many "hidden" assets — such as pension benefits and life-insurance values — that you might not normally consider without this kind of formal review.

Assets:		
Cash	$	300.00
Savings account		2,250.00
Investments		2,700.00
Value of house		25,000.00
Home furnishings		2,500.00
Automobile		1,600.00
Cash value of life insurance		700.00
Pension holdings		3,100.00
Total Assets		38,150.00
Liabilities:		
Mortgage		18,500.00
Car payments		1,100.00
Other debt		2,000.00
Unpaid bills		370.00
Total Liabilities		21,970.00

NET WORTH
(38,150.00 minus 21,970.00)
equals $16,180.00

When to calculate

When is a good time of year to calculate your net worth? Year-end is one logical possibility. And April is, of course, income tax month. You may long for relief then from money computations. But financial figures are fresh in your mind and important papers are already gathered and close at hand.

One last word of advice: set up a special folder for your net worth computations, and then put it in a safe place where you know you will be able to find it. This way you can go back each year and see how you calculated in the past and also compare your new net worth figure with previous years.

Chapter 2

Saving without risk

One of the basic cornerstones of personal financial management is the creation of a family savings account, generally at a bank or savings & loan association. Establishing such an account — eventually in the range of perhaps $2,000 to $4,000, depending on your particular needs — should be a matter of high priority.

The term "savings," as we use it here, means any risk-free mechanism for setting aside cash at a reasonable rate of return.

It is important to note right at the start that savings accounts are most useful when you discipline yourself to deposit specified amounts — perhaps $25, $50 or even $100 a month — on a regular basis. This can be accomplished through payroll deductions at work, automatic transfers from your checking account, or regular deposits on your own. You will be able to build a substantial savings reserve in just a few years this way.

What are "savings"?

If, for instance, you were to deposit $50 a month, after five years you would have $3,368 and after ten years $7,581. This includes interest paid at the rate of 4½ per cent a year and compounded quarterly. A higher interest rate would give you even more.

WISEGUIDE

Savings accounts have certain specific advantages, as well as two major drawbacks.

Advantages of a savings account:

• Savings accounts are safe. Accounts at almost all banks are automatically insured for up to $20,000 by the Federal Deposit Insurance Corporation, a government agency, in the event the bank gets into financial trouble and goes out of business. Similar insurance coverage is provided at most savings & loan associations by the Federal Savings & Loan Insurance Corporation. (Make sure, however, that the bank where you are placing your money is actually insured.) If your account starts approaching the $20,000 insurance limitation, you can simply open a second account at another bank and be fully insured at both.

Safety

• Savings accounts are convenient. You can either put money in or withdraw it immediately, whenever you want. And there is no limit to the amount you can withdraw (up to the size of your balance in the account, of course). Theoretically, banks and other savings institutions have the option of delaying payment of a requested withdrawal for up to 30 days. But in reality this option is rarely if ever exercised by these institutions. Savings accounts, therefore, are an ideal haven for an emergency cash reserve that you want to be able to tap on short notice.

Convenience

Saving without risk

Interest payments

Savings accounts pay interest. Getting a 6 per cent return (or whatever rate) is certainly a lot better than hiding your cash under a mattress or leaving it, at no interest, in your checking account.

Disadvantages:

The drawbacks:

Not the best rate of return

The yield, while good, is not great. A number of other investment mechanisms provide higher rates of return. High-quality corporate bonds, for instance, have recently been yielding as much as 9 per cent a year. They have drawbacks of their own, however, which we discuss in Chapter 12.

The effects of inflation

The typical 5 or 6 per cent interest rate on a regular savings account is actually, in one way, a *negative* rate of return.

Let's explain that second point. Everybody is aware of how badly their purchasing power has been undermined by inflation in recent years. In fact, the prices you pay for food, clothing, medical care and other products and services have been rising at a rate of nearly 5 per cent annually. Just to keep even with this price inflation, so that your dollars will be able to buy the same amount of goods in the future that they buy today, you would have to earn 5 per cent annually, after taxes, on your savings account. And what did we say? Five per cent is actually a fairly typical rate of return on savings. And that 5 per cent is *before* the Internal Revenue Service takes its bite of your interest income each April 15, not after.

The result: You are falling behind if you only earn 5 or 6 per cent.

Why you should have a savings account

In subsequent chapters, we discuss ways to try to beat inflation by earning more from your cash. Our message here is that you should have adequate savings primarily because of the safety and because of the convenience of withdrawal.

WISEGUIDE

Once you have established an adequate savings reserve, you should consider putting your additional excess cash into forms of investment that are potentially more rewarding *(see Chapters 12 and 13)*.

How much in savings do you need?

What is an adequate amount of savings? There are two ways of answering that question:

Some financial counselors advise that an average family should regularly set aside between five and 10 per cent of its pre-tax income for savings and investments. Although many individuals find this impossible, it really is quite realistic, as indicated by the chart on page 25. This chart (which is based on after-tax income rather than pre-tax) shows that Americans as a group actually set aside anywhere from five to eight per cent each year for savings.

These same counselors suggest that, in terms of total size of your savings account, it probably should be equivalent to at least three to four months worth of your pre-tax salary. If you earn

Systematic saving

$1,000 a month, then your goal should be a savings reserve some-where in the range of $3,000 to $4,000. Of course, your individual circumstances might dictate a somewhat different amount. For instance, if you are single, with few financial obligations, you might want to put less into savings and more into riskier (but potentially more rewarding) types of investments. If, on the other hand, you have a big family and work at a job where you could be laid off without notice, you should build as large a savings reserve as possible.

Another important factor is the size of your insurance coverage, both life and medical. If the amount is great, there is less need for a large emergency savings reserve.

WISEGUIDE

Besides providing basic financial protection, a savings account can be a convenient method for accumulating money to meet a specific family goal.

Saving for a specific goal

Maybe you want to buy a vacation home. Regular deposits in a savings account will eventually give you enough cash for the down payment. Similarly, money can be accumulated for sending your children to college or for your retirement.

The two main advantages in using a savings account to accumulate this kind of nest egg are:
1) you can make small, systematic deposits, and
2) your money is safe. You know that all the cash will be there, plus interest, when you want it. The great disadvantage is that you probably could get a better rate of return elsewhere — at the risk, however, of possibly losing some of your money.

Safety and systematic deposits

In the final analysis, you will just have to decide for yourself whether you prefer to use a savings account to accumulate your basic family nest egg — as opposed to an emergency savings re-serve — or whether you want to invest in something riskier in an attempt to build a family fortune. The overriding consideration is this: Do you feel comfortable taking a risk? If so, read Chapters 12 and 13 about common stocks, mutual funds and other forms of investments. If not, a savings account is for you.

There are all sorts of different vehicles for creating a savings re-serve — regular savings accounts in banks and savings & loans, long-term savings certificates, credit union accounts, government savings bonds, etc. As recently as a decade ago, it was possible to say with a sense of certainty that savings & loan associations paid the best rate of return, and that you should put your money there if you wanted the best yield.

A variety of savings plans

That is no longer true. Interest-rate differentials between various types of savings institutions aren't nearly as great today. Now you have to shop around a little, comparing various types of savings plans and weighing the advantages and drawbacks of each. The key is to get the best deal in light of your particular needs.

Shopping around for the best yield

Saving without risk

It isn't at all important whether you put your money into a commercial bank, a savings bank, a savings & loan, a credit union or whatever. What is important is that you get a good deal.

Saving by mail

Often, a local bank may not offer the best rate of return. This is particularly true in rural areas, where dividend rates on savings accounts tend to be lower. In that case you may want to look into the dividend rates at savings institutions in the nearest major city, and then open an account at one of them by mail. You generally can track down these institutions by looking for their ads in the local newspaper.

Five types of savings institutions

There are five major types of savings institutions. Maximum interest rates that can be paid to depositors are specified, in each case, by the government.

Commercial banks:

Regular accounts pay maximum of 5% interest; very small minimum deposit

Ninety-day accounts pay maximum of 5½%; minimum deposit of $500

Savings certificates of one to two-and-a-half years length pay up to 6%; minimum deposit of $500

Savings certificates of longer than two-and-a-half years length pay a maximum of 6½%; minimum deposit of $500

There is no maximum interest rate of savings certificates of four years or more; minimum deposit of $1,000 required

These are the full-service banks that exist in every city and town in the country. They offer a wide array of services — checking accounts, loans, safe deposit boxes, etc. And, of course, savings accounts.

In past years, commercial banks have tended to pay much lower interest on savings than other types of insitutions. But millions of Americans left their money there anyway because of the convenience of one-stop banking. In fact, with an estimated 42 per cent of all savings dollars, commercial banks are the largest kind of savings institution in the country.

On regular savings accounts, commercial banks are prohibited by federal regulations from paying more than 5 per cent annual interest. This is the lowest ceiling among the various types of savings institutions. But there are other forms of special accounts on which commercial banks can pay up to 6½ per cent or more.

Is it for me? Should I save at a commercial bank?

For
- Many other financial services offered.
- Extra convenience may make it worthwhile accepting the lower interest rate, especially for the smaller saver.

Against
- Lower interest rate than other savings institutions, unless you commit your money over a long period.

Savings & loans:

Regular accounts pay a maximum of 5¼%; very small minimum deposit

90-day certificates pay up to 5¾%; minimum deposit of $1,000

One-year savings certificates pay up to 6½%; minimum deposit of $1,000

Four-year certificates pay up to 6¾%; no minimum deposit

There is no maximum interest rate on four-year certificates of $1,000 or more

Savings & loan associations, with approximately 36 per cent of all savings dollars, are the second largest factor in the savings market. Like commercial banks, they can be found in all 50 states.

There are a number of technical differences in the structure of savings & loans versus other types of savings institutions, but these are meaningless to the saver. Let it suffice to say that savings & loans are mortgage-lending institutions. They seek your deposits in order to raise funds for granting mortgages to homeowners. Their current maximum dividend rate on regular savings accounts is 5¼ per cent, and on special long-term accounts it is 6¾ per cent or more.

Savings banks are similar in purpose (though different in technical structure) to savings & loans. They exist in only 18 states, primarily in the Northeast.

Current maximum divident rates are the same as those at savings & loans: 5¼ per cent on regular accounts, up to 6¾ per cent or more on certain types of long-term accounts.

For

- Rate of interest higher than commercial banks.

Against

- Lack the wide range of service given by a commercial bank.

Credit unions can be found nationwide. They might be described as "cooperative" organizations that restrict themselves to serving the savings and borrowing needs of their members. They aren't allowed to deal with the general public. Membership in each credit union is limited to a specific group of people, such as the employees of a particular corporation or the members of a trade union.

All federally-chartered credit unions are insured through a program of federal share insurance, similar to the insurance coverage at banks and savings & loans, for up to $20,000 per account. The situation at state-chartered credit unions varies from state to state; it is important that you look into the specific rules in your own state before putting any money into a state-chartered credit union.

Credit unions pay anywhere from 4 per cent (and sometimes even less) up to 6¼ per cent on savings. Ultimately, the amount depends on the abilities of the individual credit union's management. This is a point that cannot be emphasized too much. If you are eligible for membership in a credit union that is well run, it might be worth your while to save and borrow there rather than at a bank. But keep away from any credit union that lacks effective management.

For

- Interest rates at the best credit unions are good.
- Getting a loan can be easier than from other sources.

Against

- Rate of interest depends upon effective management.
- You must be a member of a specific group to be able to join.

U.S. savings bonds aren't really a savings "institution" in the same sense as a bank or savings & loan. But they are directly competitive with accounts there. When you buy a savings bond you are lending your money to the U.S. government.

There are two types of savings bonds — Series E and Series H. Series E bonds, by far the more important of the two, pay 5½ per cent interest when held to full maturity of five years, ten months. However, you receive much less (4.01 per cent in the first year, for instance) if you cash them in before then. This is a real drawback.

Savings banks: Account rates essentially the same as savings & loans (above)

Is it for me? Should I save at a savings & loan association or savings bank?

Credit unions: Rates and rules vary from state to state and among individual unions; some can pay a maximum of 6¼%, others less; minimum account size usually is very small

Is it for me? Should I save at a credit union?

U.S. savings bonds: Series E bonds pay 5½% when held to maturity of five years ten months, less when held for shorter periods; minimum purchase is in units of $17.50; maximum permissible holding per individual is $5,000

Saving without risk

Series H bonds pay 5½% when held to maturity of ten years; minimum purchase is $500, maximum purchase is $5,000

Series H bonds are much less attractive to the small investor. They come in minimum denominations of $500 and pay a full 5½ per cent only if held for ten years.

Series E bonds have certain mild advantages over other forms of saving:

1) they are the safest form, since they represent a direct obligation to repay by the government itself;

2) they can be purchased in small amounts on a regular basis through payroll deduction;

3) you don't have to pay income taxes on the interest until you cash the bonds in (income taxes on interest from a bank savings account, on the other hand, must be paid each year as the interest is credited to the account).

But the rate of return on savings bonds, although increased considerably in recent years, still doesn't stack up too well against other forms of long-term savings. In that sense, savings bonds are one of the poorer choices a saver could make.

Is it for me? Should I buy U. S. savings bonds?

For
- The safest form of saving.
- Series E bonds are good if you find it difficult to save — this can be done through payroll deductions.

Against
- Money has to be tied up for a long time to get a reasonable rate of interest.

WISEGUIDE

The best opportunities for earning the highest returns probably can be found at savings & loans and savings banks, the worst at commercial banks and in U.S. savings bonds.

The variety of accounts

It would be impossible for us to review every single type of savings account and tell you its advantages and disadvantages. There simply are so many different types available today that there isn't enough space on these pages to analyze them all in detail. One big New York bank, for instance, boasts the following different types of savings plans: regular savings accounts (4½ per cent interest); Christmas, vacation and special goal clubs (4½ to 5 per cent); golden passbook accounts (5½ per cent); systematic savings accounts, with money automatically transferred from your checking account on a regular basis (5 per cent); golden growth bonds (6 per cent); various types of long-term investment certificates (6½ per cent and more); and savings plus life insurance, with the insurance premiums deducted automatically from savings-account interest.

Some basic guidelines

What we can do, however, is give you some general guidelines for analyzing just how profitable each type of account will be for you.

There are two major factors you should consider when opening a savings account:

● How long are you willing to commit yourself to leaving your money in the bank? The longer you are willing to commit, the greater the interest rate you are likely to be able to earn.

To maximize your yield, it might be worthwhile to sit down some evening and sort out your savings goals. What funds can you shift into long-term certificates to earn the extra rate? You wouldn't want to put *all* your savings into these certificates, of course, since it would leave you without any short-term savings to tap in case of an emergency. But if you can see your way clear to leave $500 or more at the bank for at least the next two years, certificates offer a definite advantage. And if, by some unforeseen chance, you must collect your cash before the certificates come due, you can just tell the bank you want it back — generally, however, at a penalty in the form of reduced interest.

As we mentioned, you can earn up to 6 per cent annually on certificates of two to five years' length versus the maximum 5 per cent on regular accounts. Let's look at the difference this would make on a $1,000 account, with interest compounded annually:

	Original deposit	After one year	Two years	Three years	Four years	Five years
5% interest	$1,000	$1,050	$1,103	$1,158	$1,216	$1,276
6% interest	$1,000	$1,060	$1,123	$1,191	$1,262	$1,338

Not a tremendous disparity, as you can see, but still worth going for the larger amount. Also, it should be noted that the difference tends to widen as the compounding of interest becomes more frequent.

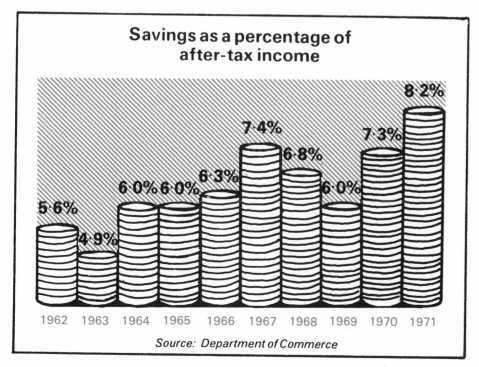

Savings as a percentage of after-tax income

1962	1963	1964	1965	1966	1967	1968	1969	1970	1971
5·6%	4·9%	6·0%	6·0%	6·3%	7·4%	6·8%	6·0%	7·3%	8·2%

Source: Department of Commerce

"Compounding" of interest

• That gets us to our second point — "compounding" itself. The term refers to the process of calculating interest payments on your account. If interest is compounded annually, the bank calculates interest once a year (at the end of the year). If, on the other hand, interest is compounded quarterly, payments are credited every three months, at a quarter of the bank's annual dividend rate each time.

Surprisingly, this does make a bit of a difference in terms of how much cash you receive. A simple example is that five per cent, compounded annually, adds up to $5 a year on a $100 account. But five per cent, compounded quarterly, adds up to something like $5.09, depending on the exact method of computation.

The reason for the difference is what can be termed "interest paid on interest." When interest is compounded quarterly, in the first quarter you are only credited with interest on your original deposit. But then in the second quarter you receive the small additional bonus of interest paid on the first quarter's interest, which has become an integral part of your account. In the third quarter, interest is paid on the previously-credited interest from *both* the first and second quarters, as well as on your original deposit. And so on, as this "interest paid on interest" gains momentum. Over a period of 20 years or so, this can make a substantial difference.

When interest is compounded annually, on the other hand, you don't receive any "interest on interest" until the end of the end of the second year.

A general rule of thumb, then, is this: the more frequently interest is compounded, the more you stand to earn.

WISEGUIDE

But the *rate* of interest is still more important than the frequency of compounding. Five per cent compounded annually is better than 4½ per cent compounded daily.

Deposit and withdrawal rules

Besides the length of your savings deposit and the frequency of compounding, a third major factor is the individual bank's rules regarding how interest payments are affected by deposits and withdrawals. If you are simply leaving a previous savings deposit in the bank with no thought of withdrawing it or adding more cash, the rules will make little or no difference in terms of how much interest you receive. Complications enter, however, when you put money in or take it out.

Here are some of the basic rules you should be aware of:

The "low balance" method

• Computation of interest on the "low balance" method. What this means is that you receive interest only for the lowest balance in your account during the interest computation period. Let us suppose, as an example, that interest is paid quarterly and you start off the quarter with a balance of $1,000. Then you deposit a second

$1,000, but withdraw this just before the quarter ends. You should receive at lease some interest on the second $1,000. Right? Wrong.

Under the low balance method, you wouldn't receive any interest whatsoever on the second $1,000. This is because the lowest amount in your account during the full quarter was the original $1,000 — you never went below that figure. Furthermore, if you had withdrawn $1,500, leaving yourself with an end-of-quarter balance of $500, you would have received interest only on that amount. And if at any point during the quarter you had taken all your money out — even for one day — you would receive absolutely nothing in interest payments.

Obviously, this is a terrible method of interest computation from the depositor's viewpoint. Yet it is fairly common. If a bank doesn't specify what method it uses for figuring interest payments, chances are it may use the low balance method. This is worth checking into, and avoiding, before you open an account.

• **Day of deposit to day of withdrawal.** This method is just the opposite of low balance. You receive pro-rated interest credit for any money you put into the account, regardless of how long you leave it there. In most cases, the only requirement is that you leave some sort of small balance, usually about $5, in the account until the end of the quarter. This type of payment rule is particularly attractive if you have "active" funds — that is, if you make lots of deposits and withdrawals.

Day of deposit to day of withdrawal

• **Grace days.** These "bonus" days allow you to earn interest on money you haven't yet deposited. For instance, a bank might specify that any money you deposit during the first 10 days of each quarter will earn full interest from the very beginning of the quarter. Likewise, it might also designate the last three days of the quarter as grace days — meaning that you can withdraw money then and still earn full interest on the funds to the very end of the quarter.

Grace days

Some banks in major cities are now offering grace days at the beginning of every *month*. This can be particularly valuable if you make regular deposits in your account, and the deposits are made toward the beginning of each month. You can pick up a lot of extra interest income under these circumstances with a grace-day account.

The ultimate would be interest from day of deposit to day of withdrawal, monthly grace days, interest compounded daily and paid quarterly, and a high basic interest rate — all in the same account.

WISEGUIDE

Saving without risk

Actually, in some big cities where banks are actively trying to outdo each other in their efforts to attract new savings accounts, there are a few banks that do offer all these features packaged together in a single type of account. But you have to do some searching and read all the fine print to make sure you have found one.

Chapter 3

Borrowing

Borrowing at the lowest cost

America has become a nation of borrowers. Since the end of World War II, total consumer credit has increased an astonishing 2,500 per cent, from $5.7 billion in loans outstanding in 1945 to roughly $160 billion in 1972 (as shown by the chart on page 30). These figures, by the way, don't even include home mortgages, which add another $375 billion or so to the latest total.

(Mortgages are discussed in detail in Chapter 6. Other specific types of loans that are dealt with in subsequent chapters are automobile loans, Chapter 8; educational loans, Chapter 11; and loans for investing in the stock market, Chapter 12.)

At any point in time, approximately half of all American families owe money on some form of installment loan — that is, a high-cost loan that is repaid in regular installments, usually monthly. Countless others hold other types of loans.

Half of us are in debt on installment loans

The post-war growth in borrowing has been particularly great in the following areas: automobile loans, loans to finance the purchase of other "durable goods" (such as refrigerators, TV sets and furniture), and unsecured personal loans. There also has been considerable growth in the amount owed on credit cards.

These statistics would seem to raise a basic question. Have we gone overboard in our use of debt? Certainly some individuals have gone off the deep end, borrowing more than they can ever hope to repay comfortably. But, on the other hand, the spectacular growth in consumer credit isn't necessarily a bad thing.

Debt has its good side, too

Intelligent borrowing has its definite strong points. In particular, it enables you to buy things you need before you save up the money. A car, for instance, is essential to most Americans, yet many would be unable to afford one without a loan. Similarly, some people borrow for vacations that they otherwise couldn't afford.

Borrowing is like a modern drug. Used as directed, it can be highly beneficial. But misuse can bring on disaster.

WISEGUIDE

Just what is "proper use" of debt? Here are some guidelines. These are all couched in essentially negative terms because caution is the best course when it comes to going into debt, particularly until you are sure of what you are doing.

Some rules for using credit

• One New York bank suggests that a family's monthly credit repayment obligations should never be more than 25 per cent of its

1945	$ 5.7 billion
1950	21.5 billion
1955	38.8 billion
1960	56.1 billion
1965	90.3 billion
1970	126.8 billion
1972	157.6 billion

after-tax income. However, 10 to 15 per cent probably is more realistic for most families. A simple rule of thumb is to borrow the least you need rather than the most you can get.

• Regardless of the limits mentioned in the previous guideline, be careful not to borrow so much that an unexpected illness or lay-off from work will jeopardize your financial standing. You should have a plan in mind for meeting repayment schedules in the event of an emergency, and should only borrow within the limits of this plan.

• If you do get into trouble and cannot repay your borrowings on schedule, talk it over face to face with your creditors. Silence, in this case, is *not* golden. After all, your creditors want more than anything else to get their money back and would rather work out a new repayment schedule than risk losing all. They get very nervous if you fall behind and they don't hear from you.

• Avoid so-called "debt consolidation loans," which are designed to give you funds to repay existing debts. They sometimes end up costing you much more than the loans they replace. They are often great for the lender, but not for you.

• Before buying anything on credit, ask yourself these questions: Is the merchandise or service really worth buying? Would I part with my own out-of-pocket cash to buy it? If not, don't buy on credit. "Easy" payment terms, advertised by merchants throughout the nation, often turn out to be very expensive.

• Finally, before signing any commitment to take out a loan, make sure you have shopped around for the best available terms.

This last point is extremely important — perhaps the most important point in this chapter. It is an area where many people make bad mistakes.

WISEGUIDE

Credit costs vary tremendously from place to place. Failure to spend an hour or two finding the most reasonably-priced loan can be very expensive.

What credit is

Credit is the use of someone else's money. As such, it is a service that you buy and for which there is a charge. The charge is usually called "interest." It can be lumped with overhead costs and called a "service charge," "fee," "carrying charge," "finance charge" or something similar. The credit itself can be in the form of a loan, a charge account, a revolving credit arrangement or a mortgage. There are various places where credit can be obtained, such as banks, department and retail stores, automobile dealers, finance companies and credit unions.

The best way to compare credit costs

The best way to compare the cost of credit from different sources is to ask for the "true" annual percentage rate of interest, which

must be given to you under the federal Truth in Lending Law of 1968 *before* you sign any agreement. Make absolutely certain it is.

Another way to compare costs is simply to sit down with pencil and paper and add up the amounts of all the payments you will make over the term of the contracts, including the initial down payments. Subtract the price-tag figure of the merchandise to obtain the cost of the credit in dollars.

A second way to compare costs

WISEGUIDE

The variations between costs of short and longer-term plans should not obscure the central fact you want to determine: how much will this credit plan cost me in dollars, as compared with other credit plans?

One more point: when you buy on credit, you are not being done a favor. You are a paying customer buying the use of money. The lender probably stands to make a good-sized profit for himself from the transaction. This difference in attitude is what makes it easy, and logical, for you to shop around frankly for credit at the lowest price.

Remember — you aren't being done a favor

Since rates vary so widely, just how does a lender go about deciding how much to charge you for a loan? There are four basic factors:

How a lender decides how much to charge

• First, to some extent both you and the lender are at the mercy of forces beyond your control — namely, the condition of the national economy and the behind-the-scenes activities of the Federal Reserve Board. The "Fed" is an independent government agency with the legal responsibility for manipulating the general level of interest rates upward or downward, depending on its assessment of the nation's needs. It does so actively. On many types of loans, particularly mortgages and securities loans, you end up paying essentially what the state of the economy dictates and the Fed thinks you should pay.

The "Fed"

• Second, every one of the 50 states regulates lending rates within its borders, specifying the maximum rates that can be charged on certain types of loans. Most of all, this affects loans by finance companies and interest rates on credit accounts at department stores. Chances are you will pay the ceiling rate on these high-cost loans, regardless of any other factors. That's because most finance companies and department stores always charge the maximum that each state will allow.

Regulations

• As indicated by the two previous factors, the type of loan you want has a direct bearing on the cost. A home mortgage, for instance, might typically cost about 7 to 8 per cent annual interest, while a debt consolidation loan might go for 18 to 36 per cent or more. Similarly, every other type of loan has its own rate range.

Type of loan

• Finally, the lender tries to assess your ability to repay. The better he views your ability, the better your chances for getting a cheaper type of loan.

How you measure up

Borrowing

How a lender determines your "creditworthiness"

This final factor deserves further discussion. Lenders prefer borrowers with stable jobs and stable family relationships, and with a demonstrated ability to handle their financial obligations honestly and efficiently. Somewhere — probably in a number of different places — a credit rating bureau has a file on your personal spending habits, your job record, your salary level, your past performance in repaying loans, etc.

WISEGUIDE

Whenever you apply for a loan, the lender will automatically check with one or another of the credit rating bureaus to review your file.

What to do about erroneous data in your file

If your file is essentially favorable, getting a loan should be no problem. But what happens if there is erroneous information in your file, and the lender turns you down because of it? Under a recent law change, you are supposed to be able, on written request, to find out what information was used against you and, if it turns out to be inaccurate, require that your file be corrected.

In theory, this law is a big step forward in protecting borrowers' rights. But many credit rating bureaus aren't complying as enthusiastically as they should. If you end up in a battle over erroneous information, it might be well worth your while to retain a lawyer to help make sure your file is straightened out. After all, if the record isn't set straight now, the erroneous data may haunt you the rest of your life whenever you apply for a loan or even for a job.

Your first loan helps establish your credit rating

One final point about how lenders determine your "creditworthiness." A totally clean financial record — one where you have never resorted to a loan in the past — is actually a negative factor. Banks and other lenders would rather see that you have borrowed previously and repaid on schedule. To them, this is the best assurance of all that you are a good risk. So there is something to be said for taking out a bank loan early in your adult life and then repaying on schedule. This will help you establish a good credit rating and set yourself up for future borrowing needs at relatively low interest rates.

Five basic types of loans

There are all sorts of different kinds of loans. They vary from institution to institution. Here are a few of the more basic types that you should know about, with approximate interest costs for each.

1. Installment loans

These are far and away the most widely-used kind of consumer loan. They can be obtained from commercial banks, finance companies, automobile dealers, furniture and appliance stores, mail-order houses and similar sources. They are called "installment" loans because repayment is made in regular monthly installments, usually over a period of anywhere from one to three years. When the interest cost for an installment loan is stated in terms of dollars per $100 of loan, the "true" interest rate is approximately double the stated

32

dollar rate. For example, a stated rate of $6 per $100 of loan would actually work out to a true interest rate of approximately 12 per cent.

There are three types of installment loans:

• Collateral loans are used to finance the purchase of a specific **Collateral** piece of merchandise — a car, a refrigerator, a TV set, a new sofa, etc. They generally cost roughly 10 per cent true annual interest when obtained from a bank, much more at finance companies and other sources. In most cases, if you fail to meet your payments the lender has the right to take back the merchandise (more on this in Chapter 18).

• Unsecured personal loans are the same as collateral loans, except **Unsecured personal** that they aren't secured by any specific piece of merchandise or property. They often are used to finance vacations, medical expenses and similar personal expenditures. You generally must have a fairly decent credit rating to get one of these loans. Interest tends to be somewhat higher than on collateral loans.

• Home improvement loans generally have a longer term of re- **Home improvement** payment than other types of installment loans — usually about five years.

These are similar to installment loans in that regular repayments **2. Revolving credit** must be made. They can be found at commercial banks, credit-card **arrangements** companies and department stores. Essentially, this kind of loan is a "line of credit," giving you the power to borrow up to a predetermined limit any time you want.

Many banks, for instance, offer "overdraft" checking accounts that enable you to write a check larger than your cash balance; the excess is charged against your account as a loan, usually at an annual interest rate of about 12 per cent. Interest rates on credit-card borrowings, at department stores and mail-order houses, on the other hand, are generally 18 per cent annually.

These are available at most commercial banks. They usually are **3. Demand loans** reserved for the bank's best customers, such as businessmen whose companies have some sort of client relationship with the bank. They are offered mainly on a short-term basis — in the range of 30 to 180 days. When the term is up the bank can either renew the loan or demand repayment. A good credit rating is required. This is one of the less expensive types of loans, with interest roughly in the range of 7 to 9 per cent.

Passbook and insurance loans are available at savings banks, some **4. Passbook and** savings & loan associations, and life insurance companies. You **insurance loans** must already be a customer to borrow, and you can only borrow up to the amount of money you already have left on deposit or, in the case of insurance companies, the cash value of your life insurance policies. These loans are very inexpensive — generally in the area of 5 to 7 per cent true annual interest.

5. Second mortgages

These high-cost loans are resorted to mainly by people who can't get any other type of loan. The lender gives you the money in return for a "second lien" against your house — that is, if you cannot repay he stands second in line behind the holder of your first mortgage in terms of collecting his cash from the forced sale of your home. One aspect of second mortgages that is particularly troublesome is the so-called "balloon clause," under which you make small monthly repayments only to be faced with a huge "balloon" payment at the end of the loan's term. If you don't have the money to meet this final big payment, you could end up in bad financial trouble.

Types of lending institutions

Now that you know what to look for in shopping for a loan, just where do you go looking?

Where to shop for a loan

The following list of major types of lending institutions is arranged in approximate order from least expensive to most expensive. You should start at the top of the list and work your way down in your search for the best terms.

WISEGUIDE

If you get all the way down to the finance companies and still don't have your loan, you should ask yourself whether you really need the money. One answer may be that people who have to resort to finance companies and other high-cost lenders shouldn't be borrowing at all.

"Free" loans

"Free" loans come from a variety of places — advances on your office expense account, purchases on a credit card or a department store credit account (which you don't have to pay until you are billed), and, in some cases, purchases by mail order. You can, in effect, write yourself a free loan for 30 days or so this way, since you are usually given about that much time to repay without being charged interest. But be careful not to let yourself get so suckered into this handy way to shop that you end up over-committing yourself financially or buying merchandise you don't really need.

WISEGUIDE

Make use of any truly free loans which you can obtain.

Life insurance companies

Life insurance companies are one of the few real bargains left in the world of borrowing. Most "cash-value" life insurance policies specify that the holder has the right to borrow the value of his policy from the company. Older policies generally specify a 5 per cent interest rate, ones issued in the last three or four years a 6 per cent rate. And the biggest bargain of all can be found in GI-benefit policies, with a 4 per cent interest rate to borrowers.

In fact, if you have a good-sized cash value in life insurance and you haven't borrowed against it, you may be making a mistake.

Money borrowed from life insurance companies is so inexpensive in relation to today's general interest-rate levels that you could take the cash and probably reinvest it elsewhere at a higher rate, for a net profit.

By the way, unlike almost all other types of consumer loans, you **You repay if and when** don't even have to work out a repayment schedule on insurance **you please** borrowings. You are billed the interest, and you repay the loan itself whenever you want. Also, you can use the money for any purpose.

Some people are still cautious about borrowing on their life insurance, because this reduces the amount of cash payment to the family in the event of their death. Certainly, this is a bit of a drawback, especially in comparison to most bank loans. Bank loans generally carry automatic insurance protection for repaying the full loan if you die, rather than leaving the loan as a liability that must be paid out of your estate. But this extra protection hardly seems to justify the much higher interest rate you would pay the bank.

So, if you must borrow, why not borrow against your insurance **WISEGUIDE** and enjoy the benefit of paying the lowest interest rates around?

Savings banks and some savings & loan associations provide a **Savings institutions** similar advantage: you can borrow against your own assets. In this case, however, the assets involve savings accounts rather than insurance policies. As with life insurance borrowings, the interest rates are quite cheap — in most cases around 7 per cent.

But even the 7 per cent is, in one sense, a bit high. Since savings rates are now in the 4½ to 6 per cent range, it would actually be cheaper to withdraw your savings than to borrow against them and pay the difference.

But that doesn't necessarily mean that taking out a loan against **The net cost is actually** your own savings is wrong. The net dollar cost of such borrowings **quite low on passbook** will actually be very low — a difference of roughly $10 a year be- **borrowings** tween your savings income and borrowing costs on a $1,000 loan, for instance, and chances are that you would be more likely to repay a loan than to restore your savings account to its original size if you took the cash directly out of it. So the small extra cost of borrowing may be worth paying, after all. Incidentally, passbook loans are like insurance-policy loans in that they are general-purpose borrowings that you can use for whatever you want.

Passbook loans are inexpensive, but you must have savings. **WISEGUIDE**

Borrowing

Credit unions

Credit unions account for roughly 11 per cent of all installment loans. They tend to be a relatively inexpensive source of funds — generally at less than 10 per cent annual interest. As we discussed in the previous chapter, these are "cooperative" organizations that serve the savings and borrowing needs of members. The drawback is that unless you are a member you aren't allowed to borrow from a credit union.

Most credit union loans are earmarked for a specific purpose — to finance the borrower's new car and for educational expenses, in particular. Usually they are made in the form of installment loans, with repayments sometimes deducted automatically from your paycheck.

WISEGUIDE

Credit unions can be quite useful, but you must be a member.

Commercial banks

Commercial banks are the biggest lenders of all. They are the source of about 40 per cent of all installment credit in the nation, and they also make a variety of non-installment types of loans. If you want to borrow money for any legitimate purpose whatsoever, chances are a commercial bank has the right type of loan for you.

There is only one disadvantage to borrowing from a commercial bank: rates there aren't the cheapest. Unfortunately, however, all the cheaper sources of money (insurance companies, savings institutions and credit unions) require that you already have some sort of basic business relationship with them before they will lend you a penny. So if you have no such relationship, a commercial bank should be the first stop on your shopping list for a loan.

There isn't one single rate at a commercial bank

There are all kinds of different rates on different types of loans at commercial banks. In fact, the rates also vary a bit from bank to bank. On installment loans, the true annual interest tends to be in the range of 10 to 12 per cent. This certainly isn't a bargain, but it isn't ridiculously high either.

One last note on borrowing from a commercial bank: it helps if you are already a customer of the bank.

WISEGUIDE

A checking account at a bank, for instance, will be a point in your favor when you apply there for a loan. But this is by no means essential. Feel free to apply for a loan even if you have never done any business with the particular bank before.

Retail credit

Most department stores and mail-order houses offer extended credit terms on merchandise you purchase from them. This is either in the form of a charge account or a specific loan arrangement. On charge accounts, interest rates generally are 1 to 1½ per cent a month

ZIP SCORING CHART

DIRECTIONS FOR ZIP SCORING

Circle the number on each line that describes you and enter it in the blocks to the right. Total your score. If you have scored 19 points or more complete the additional information and mail today.

SAMPLE LINE

21-25	26-35	36-45	46-64	65 & Over	
1	2	2	2	1	

A AGE

21-25	26-35	36-45	46-64	65 & Over	
1	2	2	2	1	

B MARITAL STATUS

Single	Separated	Divorced	Widowed	Married	
1	1	1	1	2	

C DEPENDENTS (Include yourself.)

One	Two	Three	Four	Five or More	
2	2	2	1	1	

D LIVING FACILITIES

With Parents	Rent: Furn.	Rent:Unfurn	Own: Mtg.	Own:NoMtg	
1	1	2	4	5	

E YEARS AT PRESENT ADDRESS

Under 1 Yr.	1-2 Yrs.	3-5 Yrs.	6-10 Yrs.	Over 10 Yrs.	
1	1	1	2	2	

F YEARS AT PREVIOUS ADDRESS

Under 1 Yr.	1-2 Yrs.	3-5 Yrs.	6-10 Yrs.	Over 10 Yrs.	
1	1	1	2	2	

G TOTAL MONTHLY INCOME

Under $400	$400-$600	$601-$800	$801-$1000	Over $1000	
1	1	3	5	7	

H YEARS WITH PRESENT EMPLOYER

Under 1 Yr.	1-3 Yrs.	4-6 Yrs.	7-10 Yrs.	Over 10 Yrs.	
1	2	3	4	5	

I TOTAL MONTHLY OBLIGATIONS (Exclude Rent or Mtg. Pymt.)

Under $75	$75-$125	$126-$200	$201-$300	Over $300	
2	2	2	1	1	

J OCCUPATION

Part-Time	Unskilled	Skill.-Equiv.	Exec.-Super.	Profess.	
1	2	3	4	4	

K BONUS POINTS (Circle all that apply and enter the total in box)

Have a Phone In Your Name	2	Loan With This Bank	5	Checking or Savings With This Bank	5	Loan Exp. With Other Bank	3	

IF YOU SCORE 19 POINTS OR MORE, MAIL TODAY! The right of final loan approval is reserved by this bank. **TOTAL SCORE**

©MOTIVATIONAL SYSTEMS, INC., NEW YORK, N.Y. 1972

Do you qualify for a loan at a commercial bank?

To find out, fill in this simple rating chart. Developed by a marketing organization in New York, this particular chart is used by a number of banks across the nation to screen loan applications. It gives you an idea of the factors that go into evaluating whether or not you will be granted a loan. One warning: while the chart here specifies a minimum total of 19 points to qualify for loan consideration, some banks actually set a somewhat higher minimum — in the range of 20 to 26 points.

on the unpaid balance, for a total of 12 to 18 per cent a year. The specific figure varies from state to state. If you are making a big purchase with the idea of paying if off through your charge account over the next few months, you certainly would be well advised to arrange a lower-cost loan at a bank instead.

On installment loans to finance specific purchases — such as TV sets and furniture — the rates tend to be even higher, in the range of 18 to 36 per cent and more. These loans, unless you really want the goods and have no alternative source, should be avoided. It's rare indeed that any merchandise or service is worth paying that much in interest costs.

Retail credit can be expensive. Check the rates before you buy.

WISEGUIDE

Borrowing

Finance companies

We have mentioned finance companies several times. These are sometimes referred to as "small loan" or "personal finance" companies. They're the organizations that run those cheerful jingles on radio and TV, telling how anxious they are to do business with you. They should be, at the rates they charge!

WISEGUIDE

Finance company loans are very expensive. Avoid them if you can.

Pawnshops

The final lending source is that old standby, the neighborhood pawnshop. Rates, as you might suspect, are high.

WISEGUIDE

Pawnshops should be thought of as a last resort.

The dangers of co-signing

Some day, a friend or relative may approach you with what seems like a basically simple request: would you co-sign a loan agreement for him or her? Perhaps he'll say the lender wants a co-signer as a routine matter, and that you will be doing a favor that will entail little or no liability on your part.

Take care!

Beware of this "simple" request. You should know that when you co-sign any loan contract, you become just as responsible for repaying as the person who gets the money. If the borrower doesn't pay it back, chances are that you will have to do so yourself.

What is a "co-signer"?

That's what a co-signer is — a signer for a loan, other than the borrower, who agrees to take full responsibility for the loan's contract terms if the borrower fails to live up to them. This is not a matter that should be taken lightly.

A co-signer is a fairly common requirement these days. For instance, a co-signature might be required on the contract before a loan is granted to a young person who hasn't borrowed before, a woman who is likely to become pregnant and quit her job, or an individual with a poor financial record or with an already-heavy debt burden.

WISEGUIDE

Agreeing to co-sign for a friend's loan is a serious matter. Make sure you understand exactly what you are getting into before you put your John Hancock on the dotted line.

Bank Loans

Commercial banks grant more loans than any other lender.

Worth trying for.

Finance Companies

Very expensive. Best to avoid.

Pawnbrokers

Only if all else fails.

Life Insurance Companies

Very low interest rates. Repayment can be delayed indefinitely.

Savings Banks and Savings & Loans

You can only borrow against your own savings. Attractive terms.

Auto Dealers and Appliance Stores

Expensive. Always read the fine print before signing.

Charge Accounts

O.K. it you pay within 30 days. Expensive after that.

Second Mortgages.

High interest rates. Know what you're doing.

Credit Unions

A good place to borrow. You must be a member, though.

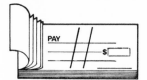

Chapter 4

Banking

Checking accounts and other services

In the two previous chapters, we discussed saving and borrowing. These are at the heart of a commercial bank's operations. Each bank's main purpose in life is to serve as a middleman in the handling of money, taking in cash from savers and then turning around and parceling it out to borrowers.

A variety of services
But banks also provide a variety of other services that you should be aware of. These break down into two broad categories:

* Money transfer services, particularly checking accounts.

* Other financial services, such as safe deposit boxes and management of your investments.

The "proper attitude"
To start, it is important that you approach a bank with the proper attitude. Although banks were once considered aloof institutions that looked down on their customers, that no longer is true — or at least it shouldn't be. Most banks are very anxious to get your business — whether it be savings, borrowing, checking or anything else. You should go there with this in mind. Don't let yourself be intimidated.

WISEGUIDE

You have every right to expect efficient, courteous service from your bank. If you don't get it, there will be another bank nearby that will treat you like a valued customer.

What is a "commercial" bank?
We want to differentiate at this point between commercial banks (the only type of bank we will be discussing in this chapter) and savings institutions — namely savings & loan associations and savings banks. Commercial banks are sometimes referred to as "full service" banks. In other words, they are the only kind of banking institution that offers all banking services — checking accounts, trust services, credit cards, etc. Savings & loan associations and savings banks, on the other hand, are limited by law mainly to taking in savings and giving out loans.

Commercial banks take their name from the fact that they used to cater almost exclusively to large corporations and the rich. Corporate accounts are called "commercial" banking.

The post-war growth in retail banking
After the end of World War II, however, many commercial banks began seeing the possibilities for expanding their operations by dealing with the mass public as well. This is called "retail" banking.

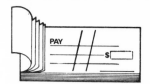

As we have mentioned, saving and borrowing are two primary parts of retail banking. A third is checking accounts.

A checking account, as millions of Americans have discovered, can be an extremely valuable aid in handling family finances. There are two main benefits, in particular:

The advantages of a checking account

● A checking account provides a safe and convenient way to pay your bills. In most cases, checks can be used as freely as cash. But unlike cash, only the person to whom the check is made out can get the money.

● A checking account helps you maintain orderly financial records. Canceled checks are legal proof of payment.

Bank checks have, in fact, become by far the most common method for transferring moderate to large sums of money in the United States. Our national economy simply couldn't function without them. More than 24 billion checks are now written each year by individuals and business organizations. That's over 100 checks for every person in the United States per year!

24 billion checks a year

To facilitate the processing of all these checks, a highly-structured system has been built up within the banking community. Here is how it works:

Assume you owe your dentist $20

1) Instead of going to his office and handing over that amount in cash, you write a check. It is, in fact, no more than a written instruction to your bank to pay $20 on your behalf, deducting the amount from the balance in your checking account.

2) Because you have written your dentist's name on the check, he is the only person who can legally receive payment. Therefore it is perfectly safe to send the check through the mail. Even if it is stolen, it is unlikely that it could be cashed. The thief would first have to prove to a bank that he actually is your dentist — something he probably couldn't do without also stealing identification papers.

3) On receiving the check, your dentist will take it to his own bank, which will credit $20 to his account.

4) The check will then be "cleared." It would be ridiculous for, say, First National City Bank to have to pay separately for every check written by one of its customers and receive separate payment for every check credited to one of its customer's accounts. So the system is centralized: all the checks are added up and each bank makes or receives just one daily payment to or from its competitors. Large banks within the same city usually do this through a bank-sponsored "clearing house." Large banks in different cities usually work through the Federal Reserve. Some smaller banks, on the other hand, clear all their checks through "correspondent" banks in major financial centers.

5) When the check has been cleared, it will be returned to the branch of the bank on which it was drawn — your branch, in other words. There, your account will be reduced by $20 — assuming, of

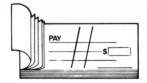

course, that there is at least $20 in the account in the first place. If not, the bank either will allow you to become overdrawn and go into the red or will refuse to honor the check. If it chooses the latter, your check will be returned by way of the same "clearing" route back to the dentist. It then becomes his job to take up the matter with you directly.

WISEGUIDE

To keep good relations with both your bank and with those to whom you have to pay checks, it is essential that you never go into the red unwittingly.

What does a checking account cost?

The only real drawback of using a checking account — if there actually is a drawback — is the cost. But this probably will be fairly small, particularly in major cities where the leading banks are competing actively for checking account business.

It would be impossible for us to tell you what rates you should expect to pay, since they vary from city to city and bank to bank. Usually, however, banks are relatively straightforward about what they charge, so you can figure out specific rates on your own.

Two basic types of accounts

Most banks offer two basic types of checking accounts — regular and special. The major difference is in the size of the minimum balance required and the way fees are calculated.

Regular accounts

• On a regular account, the service charge usually is based on "activity"— that is, the number of checks written, deposits made, and the average or lowest balance during the month. For instance, there might be no charge as long as your average monthly balance doesn't fall below $500. In that case, the bank will make money from your account by having free use of the $500. Regular accounts tend to be best for people who generally leave at least a few hundred dollars in their checking account and who write a lot of checks.

Special accounts

• A special account, on the other hand, typically costs about 10 cents a check, plus in some cases an additional monthly service charge, perhaps in the range of 50 cents to $1. No minimum balance is required. Special accounts are best for people with low balances and light to moderate activity.

Three other types of checks

In addition to writing out an ordinary check against your own account, there are three special kinds of checks that you might make use of at one time or another:

Cashier's checks

• These are the bank's own checks, made payable to the person you specify. To obtain a cashier's check, you simply pay the bank the face value of the check plus a small service charge. Or you could buy a money order from any branch of the Post Office; postal money orders are essentially the same as bank cashier's checks.

Travelers checks

• Most banks sell these special checks, which may be cashed readily when you are away from home. They require no identifi-

Some Handy Hints About the Use of Checks

Never cross out or change anything on a check. If you make an error filling one out, write "canceled" across its face and file it with your canceled checks.

If the amount in figures on the face of a check disagrees with the amount in words, the words determine the value.

Always keep your blank *and* canceled checks in a safe place. Canceled checks, if stolen, can be used by a forger to copy your signature.

If you send out a check and then, for whatever reason, don't want to make payment after all, you can issue a "stop payment" order to your bank. The bank will then refuse to honor the check (and will charge you a small fee for doing so). You must notify the bank quickly, however.

There are no secrets in a checking account! Under a recent law change, banks are required to maintain a record of all transactions in each checking and savings account. The government can then, under a number of different circumstances, gain access to the data. The law is being challenged in court, however.

A joint checking account works well for some couples, but for others it's a fiasco. Separate accounts may be worth the extra expense.

Nowadays, many teenagers have their own checking accounts. It's perfectly legal.

Checking accounts are insured for up to $20,000 by the Federal Deposit Insurance Corporation in the event the bank gets into financial trouble. But if your combined checking and savings accounts in a single bank exceed that amount, the insurance coverage applies only to the first $20,000 of the total.

Never accept an old check in payment without first getting in touch with the bank on which it is drawn.

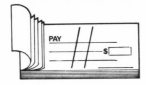

cation to cash except a comparison signature at the top that matches your signature at the bottom. If lost or stolen uncountersigned, your money will be refunded. This is one of the safest ways to carry funds while traveling. There are three major domestic brands of travelers checks: American Express, First National City and Bank of America.

Certified checks

These are simply your own checks, with "certified" stamped across the face by your bank. The bank is guaranteeing that you have the funds in your account to cover the check. Therefore, when it certifies one of your personal checks it sets the cash aside from your account to make sure it will be there.

WISEGUIDE

Never destroy a certified check. You will have a terrible time getting the funds transferred back into your account. If you decide not to use a certified check, return it to your bank.

Check-cashing cards

To make it easier for you to use your own checks — either by cashing them at a bank or to pay for merchandise at a shop — many banks provide a free check-cashing card. These are a form of identification under which the bank guarantees payment of your checks up to a certain limit, usually $100.

WISEGUIDE

A check card provides a guarantee of your creditworthiness. Try to get one.

Credit cards

But while check-cashing cards are useful and valuable, there is a second kind of card that the banks have promoted much more aggressively — the credit card. Everybody is familiar with these little plastic cards and is aware of how the banks flooded the mails with them in the late Sixties. It was, in fact, a real fiasco, as banks sent out unsolicited credit cards to millions of customers. Many of the cards were lost or stolen, and the resulting losses from fraud were huge.

The mailing of unsolicited cards has now been made illegal, and the banks have finally settled down in their promotions. Out of the whole mess only two major bank credit card systems have survived — the BankAmericard and its competitor, Master Charge. Each is available at hundreds of different banks across the country, and either is worth obtaining, particularly since they are free.

WISEGUIDE

The advantages of using a credit card to travel, dine and shop are obvious: convenience, elimination of the need to carry large amounts of cash, and the fact that payment can be delayed until after you receive your bill.

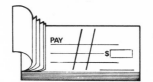

There also is a major disadvantage, however: if you are a compulsive spender, a credit card only makes it easier for you to buy things you don't really need.

Are you a compulsive spender?

Besides the two major bank sponsored-credit card systems, there are three main independent systems — Amerian Express, Diners Club and Carte Blanche. Actually, the American Express card is available at some banks, although most subscribers get their cards directly from American Express itself. Unlike the two bank-sponsored cards, there is a $15 annual fee for each of these three cards.

Even though you have to pay to obtain an American Express, Diners Club or Carte Blanche card, it probably is worth it if you travel a great deal. In particular, these cards are much more useful overseas than the bank-sponsored credit cards.

Why pay?

Another major difference between the bank cards and the independent cards is that the independent card companies are fussier about their customers. For instance, American Express, largest of the three, specifies that you must earn at least $8,500 a year to qualify for a card. The bank cards are issued much more freely.

Note that you have very little personal liability in the event that your credit card is lost or stolen. Under a recent change in federal law, you can only be held liable for the first $50 of unauthorized charges on your card. After that, the credit card company itself must absorb all unauthorized charges.

What happens when your credit card is lost or stolen

Another important bank service is the safe deposit box. A safe deposit box is nothing more than your private little vault at the bank, to which only you have access (except that in some states creditors can put a lien on the contents of your safe deposit box if you owe them money and don't repay).

Safe deposit boxes

Approximately 15 million American families use safe deposit boxes to store their valuables. If you have any important papers — such as stock certificates, life insurance policies, home deeds, etc., or even such possessions as jewelry and silver — a safe deposit box may be for you. You can just drop by your bank and rent one. Typical fee is $10 a year for a box 2 inches by 5 inches by 24 inches.

But there are certain things you should *not* keep in a safe deposit box — namely cash, the deed to your cemetery plot and your will (although it is OK to leave a duplicate copy of your will inside).

WISEGUIDE

The problem is this: in the case of the cemetery plot deed and your will, your family may need access to them immediately after you die. If they are in your safe deposit box, however, it may take several days to get a court order permitting your spouse or children to open the box. In the case of cash, some people leave a few thousand dollars in their safe deposit box on the mistaken notion that their family will be able to get at it quickly without having to pay inheritance taxes. The truth is that the state will probably inventory the

When you die, the state will inventory your box

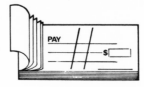

contents of your safe deposit box and find the cash, lumping it into your taxable estate.

Trust and investment services

One last note on bank services: banks provide a variety of investment management and personal trust services. These are designed essentially to help you manage your security portfolio and to help you build up the value of your estate. As part of this, you can designate the bank to be the executor of your estate when you die and to administer money in trust for your spouse or children.

The advantage of retaining a bank for these services is that there is a certain stability associated with such an institution. You know that the bank will always be there and will act in a sensible, conservative way — if that is what you are looking for. These services generally are available, however, only to persons with substantial sums of money. You should check with your bank if you are interested.

Chapter 5

Buying a house

Sooner or later, every American family is faced with these important questions: Are we ready to buy a house? Can we afford it? If so, how much can we afford? What kind of house? New or used? Big or small? Where? How do we make sure we've found the right one?

Getting at the proper answers is extremely important, since the purchase of a home will probably represent the single greatest expense of your life. This chapter will help you analyze your situation and needs, and will outline the basic steps in buying a house. In Chapter 6 we will discuss how to find a mortgage loan to finance your purchase, and Chapter 7 deals with protecting your home and its contents with proper insurance coverage.

Home-buying is a time-consuming process

Buying a home should be recognized for what it is — a time-consuming process. Taking the time to shop around carefully is the only sure way to find the right home for your needs at the best price. The more homes you look at, the greater your ultimate range of choice and the better your feel for, construction, neighborhoods, prices, etc.

In some ways, buying a house is like getting married. Few marriages are made in heaven. The same is true of houses. You should be realistic about what you are getting into. In looking at a prospective home, you should review both the good and bad points and then balance them off in relation to your family's needs.

A warning: try not to become overly emotional

Perhaps the most common mistake is to let home-buying become a highly emotional process. Some degree of emotion is bound to creep in. But there is tremendous danger in letting yourself become so swept away by the beauty of a particular house — your "ideal" home, so you think — that you become an easy target for high-pressure sales tactics. Only after you have signed on the dotted line will you begin to see all the faults — a leaky roof, a dilapidated furnace, shoddy workmanship in the bathroom or whatever.

The first rule of home-buying is to avoid becoming overly emotional in your search for the right house.

WISEGUIDE

The deposit: a point of no return?

In particular, don't let yourself be rushed into handing over a deposit. If you do, it may turn out to be a point of no return. Unless you are sure of what you are doing, you could conceivably find that you have committed yourself to going through with the deal regardless of whether you want to or not. Be sure to consult a lawyer before handing over any money or signing any sort of contract or "letter of intent."

Buying a house

A common pressure tactic on the part of sellers is to hint that there is a large group of other prospective buyers, any one of whom could sign a contract in the next few hours if you don't sign up immediately and leave a deposit yourself. This may or may not actually be true. Your best approach is to take the chance that it isn't. Remember that other equally attractive houses are bound to come along if you don't get this one.

If you let yourself be deceived into thinking that you have found your one and only "dream house," you will be at the seller's mercy.

How to keep your emotions in check

One real estate agent offers this advice for couples who tend to become emotional about home-buying:

If you immediately fall in love with the charm of the kitchen or family room or backyard garden, stop looking in that particular area of the house. You already know that you like what you see there; there is no real need to look further. If you do linger on, there is a danger that you and your spouse will rhapsodize back and forth about that particular feature and, as a result, end up talking yourselves into buying the house solely on the basis of it. Go down to the basement and then up to the attic and look for cheap construction and other faults. If you don't find any major problems, the house might be just right for your needs. If you do find some, feel lucky that you looked before being suckered into a deal.

Be systematic in your search

The point is that if you go about your search slowly, systematically and wisely, you probably will end up with a reasonably-priced home that will be a pleasure to your family for years to come. If not, you may end up with little more than years of frustration.

Initial decision

The basic initial decision boils down, of course, to whether you should buy or rent — a decision that only you yourself can make. This decision should be based as much on personal taste and lifestyle as on financial considerations. Of the two choices, buying is clearly the more popular in the United States.

Approximately 63 per cent of all American families own their homes — an indication of how important home ownership has become in this country as way of living and a form of investment.

The advantages of renting

Renting and buying each has its own basic advantages. These are some of the virtues of renting:

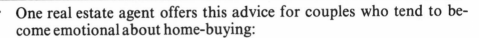 You maintain flexibility. If you are young and childless, you may want to hold open the option of moving again in the near future without having to go through the drawn-out process of

selling your house and buying a new one. This is particularly important to single people and to young marrieds whose careers might involve frequent job transfers.

● There is less risk involved in renting. If it turns out that you don't like what you have chosen, you can simply move out after the lease is up and wash your hands of the place. And a temporary reversal in your financial affairs won't endanger the equity you might have acquired through home ownership.

● Initially, at least, renting is cheaper than buying. There is no need for a down payment. Furthermore, you stay out of debt. A mortgage, if you buy, entails responsibility to meet payments over a period of 15 or 20 years or more.

● You are free from the worries of mowing the lawn and wrestling with tax collectors, repairmen and plumbers.

Buying, on the other hand, offers advantages of its own:

● You are king of your own castle. There is no landlord poking around, telling you what you can and cannot do.

● You have more living space. Most homes are considerably more spacious than apartments.

● There's a sense of permanence of residence. You don't have to worry about what will happen when your lease expires, as you do with an apartment. And you are in a better position as a homeowner to participate in neighborhood and community activities.

● Mortgage interest costs and real estate taxes are deductible on your federal tax return. Rent payments, by contrast, usually are not. Given a situation where the total monthly costs involved in buying a particular home or renting a particular apartment are roughly the same, buying is actually the less expensive of the two since it provides you with the "hidden" benefit of these tax deductions. To find out exactly how much less expensive, add up your annual real estate taxes and mortgage interest costs for your house, and then multiply this total by the income tax rate in your federal tax bracket. For example, if your annual real estate taxes are $700 and the current year's interest payment on your mortgage is $800, the total is $1,500. Then, if you are in the 25 per cent tax bracket (your own bracket can be determined by checking your latest federal tax return), you would multiply 0.25 times $1,500. The answer in this case is that home ownership provides you with $375 in tax savings each year.

● Perhaps most importantly of all, a home may turn out to be a profitable investment. When the mortgage is finally paid off, the house will be yours free and clear. Rent payments, in this sense, are money down the drain.

This last point deserves further discussion. The prices of existing homes have been rising approximately 6 per cent a year over the

The advantages of buying

Home prices are rising 6 per cent a year

last five years. Of course, you might do better by investing in the stock market than by using your cash to make a down payment on a home. But unless you are an absolute wizard in the stock market, there is a certain assured steady growth in the value of most homes that you simply cannot find in stocks.

WISEGUIDE

A home is an excellent long-term investment for most families. Unless you have specific reasons for renting, you probably will be better off financially if you buy.

New homes tend to be best as investments

You would never want to buy a home strictly on the basis of whether it is a good investment. After all, your main concern is to find a comfortable place to live. But some consideration should be given to the investment potential of a house. New homes, in particular, stand to gain in value year after year. Large, older ones tend to be less attractive. The quality of construction and the dynamics of the neighborhood — is it on its way up or on its way down? — also are crucial to the future value of a house.

An interesting sidelight is that home values actually vary quite widely from region to region. The following table is based on data from the last two U.S. censuses:

Median Value of Owner-Occupied Homes

Region	1960	1970	Percentage Increase
Northeast	$13,300	$19,400	46%
North Central	12,100	16,700	38
South	9,500	13,600	43
West	13,700	20,500	50
Total U.S.	11,900	17,000	43

How expensive a home can you afford?

Just how much money is needed to "afford" a house? There are three widely-used rules of thumb, each of which is important to your ultimate decision:

1. Down payment

● First, you must have enough cash to meet the required down payment. Generally, the down payment will be about 20 to 30 per cent of the total price, although in some cases it may be much less. The other 70 to 80 per cent usually can be financed with a mortgage loan.

2. Total price

● Second, the total price should be no more than about 2½ times your annual salary. In other words, if you earn $10,000 a year you probably can afford a house worth about $25,000 without becoming financially overextended. Similarly, if you earn $15,000 you can expect to be able to afford a $37,500 home. This is not a strict rule. Some flexibility is in order if, for instance, you have a large savings account that will enable you to make a big down payment or if there

Here is a checklist of specific things to look for in various parts of the house

Bathrooms
Are there enough? If you have a large family, you will want at least two. Are the tiling and caulking in good condition? Is there sufficient water pressure and drainage in the sink and tub? Flush the toilet. Does it sound cheap, or is it relatively silent and smooth-running? Are there trademarks on all the fixtures? If not, they may be second rate. Are there sufficient electrical outlets? Do they work?

Bedrooms
Are there enough? Will your furniture fit? Is there adequate closet space? Are noise levels low at night? Is there sufficient privacy? Is there adequate ventilation?

Outside of house
Does it need painting? Check all leaders and gutters. Note the condition of the roof. Are there broken or missing shingles? Are there signs of leaks in the attic? If possible, inspect the attic during or right after a rainstorm. Note the condition of lawns and landscaping. Are walks and driveways in good condition?

Kitchen
Check the capacity and condition of all appliances. Are there warranties that are still in effect? How are pressure and drainage in the sink? Are there sufficient electrical outlets? Are they conveniently placed? Is there sufficient storage and counter space?

Living room
Is it attractive and spacious? Is the lighting good? Is there adequate privacy? Does the front door open directly into the living room? If so, consider this a negative factor. Is walk-through traffic minimized by proper room arrangement?

Windows and doors
Do all windows and doors open and close easily, yet fit snugly? Are they weather-stripped? Is hardware in good condition? Are screens, storm windows and storm doors provided?

Dining room
Is it large enough for entertaining? Is it close to the kitchen? Will your furniture fit in? Will furniture interfere with traffic?

Basement
Check foundation walls, particularly around the windows. Is there evidence of cracks or repairs? If so, this may indicate excessive foundation settlement. Check the heating system and pipes. Is all piping fully insulated? Are water pipes made of copper or brass? If so, they will be more durable (although plastic also is beginning to gain some acceptance). Are there signs of dampness? Is there adequate ventilation and light? If the ceiling beams are exposed, are there any signs of sag or rot?

Floors and walls
Are all floors level, properly laid and finished? Do you feel any cracks in the floor when walking? Are they any spaces between floors and baseboards?

General observations
How do you rate the layout of the rooms? Are bathrooms conveniently located? Are there adequate electrical outlets? Is there adequate storage space? If there is a fire-place, does it work? Is the water heater large enough for your family's needs?

is every reason to believe that you will be given a big salary increase at work in the near future. Also, consideration should be given to individual tastes, lifestyle, family needs, etc.

3. Monthly costs   • Third, your total monthly housing cost and other debt repayment obligations — that is mortgage payments, taxes, repairs, auto loan costs, etc. — should not exceed 25 per cent of your pre-tax monthly income or 33 per cent of your take-home pay.

How to determine the full cost of owning a home   How do you determine "total monthly housing costs"? The term may seem confusing, but the arithmetic is actually quite simple. The following list shows the basic costs of homeownership that you must take into account before you buy:

1. Local real estate taxes can be expensive. Generally, they come to roughly 2 to 3 per cent per year of the total value of the home. Check this out carefully in advance, and make sure you also ask about "special assessments," such as for the local school or sewage district. In addition, try to get a sense of whether tax rates are likely to be increased, and by how much, in the next year or two. A brief visit to the local tax assessor to discuss these matters may be worthwhile before you finalize the deal.

2. Fire and theft insurance costs probably will add another one-half of 1 per cent of the home's value to your annual operating costs.

3. Upkeep, not including utilities, should be figured at about 1 to 2 per cent per year for a relatively new house, more for an older one.

4. There is no generalized guideline for utility costs — that is electricity, gas, water and telephone. You should check this out and make your own estimates.

5. The final, and usually the largest, cost in owning a home is the mortgage payments. This is discussed in detail in Chapter 6.

WISEGUIDE

In total, you can figure that the cost of owning a home is roughly 4 to 5 per cent of its value per year, not counting mortgage payments.

"The search"   Now, let's discuss "the search" — the actual process for finding the right house. You can skip some steps and take short-cuts if you like, but make sure you know what you are doing. As we mentioned previously, house-hunting is a time-consuming process. It is better to just accept this fact than to fight it.

To start, it's a good idea to take the time to visualize your ideal home. Talk it over with your spouse. What's important to the two of you — privacy, convenience to shopping areas, good schools, plenty of living space, a friendly neighborhood, quality construction that will eliminate most maintenance headaches, old-style charm, good resale possibilities, a modern kitchen? Get a sense in your own mind of just what you want.

Perhaps you can't afford your ideal house right away. But you can **Your "ideal" home:** set an objective to reach it in stages, first buying an acceptable home **a long-range goal?** that you are able to afford now, and then working your way slowly up to your ideal. (Incidentally, federal tax laws are specifically structured to encourage this kind of gradual step-up. These laws work this way: normally, your profit from the sale of a house — that is the difference between your original purchase price and the money you receive from selling the house — is taxable on your federal income tax return. But there is an important exception. Federal tax rules specify that you don't have to pay income tax on the profit if you put all the money back into another house within 12 months, or within 18 months if you are building a new home. So long as you keep moving up to houses that are always more expensive than the last, no tax payment is required. You can defer the taxes indefinitely this way. But if the day ever comes when you sell and buy a less expensive house or no house at all, watch out! All the untaxed profits that have been accumulating over the years are suddenly subject to taxation.)

Once you are settled in general terms on the type of house you are **Finding the right** looking for, you can start reviewing the possibilities in terms of **location** location. Don't run all over the place, looking at one house here and then another one way over there.

Almost all the experts say the best way to approach your search for a house is first to find the general neighborhood you want, and then to zero in on specific houses within that neighborhood.

An item of particular importance is the neighborhood's zoning rules. **Zoning rules** Few home-buyers know what this means, let alone look into it. Zoning rules are locally enacted ordinances that specify what kind of structure can be built in each neighborhood and how the buildings in that neighborhood can be used. Is it possible for someone to build a gas station down the street from your new home? The zoning ordinances should give the answer. Can the fellow next door turn his house into a funeral home or a boarding house? Again, the zoning ordinances should specify.

Good, fairly-enforced zoning rules are your ultimate assurance that the neighborhood will age gracefully and won't go sour with commercial development. Of course, in the past some zoning rules have been concocted solely to serve as a shield for keeping minority groups out of all-white neighborhoods. New federal anti-discrimination laws now make this kind of use illegal although, despite these laws, it certainly still exists.

It cannot be emphasized too much that the time you take to look into local zoning ordinances is time well spent.

How to check out the zoning rules

You can either check out a neighborhood's zoning rules with a lawyer or by visiting city hall. Real estate agents and, in some cases, banks will tend to dismiss your questions in this area by assuring you that everything is all right. They are not a particularly good source of information.

Not only is it important to know just what kind of building use and construction the zoning rules will permit in a neighborhood, but you also should find out how vigorously these rules are enforced. Most zoning ordinances permit the granting of "variances" where appropriate. Is every Tom, Dick and Harry given a variance to build whatever he wants? Or are variances given out sparingly? Ask your lawyer.

Other important factors in choosing a neighborhood

Besides zoning ordinances, there are a number of other factors you should review in terms of settling on a specific neighborhood where you will look for your house:

- Convenience to transportation.

- Convenience to shopping.

- Location and quality of schools.

- Availability of play areas for children.

- General attractiveness of the community.

- Absence of excessive traffic noises.

- Absence of smoke or unpleasant odors.

- Fire and police protection.

- Adequacy of garbage collection, sewerage and other municipal services.

- Present and anticipated real estate tax rates.

What you should know about tax rates

A note on this last item: Each community sets its own tax rate. Thus, in the same geographical area you may find one town with a $5 rate per $100 of assessed value and another town close by with a rate of $10 per $100 of assessed value. In addition, some communities may charge taxes on only 50 or 75 per cent of the assessed value, while others may charge on the full amount.

To confuse matters further, "assessed" valuation is not necessarily the same as "market" value, or the actual price you pay. Generally, however, all communities within a given region do follow the same uniform assessment procedures. Thus, all the communities may assess property at 50 per cent of market value or at some other agreed-on rate.

An example

For example, let's take a theoretical $20,000 home with an "assessed value" of $10,000. In a town with a $5 rate on 100 per cent of assessed valuation, taxes would amount to $500 per year. In a nearby town with a $9 rate on 100 per cent of assessed valuation, they would amount to $900. In another town with a $3 rate on 50 per cent of assessed valuation, they would amount to $150. And in still another

town with a $4 rate on 75 per cent of assessed valuation, taxes would come to $300 a year.

Our point is that you should make a thorough check of the tax rate in each of the communities where you are considering looking for a home. To go one step further, when looking at a specific house you should ask to see the owner's recent property tax bills. This will enable you to confirm your understanding of the local tax rate and will help you determine exactly how the rate applies to that house. Furthermore, you should try to get a sense of whether a big tax increase is in the works.

In older towns, the possibility of large rate increases usually is small. You should keep in mind, however, that in younger communities there is always the danger of a big tax increase to finance new schools or other municipal programs.

WISEGUIDE

Finally, in terms of type of neighborhood, you might want to consider a home in a planned residential community. Such communities are designed with churches, schools, shopping facilities, controlled traffic streets and community centers all in mind. And they usually are protected by strict land-use covenants and zoning ordinances. Of course, you may be turned off by the prospect of what you consider to be "sterile" living. But planned communities sometimes offer greater housing value for your money, and the homes in these communities usually work out to be fairly good long-term investments.

Is a "planned residential community" for you?

Almost every prospective home-buyer nourishes the hope, deep down inside, that he will find a fantastic bargain that everybody else has overlooked, particularly in a quaint older house. There aren't many. That's a dream you had better not count on coming true. You might as well be realistic and look for something nice that is priced within reason.

Which gets us to the next step in "the search." Once you have found the neighborhood or neighborhoods you want to concentrate on, it's a matter of finding the right house. You must get out and see what's available. A lot of legwork is called for. Real estate brokers and agents can offer you valuable leads. After all, their business is to know exactly what's on the market. But remember that they are salesmen who will make a commission from selling you a house. Don't let them rush you into something that isn't right.

Now the real legwork begins

On the other hand, some home buyers try to avoid agents and brokers altogether, figuring they can deal directly with the seller and save the 6 or 7 per cent brokerage commission. It is the seller, of course, who must pay this commission. But the theory goes that where there is no commission payment to inflate the price, the buyer is bound to get a break as well. This theory doesn't always work out in practice, however.

Should you avoid brokers and agents?

55

Buying a house

Many houses that are up for sale without an agent or broker are grossly overpriced to start with, more than offsetting any savings that might arise from elimination of a brokerage commission.

Something new or something old

Essentially, you have to choose between buying a new home or an older one. Terminology gets a bit foggy at this point, particularly when it comes to houses that are only two or three years old. Are these recently-built houses "new" or "old"? Real estate men get around the problem by listing two distinct categories: "brand new" homes, and "existing" homes. Once someone has lived in a house — even for a day — in the eyes of the experts it falls into the "existing" category.

The advantages of new houses

New homes have two main advantages to offer:

• They are "fresh." Their full life is ahead of them. If the builder has done his job properly, repairs will be minimal in the years immediately ahead.

• From an investment viewpoint, they tend to be a better buy. Prices of new homes have risen more rapidly, on average, than those of older homes.

The advantages of older houses

Older homes, on the other hand, have this to offer:

• They have withstood the test of time. If the original workmanship was poor, there is no mistaking it. You can see the cracks in the walls or the water marks in the basement. You know whether or not you are buying a lemon.

• They are more mellow. Trees are fully grown, and the character of the neighborhood is well established.

Whichever type of home you look at — new or used — seek quality fixtures and construction. They are your best guarantee of minimal repair bills and maximum resale value.

Bargaining with the seller

Be sure to make a written notation of any problems. If you decide you are interested in buying, you can use this list in bargaining for a better price. Although prices of newly-constructed homes tend to be non-negotiable, you would be foolish to buy an older house without first trying to bargain the seller down.

Does the builder have a good reputation?

It also is a good idea to find out the name of the builder and check his reputation. A builder tends to repeat the same patterns from house to house. If his work is sloppy on one, it probably will be the same on others. If he does quality work on one, it's a pretty good assurance that all his houses are well constructed.

While you probably can decide in general terms whether a house is in good condition, it would pay to retain a technical expert to give the house a thorough going-over. Do this only after you have made up your mind that you are really interested in buying the house. Your bank can recommend an expert to you, or you can find names in the Yellow Pages under "home inspection services." **It pays to have a technical inspection made**

Typical fee for a professional inspection of a house you are interested in buying is $50 to $100.

WISEGUIDE

In addition to looking at new and used conventional houses, there are three special categories of housing that you might want to consider: **Other types of housing**

- Cooperative apartments. When you buy a "co-op," you are buying a share in the overall apartment building. This share of ownership entitles you, in turn, to live in a specific apartment in that building. It is important to note, however, that you don't own the individual apartment itself. The drawback of this arrangement is that you cannot sell your share in the building to another individual without first obtaining the approval of the other owners (residents). Buying a co-op combines many of the advantages of apartment living with many of those of home ownership. You hold an equity in your own home, rather than paying rent to a landlord. And you are king of your own castle, although certainly not in the same absolute sense as if you bought a conventional home. **1. Cooperative apartments**

- Condominiums are similar to cooperative apartments, with one important legal exception. You own your specific apartment, not a share in the overall building. This leaves you free to sell to whomever you like. **2. Condominiums**

- Mobile homes are a story in themselves. Once thought of purely as shanty-type dwellings for people who wanted to be able to take their house with them when they moved, they have suddenly gained tremendous acceptance in the past decade. Approximately half a million American families a year now buy mobile homes. **3. Mobile homes**

Although mobile homes certainly aren't as large or as comfortable as most conventional houses, their quality has come up rapidly in recent years. And prices are low — roughly around $10,000.

WISEGUIDE

Let's assume that you have finally settled on a specific house. You and the seller have agreed on a price, and everything seems to be all set. **What to do once you have agreed to buy a specific house**

From this point on, you will need the help of a competent lawyer. He will make sure, for instance, that the contract contains an escape clause in case you are unable to obtain a mortgage. And he will guide you through the treacherous process known as "the closing" — that nervous little ceremony when the final papers are signed and you become actual owner of the house.

Finding a mortgage

Obtaining a mortgage at a reasonable interest rate is probably the most important step after you have arranged the purchase. Although you may be completely worn out from all the effort you have put into searching for the home, it may be worth your while to spend just a few more hours shopping around for the mortgage. This is because long-term cost differences between various mortgage terms and rates can completely overshadow any money you may have saved on the price of the house itself by bargaining with the seller. For instance, a typical $20,000, 30-year mortgage would end up costing you approximately $45,500 in total repayments over the term of the loan if the interest rate is 6½ per cent a year and $50,400 if the rate is 7½ per cent — a difference of nearly $5,000! Mortgages are discussed in detail in the next chapter.

Make sure you have the property surveyed

For your own protection, you should have the homesite surveyed before the deal is closed. Without a survey you won't know, until it is too late, whether the building encroaches on a neighbor's property or comes so close to the edge of the lot as to violate a local zoning or building code. Your bank or lawyer can help arrange a survey for you.

"Closing costs"

You also should be aware that you will have to pay certain "closing costs" on the day of the closing. These costs, in addition to your attorney's fees, include such items as fees for the title search, surveys and preparation of documents.

WISEGUIDE

Closing costs on a home purchase generally total somewhere between $200 and $1,000.

Preparing for moving day

And, of course, you also must leave yourself enough money to pay for moving into the house. The movers will insist on being paid in full, either in cash or by money order or certified check, on delivery of your belongings into your new home.

To many people, moving is the worst trauma of all in buying a house. It need not be. Each year, one out of every five American families moves, and a highly-complex business has sprung up to service their needs.

Two kinds of moves: interstate and local

In the world of moving companies, there are two basic kinds of moves: interstate and local. Each is governed by its own rules and procedures, about which you should be fully aware.

The rules for interstate moves

If you are moving from one state to another, the moving company's fee will be based on the total weight of your possessions as well as on the distance traveled and any special equipment or services you use. Generally, the rate is a specified number of dollars per 100 pounds for a move between two specific points.

Moving companies are quite willing to send over an estimator to try to figure out the total weight of all your items and the anticipated cost of the move. Chances are, however, that different estimators will come up with different answers. To get estimates as accurate as possible, be sure to show the estimators all your heavy possessions, including those in the attic, basement and garage.

A look at the rules for interstate moves

All interstate moves are governed by Interstate Commerce Commission regulations, which give you considerable protection.

WISEGUIDE

These ICC regulations specify, for instance, that the mover must do his best to abide by his promised pick-up and delivery dates, and must let you know promptly if there is going to be a delay. His estimates must be made on forms approved by the ICC. His rates must be available for your inspection. He must tell you beforehand where he will weigh the van carrying your goods. And after the move is completed, he must give you official tickets showing what the van weighed both before and after your belongings were added.

What the ICC's rules specify

Although it isn't usually done, you can follow the truck in your car to see the weighing. Or you can demand another weighing at your destination. If the load is at least 100 pounds under the weight claimed by the mover, he must pay for this second weighing. If not, you are stuck with the bill yourself.

Before contracting with you for an interstate move, the mover must give you a copy of the ICC's booklet, Summary of Information for Shippers of Household Goods. Under ICC rules, your goods cannot be moved until you sign a statement saying you have read this booklet.

The "weighing"

For local moves, procedures are much more informal. Regulation, where it exists, is on the state and local level.

The rules for local moves are different

Most local movers charge by the hour rather than by the pound. Typical hourly rates in a big city for a truck and two or three men might range from $20 to $40.

WISEGUIDE

As with long-distance movers, most local movers will be happy to send over an estimator. Even then, however, you will only receive an educated guess as to the cost of the move, not a binding contract. But a reputable company should come within 10 to 15 per cent of

An estimate is not binding on the mover

the estimate. Get three or four estimates, and beware if one is unusually low.That company may simply jack up the price later or use inexperienced men who will end up breaking half of what you own.

Should you buy extra insurance?

Insurance protection can be a sticky area when it comes to moving. If your property is damaged or lost, the mover isn't necessarily liable for paying the full value. His liability is by the pound. In a local move, the limit generally is 30 cents a pound per article or container. Interstate, the maximum is 60 cents a pound. Stop to think about it, and you will realize that this isn't very much.

To make sure you will be paid in full, you really need your own insurance. Your homeowners policy, if you have one, may already cover your possessions in transit. If not, add a rider. Or take out special insurance through your agent or mover.

WISEGUIDE

The premium rate for insurance to protect goods being moved is roughly $2.50 to $5 per $1,000 worth of goods, or about $50 to $100 for items valued at $20,000.

How to pack

If you want, the movers will pack everything for you in barrels or cartons. But the general rule is to leave only the more valuable and delicate items to them. These include expensive china, crystal and objects of art. You can usually handle everyday dishes and the like yourself.

Movers charge extra for what they pack, but on the other side of the coin they should pay for anything in their packages that breaks. The usual packing charge is $9.25 to $10.25 per barrel. This includes both packing and unpacking.

You can buy cartons from the mover and do the packing yourself

For about $1.50 to $2 each, movers can give you large-sized cartons and heavy tape in advance. It's best to have everything packed well ahead of time to avoid last-minute headaches and delays. Leave one box open until the last moment, however, for odds and ends.

When moving day finally arrives, make sure you draw up an inventory of everything that goes into the truck, with any existing damage itemized. Give a copy to the head mover. When the truck is unloaded, check your goods back against your inventory. Don't sign a receipt until you have done this.

Filing a claim against the mover

Incidentally, in interstate moves you are allowed up to nine months after delivery to file a claim, although it's best to do so as quickly as possible. The mover must in turn respond in 30 days, and pay or refuse to settle in 120. If you feel you haven't been treated fairly, you can write to the Director of the Bureau of Operations, Interstate Commerce Commission, Washington, D.C. 20423.

Another possible problem: selling your old house

Finally, we would like to discuss the other problem that sometimes arises when a family moves: how do you sell your existing house? Here are some tips:

● If your company is relocating you, there's a chance they will retain an outside firm to help you make the sale. Some of these firms will ask appraisers to look at your home. The firm may then offer to buy your house for the average evaluation. Most homeowners go along, and it saves everybody a lot of time and work.

● At the other extreme, you could try to sell your house on your own without even using an agent. This is risky business, and can prove to be very time-consuming. You might save the brokerage commission, but you could end up underselling your house because you are unable to attract enough good prospects.

Should you avoid brokers and agents?

● If you use an agent or broker, on the other hand, he should advise you on how much to ask and should give you some worthwhile hints on how to spruce up your house for buyers. He also can serve as a buffer in any dickering over price. For a limited time — a few days, at least — list your home exclusively with one broker. This gives him a chance to make the full commission, and provides an incentive for him to work hard for a quick sale.

Typical buying costs for a $27,000 house	
Professional appraisal	$ 75.00
Homesite survey	50.00
Termite inspection	30.00
Title examination	110.00
Title insurance	60.00
Preparation of documents	25.00
Credit report	15.00
Taxes and insurance previously paid by the seller	120.00
Legal fees	350.00
Other closing costs	100.00
Down payment	7,000.00
Total	**$7,935.00**

(Moving expenses and remodeling and redecorating costs are not included)

Typical annual operating costs for a $27,000 house	
Mortgage on $20,000 at 7½% interest for 20 years	$1,933.44
Real estate taxes	600.00
Electricity, gas, heat and water	540.00
Telephone	150.00
Maintenance	600.00
Homeowners insurance	150.00
Total	**$3,973.44**

Monthly cost: $331.12

How much should you ask?   Determining the asking price can be a difficult matter. If you ask too much, most brokers won't really push the house because they know it probably won't sell. If you ask too little, you end up short-changing yourself. The best bet is to rely on the advice of professional appraisers and agents, rather than your own prejudiced judgment.

WISEGUIDE   The biggest mistake in trying to sell a house, some brokers say, is to overprice it and then refuse to budge when a prospective buyer makes a reasonable offer. It can take a long time to sell a house this way.

Chapter 6

Finding the mortgage

There are two major steps involved in buying a house: finding the right home at the right price, and then negotiating the mortgage. The previous chapter dealt with the first step. This chapter describes the second.

Although buying the house and obtaining the mortgage are two separate transactions, both are finalized at the same ceremony — the "closing." The mortgage lender gives you the money, which you immediately hand over to the seller of the house. This payment in turn enables you to assume ownership of the home.

It actually is best, however, to do your preliminary mortgage shopping before you sign a contract to buy a house. This will give you an idea of how expensive a home you can afford, the size of the down payment you will have to make, and the anticipated mortgage interest rate and repayment terms. For your preliminary talks with representatives of mortgage lending concerns, take along details of your total income, savings and other assets, financial obligations (including debts) and employment record.

Begin your mortgage shopping early

The beauty of a mortgage is that it permits you to buy a house on the installment basis, paying the cost in equal monthly sums over a period of anywhere from 5 to 35 years.

WISEGUIDE

In effect, by taking out a mortgage, you are arranging to pay for a house out of your future income, rather than being forced to save up the full purchase price in advance. Without this kind of arrangement, few American families would ever be able to afford to buy a home of their own.

Paying for the house out of your future earnings

Mortgages, like other loans, represent a personal obligation on the part of the borrower to repay. From the lender's viewpoint, however, the ultimate security that he will get his money back is not so much your personal financial condition as it is the property behind the mortgage. If you fail to repay, the lender knows that he can always protect himself by "foreclosing" — that is, by taking title to your house, selling it off and then pocketing what you owe him. Any money that is left over from the sale price becomes yours. Fortunately, foreclosures are relatively rare, as indicated by the fact that only about one-half of 1 per cent of all residential mortgages currently on the books are in the process of being foreclosed.

What is "foreclosure"?

Finding the mortgage

Average mortgage interest rates on new homes	
1968	6.97%
1969	7.81%
1970	8.44%
1971	7.60%
1972	7.70%

As with other types of loans, you pay interest to a mortgage lender for the use of his money. And at current interest rates, you pay rather dearly. Although rates vary somewhat from lender to lender, during the last two years they have averaged approximately 7½ per cent (as the chart at left shows). This is extremely high by historic standards.

With rates so steep, a basic question arises: What would be the smart move for me to make — to buy now, or to put off my home-buying plans in hopes that interest rates will decline to more reasonable levels in the next two or three years? A strong argument can be made on either side of the issue. But one major problem with waiting is that home prices are rising so fast — an average of 6 per cent a year over the last five years — that the increased purchase price could more than offset any savings you might achieve from a lower-rate mortgage. And there is no real assurance that mortgage interest rates actually will decline. The best advice, then, seems to be this:

WISEGUIDE

If you have a good reason to buy a home, don't let today's high mortgage interest rates deter you.

Buy now or buy later? Here is an example

A simple example, based on a theoretical $28,000 house, will illustrate our point. Suppose, on the one hand, that you decide to buy right now. If you pay $8,000 of your own cash and finance the rest with a $20,000, 20-year mortgage at 7½ per cent annual interest, your monthly payments would come to just over $160. Suppose, on the other hand, that you wait two years to buy and that the price of this same house rises 6 per cent a year in the interim to $31,400. Let us suppose further that during this two-year period the interest rate on a mortgage declines to 6½ per cent. Will you have come out ahead financially by waiting? The answer, in this particular case, is no. And here is why: If two years from now you make the same down payment of $8,000, it would leave you with a $23,400 mortgage. And, even after taking into account your savings from the lower interest rate, the required payments on a mortgage this large will be nearly $175 a month — about $15 a month more than if you had bought right away.

Of course, you wouldn't want to make your decision solely on the basis of this one example. For one thing, our example is based on the assumption that home prices will continue to rise as sharply as they have in recent months — an assumption that may or may not turn out to be true. But, with conditions as they are today, the risk does seem to be greater in waiting to buy than in buying now.

How to protect yourself when taking out a high-cost mortgage

Furthermore, if you do take out a mortgage at today's high rates, there are ways to protect yourself. One is to insist on inclusion of a "prepayment" clause or, better yet, a "refinancing" clause in your mortgage contract. A prepayment clause enables you to speed up

repayment of the mortgage if you find that you have enough extra cash to do so. A refinancing clause goes one step further. It specifies that if interest rates go down you can replace your existing mortgage with a lower-rate one, subject to payment of certain penalties for making the switch. Obviously, lenders are not anxious to provide such a clause, but you should at least ask. You might discuss this matter with your lawyer before negotiating final mortgage terms with the lender.

Another possibility is a variable interest rate mortgage. This is just what the name implies. The interest rate, rather than being pre-set at an unchanging figure, will vary over the years in line with the fluctuations of interest rates in general. If interest rates go up, the lender will increase the rate on your mortgage. If they go down, he will be required to decrease your rate.

Mortgages with variable interest rates

Variable interest rate mortgages are a new and exciting development. This type of mortgage will work to your advantage if interest rates decline in the next few years from their current high levels. On the other hand, if rates go up you will find yourself paying even more.

WISEGUIDE

Although almost all home mortgages now provide for repayment in installments rather than in a single lump sum, this hasn't always been the case. It used to be that most mortgages ran for a fixed length of time — 10 or 15 years, for instance — at which point the entire mortgage "came due" and the full original amount had to be repaid. If you were unable to come up with the money, you could lose your home. The lender could always renew the mortgage for another 10 or 15 years, but on the other hand he could just as easily choose not to renew. You were completely at his mercy (you probably have seen those old silent movies where the mortgage lender is a sinister-looking character, wearing a black cape and top hat, who constantly leers gleefully into the camera over the prospect of being able to foreclose on some poor fellow's home when the mortgage comes due). The folly of this arrangement became horribly clear during the Great Depression of the 1930's, when many families lost their homes or farms after the local bank refused to renew their mortgage.

Most mortgages no longer "come due" on a single day

Out of that grim experience has come the so-called "self-amortizing" mortgage — by far the most popular type of mortgage in existence today. The basic idea behind this type of mortgage is to eliminate that traumatic day when the entire mortgage comes up for repayment, and to provide instead for orderly repayment over the entire term of the loan.

The advantage of a "self-amortizing" mortgage

Repayment of a self-amortizing mortgage is made in equal monthly installments, and each installment represents a combined payment of both interest and principal.

WISEGUIDE

How the mortgage is paid off

When the last payment is made, the loan is completely wiped off the books and you own your house free and clear of all debt (unless, of course, you have put up the house as collateral for another loan besides your mortgage).

The following table shows some typical monthly repayment schedules for varying sizes and lengths of self-amortizing mortgages, at varying interest rates. The stated monthly installments in the table, it should be noted, do not include real estate taxes or fire insurance premiums, which are usually added onto the monthly mortgage payments rather than being left for separate payment by you on your own.

Monthly mortgage repayments						
Amount of mortgage	Amount per month over 20 years			Amount per month over 30 years		
	7%	7½%	8%	7%	7½%	8%
$10,000	$ 77.53	$ 80.56	$ 83.65	$ 66.54	$ 69.92	$ 73.38
$15,000	116.30	120.84	125.47	99.80	104.88	110.07
$20,000	155.06	161.12	167.29	133.07	139.84	146.76
$25,000	193.83	201.40	209.12	166.34	174.80	183.45
$30,000	232.60	241.68	250.94	199.60	209.76	220.14
$40,000	310.12	322.24	334.58	266.14	279.69	293.52

Beware! Interest costs may be huge

What the above table doesn't show is that, at today's high interest rates, a huge amount of your money goes toward meeting interest costs. For instance, on a $25,000 30-year mortgage at 7½ per cent annual interest — a fairly typical example — interest payments over the 30 years would add up to a whopping $37,900. This is $12,900 more than the amount of the loan itself! In other words, you would end up paying back a total of $62,900 ($25,000 plus the $37,900 of interest) over the 30 years for the privilege of borrowing $25,000. Interest costs on the same mortgage at 7 per cent, by contrast, would total about $34,900 — or $3,000 less.

How you can save money by shopping around

Of course, this isn't a total disaster, since the interest is deductible on your federal tax return. But our example does point up the value of shopping around for the best terms. As you can see, even a difference of one-half of 1 per cent in interest rate can make a significant difference in your total dollar interest costs over the term of the mortgage.

Who will give you a mortgage?

In shopping around for the best rate, there are six basic mortgage sources you can go to. The three most important sources are:

The six basic sources for a mortgage

- Savings & loan assocations.

- Savings banks.

- Commercial banks.

Three other potential sources, which are less important, are:

- Life insurance companies.

- Mortgage companies.

- Miscellaneous sources (most notably the person from whom you are buying the house or a friend or relative).

Each type of lender tends to have its own regulations and preferences in terms of maximum size of mortgage, length of maturity, and degree of risk that it is willing to take. In addition, mortgage lending is a very personal business. What seems to be a good risk to one lender might attract nothing more than a shrug of the shoulders from another. You might conceivably be turned away from one lender's office, only to be greeted with open arms elsewhere.

Different lenders have different rules and policies

As a general rule, the larger the down payment you make, the lower the interest rate is likely to be.

WISEGUIDE

This is because the lender's risk is reduced if you put up more of your own cash. The actual difference in interest rates between putting up a large down payment or a small one will probably be somewhere in the range of from one-eighth to one-half of a percentage point.

How this works

How do you go about finding someone willing to give you the specific mortgage you need? You can always start by visiting your local bank or savings & loan. If you already do business with a particular institution in one form or another (a savings or checking account, for instance), the people there may be a little more sympathetic to your mortgage needs. Or you can ask a friend or business associate where he found his mortgage. In addition, local lawyers and real estate brokers should know which institutions are active mortgage lenders at the moment. Formal introductions of this sort are by no means a necessity, however. After all, mortgage lenders are in the business of making loans, and, even if they have never met you before, will willingly grant you a mortgage so long as they view the deal in essentially favorable terms. Don't be shy about asking.

Who will give you a mortgage?

There are two broad factors that all mortgage lenders will take into consideration:

Two factors that lenders consider

67

- The value and condition of the property.

- Your ability to repay.

In the previous chapter, we mentioned two important rules of thumb for determining how expensive a home you can afford:
1) the house should cost no more than approximately 2½ times your annual salary;
2) the combined monthly cost of paying off the mortgage, maintaining the home and repaying your other debts should not exceed one-third of your monthly take-home pay. Mortgage lenders are well aware of these guidelines and, to play it safe, probably will not grant you a loan in excess of them.

WISEGUIDE

You also should know that mortgage lenders prefer borrowers with good, steady jobs.

What a lender looks for in a borrower

Are you in some sort of highly speculative business where you could either make a million or go broke? You may have difficulty finding a mortgage. Do you have a bad record of rent or debt repayments? Again, this certainly won't work in your favor. On the other hand, do you have a stable family life, a blemish-free financial record and a good job? Then you are just the type of person a mortgage lender likes to do business with.

What if you feel that you are being denied a mortgage on the basis of your race, religion or nationality? This is another matter altogether. This type of discrimination is illegal under the Fair Housing Section of the 1968 Civil Rights Act, and you may have grounds for legal action.

The major mortgage lenders:

Let's take a closer look at the major sources of mortgages, with an eye toward the particular preferences of each.

1. Savings & loans

Savings & loan associations are by far the biggest factor in mortgage lending, accounting for approximately 40 per cent of all residential mortgages in the U.S. Almost all their money is channeled into granting mortgages to individual home-buyers, and they generally are willing to take a greater degree of risk than most other types of lenders. On the other side of the coin, they tend to charge somewhat higher interest rates.

Under federal rules, S & Ls are permitted to lend up to 95 per cent of the "appraised value" of a house (more on "appraised value" later in this chapter), up to a maximum $36,000 loan. On loans from $36,000 to $45,000, the limit is 90 per cent. Savings & loans may prove to be your best bet if you have little money of your own for a down payment.

2. Savings banks

Savings banks, like savings & loans, serve the specific function of taking in savers' funds and then redirecting the money into home mortgages. Unlike savings & loans, however, you may not be able to find a savings bank in your community. This is because savings banks are unique to 18 states, primarily in the northeast. Regulations vary from state to state, but savings banks as a group tend to lie somewhere between savings & loans and commercial banks in terms of willingness to take risk in granting mortgages.

3. Commercial banks

Commercial banks, along with savings & loans and savings banks, are the third major factor in mortgage lending. These three types of institutions combined control roughly 70 per cent of the residential mortgage lending market, and they should be your prime targets in your search.

Commercial banks are the most conservative lenders of the three, and as a result of their caution are able to charge somewhat lower interest rates on average. In turn, these banks' terms tend to be a bit more stringent. For instance, nationally-chartered commercial banks are barred from granting mortgages in excess of 30 years' maturity or from putting up more than 90 per cent of the appraised value of a house; in reality, most won't go beyond 25 years and 80 per cent. If you have the money for a large down payment and have a relatively clean financial record, you might apply for a mortgage at a commercial bank. If not, you will have to go elsewhere and probably pay slightly higher interest as a result.

4. Life insurance companies

Life insurance companies used to be fairly active mortgage lenders on residential property, but have been withdrawing from this market in recent years. A life insurance company mortgage, if you can still find one, generally offers the combined advantages of low interest and long maturity. The drawback is that most insurance companies require that you put up a large down payment. Insurance company mortgages, when available, are obtained mainly through mortgage brokers rather than directly from the insurance company itself.

5. Mortgage companies

Mortgage companies are privately-owned firms that specialize exclusively in granting mortgage loans. Terms usually are flexible, but the interest rate often is a bit higher than at other sources. It's best to avoid mortgage companies, unless you simply cannot find a mortgage anywhere else.

6. Miscellaneous sources

Finally, there is always the possibility of working out long-term financing arrangements directly with the seller of the house or of talking a friend or relative into lending you the money. This is a tricky area where you will find no clear signs along the road to guide you. You might be able to work out excellent terms, particularly if the seller is anxious to unload his house and grants you a low interest rate as an incentive to buy. The best idea is to check the terms carefully against alternative sources to find out exactly what you are getting into before you sign up. The same holds true when you are dealing through a real estate broker who offers, for your convenience, to arrange the mortgage. This can prove to be a useful and time-saving service, but don't accept the offer without checking it out. The same rule also applies to housing developments where the builder offers to arrange financing as part of an overall package deal; see if you can get better terms elsewhere before signing up.

Should your mortgage be insured? This is an important decision

To insure or not to insure? That is another question facing the prospective mortgage borrower. What we are talking about is the choice between taking out a "conventional" mortgage — that is, one without any insurance guarantee — or a government-guaranteed one. The latter category also includes mortgages that are insured by private insurance companies; this is a rather recent development, but a fairly significant one.

WISEGUIDE

Mortgage insurance is simply what the term implies; for an added fee, you buy insurance protection that guarantees that the lender will get his money back.

How mortgage insurance works

If you are unable to repay on your own, then the government agency or private insurance company that has provided the insurance must cough up the cash. You still receive your loan directly from a mortgage lender, as you would for a conventional mortgage. The only difference is that a third party — either the government agency or the private insurance company — has entered the picture, providing a guarantee that the loan will be paid off.

Why, you might ask, should you pay extra for insurance when it only serves to protect the lender and not yourself? First off, perhaps the lender won't grant you a mortgage unless you agree to take out insurance. In that case you have no choice if you want to get the loan. One example is that federal regulations prohibit federally-chartered savings & loan associations from issuing 95 per cent mortgages without insurance.

Second, in return for the guarantee that he will get his money back regardless of whether you are personally able to repay, the mortgage lender may give you a somewhat lower interest rate. Of course, you also will be paying a fee in most cases for the insurance itself. The net result probably will be a stalemate. This is because the lender's concession in terms of lower interest usually just about equals the fee you pay for the insurance.

WISEGUIDE

The big advantage of insuring your mortgage is that it enables you to make a smaller down payment and obtain longer repayment terms.

When not to use insurance

For instance, you may find it impossible to arrange a 30-year, 90 per cent mortgage unless you agree to insure. If, on the other hand, you are making a big down payment, then taking out insurance doesn't make much sense. This kind of loan generally involves a relatively low degree of risk for the lender, so he should give you his best interest rate regardless of whether you insure or not. You shouldn't pay for insurance when you won't be able to obtain better mortgage terms in return.

The most important source of mortgage insurance is the Federal Housing Authority, a 39-year-old government agency that is in business specifically to insure mortgages and thus make it easier for individuals to obtain the money to buy a home. A second important governmental agency in this area is the Veterans Administration, which insures home mortgages for present and former servicemen who meet certain eligibility requirements. VA-insured loans are sometimes referred to as "GI mortgages." **The FHA and VA**

Cost of FHA insurance is one-half of 1 per cent a year, calculated annually on the remaining unpaid balance of the mortgage. There is no charge, however, for VA insurance; this is simply a free benefit offered to qualifying servicemen and veterans. Furthermore, the VA will insure a mortgage for up to 100 per cent of the appraised value of a house, enabling the buyer to assume ownership on a no-cash-down basis. VA-insured mortgages can run for a maximum length of up to 30 years (the same as an FHA-insured mortgage). **The cost of FHA insurance**

VA-insured mortgages are one of the few real bargains left in the world of finance.

WISEGUIDE

Government insurance is not an absolute blessing, however. One of the problems is that both the FHA and VA specify that they will not insure any mortgage with an interest rate in excess of a specified amount. The current maximum is 8½ per cent (plus, in the case of the FHA, another one-half of 1 per cent for the cost of the insurance itself). In other words, if you take out a 9 per cent mortgage the rules specify that neither the FHA nor VA can insure it. This is fine in the sense that it might protect you from paying excessively high interest rates. But what happens when the general level of mortgage rates goes well above 8½ per cent? The answer is that most lenders simply refuse to issue any more FHA or VA-insured loans. These lenders realize that under these circumstances they can make more money for themselves by concentrating solely on conventional loans, where there is no limit. **What happens if the interest rate exceeds the FHA limit?**

One way out of this problem is for the lender to charge "points" on FHA and VA-insured loans when the general level of interest rates goes above the 8½ per cent ceiling. One "point" equals 1 per cent of the mortgage; on a $20,000 mortgage, for instance, one point would equal $200. If you were charged five points on a $20,000 loan, you would have to agree to pay $1,000 in order to get **Watch out for "points"**

Finding the mortgage

the loan. Charging points is a way, then, for the lender to jack up the interest rate without being in technical violation of the rate ceilings imposed by the FHA and VA.

In rough terms, each "point" that you pay is equivalent to paying an additional one-eighth of 1 per cent interest over the length of the mortgage.

Private insurance may be less expensive

Although FHA and VA insurance are by far the dominant types, a number of private mortgage insurance companies have recently been edging their way into this field. These companies still are relatively small in terms of total amount of mortgage insurance outstanding, but it is quite possible that they will prove to be a powerful force in the years to come unless the FHA does something to meet the competition. The main advantage of dealing with one of these companies, instead of the FHA, is that you avoid a lot of governmental red tape. In addition, in some cases the private insurers actually charge lower premium rates for their insurance. Your local bank or savings & loan should be able to give you more information.

How much will the lender give you?

Just how big a mortgage can you get? One consideration is the "appraised" value of the house. The lender, seeking to protect himself, will send out his own appraisers to evaluate the home's worth. And the figure the appraisers come up with may or may not equal what you have agreed to pay for the house. If it is less, you should take note that your 80 per cent mortgage — or whatever percentage amount — will not total 80 per cent of the amount you are paying but, instead, 80 per cent of what the bank says the house is actually worth. This is a point to consider in advance, since it may mean that you have to put up a larger cash down payment than you anticipated.

A second factor is that it usually is easier to obtain a large mortgage on a new home than on an older one. This is because most lenders are willing to take a bigger risk on a new home, on the assumption that it would be easier to resell if the mortgage had to be foreclosed.

Nationwide, the average mortgage on new homes comes to about 74 per cent of the value, versus about 72 per cent on existing houses.

Buying without any down payment at all

What happens if you can't afford a down payment, but you still want to buy a house? You can always ask the seller whether he is willing to let you give him a personal note to cover the down payment, or you can seek a second mortgage for the amount. But this is extremely risky business. You could end up so overextended financially that you will have no chance of keeping up your payments. If you can't afford a down payment out of your own savings, it's best to put off any home-buying until you can.

What happens if you miss a mortgage payment? First off, the mortgage lender may have the legal right to foreclose on his loan and sell your house to pay his debt. But most prefer not to, unless absolutely necessary. It's best to talk the matter over with the lender before it reaches the crisis stage. If you are unable to keep up your payments because of sickness, temporary unemployment or a like problem, most lenders will try to help you out by lowering or even temporarily suspending your monthly payments.

Missed payments — what to do

Finally, a word about life insurance. Before granting you a mortgage, most lenders will ask about the amount of insurance coverage you have in case of your death. Full coverage in an amount equal to the mortgage isn't essential, but it will be a plus factor in your favor. An alternative is take out a specially-tailored "decreasing term" insurance policy, with the coverage always equal to the latest unpaid balance of the mortgage. You can ask either the lender or your insurance agent about such coverage.

Mortgage life insurance

Protecting your home and possessions

Once you buy a house, you will become responsible for obtaining adequate insurance coverage. For one thing, the mortgage lender will insist at the very minimum that you insure the house itself against damage from fire and lightning. Additionally, you will probably want to insure your personal belongings, including the furniture and other contents of the house. Even if you rent an apartment, your possessions may be valuable enough to merit some sort of basic insurance protection.

Insurance certainly won't prevent costly accidents from happening. But it will give you the money to replace what you lose.

How insurance coverage works

The principle of insurance is the sharing of risks. Many persons pay premiums that create a large pot of cash that will be available to the few who suffer major misfortune.

Is a homeowners policy best for you?

The "homeowners" policy, introduced in the mid-50's, combines all major types of coverage in a single insurance plan. Apart from being less complicated, the efficiencies inherent in this package approach make it less expensive than buying different types of coverage separately.

WISEGUIDE

Except in unusual circumstances, a homeowners policy will prove to be the best kind of insurance coverage you can buy for your house and personal possessions.

Americans now spend nearly $3 billion in premiums a year for homeowners coverage, making this one of the most popular types of coverage in all insurance.

Four types of homeowners policies:

Just what sort of protection does a homeowners policy provide? There are actually four basic types of homeowners policies, each with its own special areas of coverage:

1. Basic Form

● Least expensive is the Basic Form policy, which is sometimes referred to as Homeowners 1 or Homeowners A. It protects your home and personal property against damage from 11 causes: fire or lightning; windstorm or hail; explosion; riots; damage from aircraft; damage from vehicles; sudden and accidental damage from smoke; vandalism and malicious mischief; theft; damage to glass

that is part of an insured building; and loss of personal property that is removed from an "endangered" building.

● Next comes the Broad Form or Homeowners 2. It protects against all 11 perils covered in the Basic Form policy, plus damage from the following additional causes: falling objects; collapse of the building; damage from the weight of ice, snow or sleet; certain accidental damage to, or resulting from, steam and water systems; and certain types of damage involving electrical equipment, including electrical appliances. Similar coverage is available to tenants, under the names Tenants Form and Homeowners 4.

2. Broad Form

● Third is the Comprehensive Form. This type also goes under a variety of other names, including Homeowners 5, Homeowners C and "all risks". As that last term implies, this is the most comprehensive type of homeowners policy available. Essentially, you are protected against everything *except* damage resulting from earthquake, landslide, flood, surface water, waves, tidal water, sewer back-ups, seepage, war and nuclear radiation (in the case of some of these exceptions — such as earthquake and flood — there are separate policies available that will provide you with protection if you want to buy it).

3. Comprehensive Form

● Finally comes Special Form, also referred to as Homeowners 3. This provides the full Comprehensive Form coverage on your house, together with the lesser Broad Form coverage on the contents.

4. Special Form

Note that none of these forms of homeowners insurance has anything to do with damage or injury resulting from an automobile accident. Automobile insurance is a totally separate matter; it is discussed in the next chapter.

Special Form and Broad Form are the two most popular types of homeowners policies. One or the other is probably best for your

WISEGUIDE

In addition to paying for damage to your property, almost all homeowners policies provide personal liability protection. This simply means that if someone is injured in an accident on your property or in an accident away from your property that is caused by a member of your family, you are insured against financial loss if the victim sues. The limit is $25,000, although you can pay an extra premium and increase this limit if you want. Did your dog bite Jimmy's piano teacher? You are insured. Did Jimmy himself accidentally break a friend's arm playing basketball, and the friend's parents have gone to court? Again, the insurance coverage applies.

What is liability coverage?

Finally, most homeowners policies also provide three other kinds of protection:

Three other types of coverage

• Medical payments, if someone outside your family is injured on your property. The maximum usually is only $500 per person.

• Damage to other people's property. An example: you accidentally knock over and break your next door neighbor's favorite Chinese vase. Chances are your homeowners policy will cover at least part of the loss.

• Extra living expenses in the event your home is damaged by fire or other disaster and you have to move into a hotel or motel while it is being repaired.

**How the insurance
company decides what
to charge for your policy**

How much will you have to pay to buy a homeowners policy? The cost can vary a lot, depending on a number of different factors. For instance, Comprehensive Form is obviously more expensive than Broad Form, and Broad Form in turn more expensive than Basic Form. Also, the location of your home will have a bearing on the cost of your insurance. If you live in a rough-and-tough, high-crime neighborhood or in a community noted for its poor fire department, you will end up paying a higher premium. The condition of your house also counts, as does the amount of coverage you take out. Finally, consideration is given to the past record of wind damage, hailstorms, tornadoes and hurricanes in your locale.

WISEGUIDE

The only real way to measure all these factors and come up with an accurate cost for a homeowners policy that fits your needs is to talk it over with an insurance broker or agent.

**The value of shopping
around for insurance**

Rates for exactly the same coverage will vary among different insurance companies, however. So it might be worth your while to do a little shopping around. It is a good idea to price your insurance needs with three different brokers.

**An important rule:
insure your home at 80
per cent of value**

One of the basic rules of thumb for homeowners insurance (or, for that matter, for fire insurance if you decide for some reason to buy only that particular coverage) is that you should insure your house for 80 per cent of its replacement cost, not counting the value of the land. This is 80 per cent of the amount it would cost you to rebuild your existing house or buy a comparable new one. In fact, with house prices rising so rapidly in recent years, you may find that you are currently under-insured. It's best to review your insurance needs every two or three years to make sure your insurance coverage is up to date.

WISEGUIDE

If you want to reduce the risk that your insurance coverage will fall behind the value of your house, you can get a special "inflation guard" provision in your homeowners policy. This will automatically increase your insurance coverage 1 per cent every three months.

Pay special attention to the personal property coverage that is provided by your homeowners policy. This coverage protects your furniture, appliances, clothing, jewelry, etc., as opposed to the house itself. Most homeowners policies protect this property in a total amount equal to 50 per cent of the coverage on the house. In other words, if your house is insured for $25,000, your personal property is insured for 50 per cent of that, or $12,500. **Do I have enough insurance for my personal property?**

Is that adequate? Only you can tell. Take an inventory, and see what sort of figure you come up with. If you find that the value of your property is far greater than the coverage provided by your homeowners insurance, contact your broker about taking out extra personal property coverage.

Insurance companies will only pay you the replacement cost, less depreciation, of any item that is destroyed or stolen. Let's take the case of a desk that is five years old and would cost $200 to replace. The insurance company would pay something in the neighborhood of $150, on the basis that the actual value of your desk had declined to that level in the five years you owned it. **What you get from your insurance**

It is extremely important that you keep good records in the event you ever need to make an insurance claim. If your house burns down, it will be easy, of course, to prove that the house is gone. But how will you prove exactly what was inside? One answer is to make a detailed inventory and keep it in a safe deposit box or some other secure place outside your home. Update it every two or three years. Also, keep all receipts for major purchases. **Filing a claim — the need for good records**

Insurance agents advise that the best way of all to prove exactly what you own is to take pictures of all your furniture and valuables and then store these pictures in your office or in a safe deposit box. **WISEGUIDE**

Certain items must be specifically listed on your insurance policy if you hope to collect from the insurer in the event of theft or damage. These include: **What items must be listed separately on my policy?**

- cameras

- expensive jewelry

- furs

- paintings and other art

- outboard-engine boats

- snowmobiles

**Protecting your home
and possessions**

It will probably cost you extra to insure these items, but it will be worth it. You will find, however, that it is virtually impossible to insure cash, and insurance companies will not pay such claims.

How to arrange for insurance
How do you go about arranging for insurance coverage? In some cases, your mortgage lender will offer to arrange all the insurance you need and to add the cost on to your monthly mortgage installments. This may be convenient for you, but it is unlikely that the lender will be giving you much of a bargain financially. Feel free to shop around for similar insurance at lower cost.

WISEGUIDE

Only insure against major losses, like your house. If it burns down you stand to lose everything. Insuring against a minor loss, such as a $50 ring with sentimental value, is a waste of money.

"Deductible" policies
Deductible-type insurance provides that, in return for a lower premium rate, you will personally assume liability for the first $50 or $100 or whatever of damage. This approach makes a lot of sense, in that it saves you money without leaving you exposed to major losses.

Are there gaps in my coverage?
Are there any major gaps in your insurance protection? Besides your basic homeowners policy, there are three other major types of insurance coverage that you might look into:

Earthquakes
● Earthquake insurance. This is available throughout the nation, although very few people actually buy it. Is there any risk of an earthquake in your particular locale? If yes, look into earthquake coverage before it is too late.

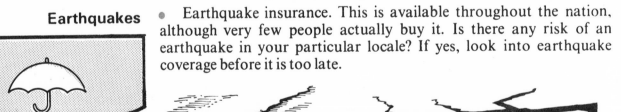

Floods
● Even more important, perhaps, is flood insurance. When a major flood strikes, thousands of homes can be wiped out. In the aftermath it almost always turns out that hardly any of the families were insured. Yet the federal government subsidizes a low-cost program of flood insurance. A policy on a single-family home valued at $17,500 and insured for flood damage up to $10,000 would cost $25 a year regardless of location.

• Personal liability insurance is another important area. Although basic liability coverage of $25,000 is included in most homeowners policies, this isn't very much. It only costs about $2 a year to increase the limit to $50,000 and about $3 a year to increase it to $100,000. This is a bargain.

Personal liability

There is always the possibility that, rather than having too little insurance, you are over-insured. This is fairly rare, but it does happen. Perhaps an overly zealous agent talked you into buying all sorts of coverage you don't need.

Am I over-insured?

Too much insurance is as wasteful as too little. No matter how much insurance coverage you buy, the insurer will never pay you any more than the amount of your actual loss.

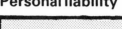
WISEGUIDE

If you want, you can insure against almost anything — so long as you are willing to pay the price. Some examples:

Other types of insurance coverage

• If you own an expensive pet, you can insure for veterinary costs or against the pet's death. This kind of insurance is used mostly for show dogs. Valuable horses and cows also can be insured. The cost is high, however.

• Some actors and actresses insure specific parts of their body. Betty Grable, for instance, insured her legs for $1 million.

• Valuable stamps, coins and jewelry are well worth insuring against theft. This is relatively inexpensive — as low as 20 cents a year per $100 of insurance — if you leave the item or items in a safe deposit box. If not, the rate can run as high as $2.80 per $100.

• You can insure against the possibility that your child will quit college or be kicked out. Most colleges will refuse to refund the tuition in that case. Insurance will.

• If you use contact lenses, you can insure them against damage or loss.

• You can even go to the extreme of insuring an expensive picnic or other outing against being canceled by rain. The high cost of this kind of coverage hardly makes it worth buying, however.

Never insure against minor losses which you could easily meet out of your own pocket. Insurance should be reserved for possibilities that would prove to be a financial hardship.

WISEGUIDE

Chapter 8

Owning a car

The Real Cost

An estimated 80 per cent of all American families own at least one automobile. Are you among them? If so, this chapter, with money-saving information about buying and maintaining a car and buying insurance coverage, is for you.

Ways to hold down your costs

If you were to sit down and figure out the full cost of owning an automobile, you probably would find that it represents the third largest item in your budget, behind housing and food. But there are ways to hold down this cost, and these ways involve a number of basic areas of decision:

- When is the most economical time to trade in my existing car for another one?

- Should I buy a new or used car?

- What is the actual cost difference between a compact model, an intermediate-sized car and a luxury model, and how should I decide which type to buy?

- Once I have chosen a car, how do I bargain with the dealer to make sure I have obtained the best possible price?

- How much will optional accessories really cost me in the long run, and which ones are worth buying?

- How can I save safely on upkeep?

- How can I save on insurance?

Each of these important questions is discussed in this chapter.

Car prices are rising rapidly

Like almost everything else, the average price of new cars has been rising rapidly in recent years. If you are about to go new-car shopping for the first time in several years, you may be in for a bit of a surprise — especially if you still expect to be able to find something in the $2,000-to-$2,500 price range.

WISEGUIDE

The average price for a new car is now close to $3,500 plus options, which can easily add another $1,000 to the bill.

How much does it really cost to own a car?

Furthermore, your initial purchase price is only part of the cost. According to a study by the Federal Highway Administration, the full cost of owning a full-sized car is approximately 13.6 cents for each mile driven, or a total of approximately $1,360 a year. This estimate is based on the purchase of a new four-door sedan with a list price of $4,400 that is driven 100,000 miles over a period of ten years and then relegated to the junk heap. (See page 93.)

Of course, chances are that you won't actually hold onto your own car that long. Additionally, you may not average anything like 10,000 miles of driving a year. But this government study of car costs will nonetheless give you a general idea of how much you probably are spending on your car and where you might be able to cut back. The study breaks down the per-mile cost of driving as follows:

Per-mile costs:

Depreciation   **4.4¢**

● Depreciation — the steady decline in your car's market value because of aging and "wear and tear" — comes to 4.4 cents per mile. This represents the original purchase price spread over the 10 years of ownership. However, approximately half of the total depreciation is squeezed into the first two years of ownership, so that if you sell your car within two or three years your per-mile depreciation costs will actually be much higher than the 4.4 cent, 10-year average. One lesson to be learned here is that the longer you hold onto your car, the lower the average per-mile depreciation.

Maintenance, accessories, parts and tires come to 2.6 cents a mile. The biggest portion occurs during the fourth through seventh years, when original parts often begin failing and have to be replaced.

Maintenance   **2.6¢**

● Gas and oil, excluding taxes, total 2.1 cents a mile.

Gas and oil   **2.1¢**

● Garages, parking and tolls come to 1.8 cents a mile.

Parking   **1.8¢**

● Insurance works out to 1.4 cents a mile. It should be noted that this is a national average. For many car owners insurance costs are considerably higher.

Insurance   **1.4¢**

● State and federal taxes come to 1.3 cents per mile driven.

Taxes   **1.3¢**

As you can see, the costs of ownership are spread fairly evenly among the six factors, although depreciation does take a somewhat bigger bite than the rest.

Why you must do your homework

The initial purchase price is one of the most important areas for potential savings. To make sure you get the best price possible, however, it is important that you do a little homework before you actually visit any dealers' car lots.

What kind of car do you need — big or small, new or used? How much can you afford to spend? Which types of optional equipment should you buy? Do you need financing, and if so where can you arrange it at the most reasonable rate of interest?

A car dealer's showroom, where you may be subjected to high-pressure sales tactics and outright trickery, is no place to make such decisions.

If you intend to be cost-conscious, you should take the time to review your needs in advance. Then you should shop around for the minimum-sized car that meets these needs.

WISEGUIDE

How to decide   Factors that you should take into consideration include the size of your family, the amount of mileage the car will be driven each year and the amount of money you are willing to spend. When you come right down to it, probably the cheapest form of transportation is to buy a run-down old car for $50 or $100 and drive it until it simply won't go anymore. But most people are willing to spend extra cash in order to buy a car that will be attractive, safe and comfortable.

Size categories: Domestic-made cars are divided into four basic size categories, each with its own price range:

1. Subcompacts

• Subcompacts include Vega, Pinto and Gremlin, as well as such popular foreign makes as Volkswagen, Datsun and Toyota. List prices, without options, generally range from about $2,000 to $2,600. For the most part, only two adults can ride in a subcompact with any degree of comfort.

2. Compacts

• Compacts include Dodge Dart, Plymouth Valiant, Ford Maverick, Chevrolet Nova, Mercury Comet, Pontiac Ventura II, Oldsmobile Omega and Hornet Hatchback. List prices are from about $2,600 to $2,900. Typically, a compact is about two feet longer than a subcompact and will accomodate two adults and two small children fairly comfortably.

3. Intermediates

• Intermediate cars include Ford Torino, Chevrolet Chevelle, Dodge Coronet and AMC Matador. List prices range from about $3,000 to $3,300. Intermediates are about 1½ feet longer and half a foot wider than compacts and are ideal for many younger families who cannot afford a full-sized car.

4. Full-sized cars

• Full-sized cars include a wide range of different models, such as Chevrolet Biscayne, Bel Air and Impala, Dodge Polara, Plymouth Fury, Ford Custom, Galaxy and LTD, Buick Le Sabre, Oldsmobile Delta 88, AMC Ambassador, Mercury Monterey and Chrysler Newport. List prices start at about $4,000.

Other differences   In addition to differences in price range and amount of passenger space, there are a number of other basic distinctions between large and small cars. Full-sized cars tend to ride more smoothly, often are safer in accidents and are more stable on the open highway.

Smaller cars, by contrast, tend to handle more easily in city traffic, usually have higher resale values in relation to original price and are much more economical to operate.

WISEGUIDE

Some experts say that the average annual cost of maintaining and operating a large luxury car is approximately twice that of a compact.

New or used?   Another basic question is whether to buy a new or used car. This is largely a matter of your personal preference and financial situation.

Can you afford a new car? If so, you probably are better going that route. But you can find some good buys in used cars two to three years old if you look carefully.

How long should you hold onto your car before trading it in for another? The latest evidence suggests two possible courses of action as most economical — change cars approximately every three years or hold onto your car for its full useful life and only trade it in when it becomes dangerous to drive or overly expensive to repair. Of course, style and comfort may outrule economic consideration. But if you want to be cost-conscious you should be aware that it generally is less expensive to keep driving a mechanically-sound old car than to trade it in. When repair costs finally get totally out of hand, however, the time has come to search for something new.

Deciding when it's time to trade in

You will find that the new-car market can be an incredibly complex place. There are about 350 American-made and 250 foreign models to choose from, each offering its own special set of optional accessories.

    The best approach is to first settle on the size car you need, then focus on two or three models within that size range, and finally shop around at various new-car showrooms of authorized dealers in those particular cars.

Buying a new car

You must be prepared to bargain over the price of a new car.

WISEGUIDE

Almost every new-car dealer asks a high price to start. If you don't go along with the bargaining game, you will undoubtedly end up paying much more than is necessary.

    Federal law requires that every new car carry a sticker listing the manufacturer's suggested list price as well as the dealer's charges for optional equipment, freight and dealer preparation. If the sticker is not on the car, demand to see it. It is your main reference point for price.

    However, you should consider the official sticker price as the starting point for your negotiations, not as the final price. (In the case of some foreign cars, however, you will find that dealers are unwilling to go below the sticker price.) In fact, only 18 per cent of all new car buyers end up paying anything close to list price.

The dealer's initial asking price will be high

How much did the dealer actually pay the manufacturer for the car? That is perhaps the most important question of all in your negotiations. If you know just how much the dealer paid, then you will have a pretty good idea of how far you can bargain him down. You should never negotiate to buy a car without knowing this price.

The manufacturer's price — the key number in your bargaining

There are two basic ways for determining the manufacturer's price:

How to determine the manufacturer's price

• First, you can calculate it yourself by taking the bottom figure on the official price sticker and then subtracting the transportation charge that is listed on the sticker. For a subcompact or compact car, multiply the resulting figure by 0.85 to come up with the approximate manufacturer's price. For intermediate cars plus Plymouth Fury and Dodge Polara, multiply by 0.815. And for all other full-sized cars, multiply by 0.78. Finally, add back the transportation charge, and you will have a pretty good idea of what the dealer has paid the manufacturer.

• A second way is to look up the exact price in a standard reference work. At least two organizations — United Auto Brokers and Masterson Fleet Auto — will sell you a computer printout of detailed price data on any car for about $7. There also are a number of books that list this same information. Perhaps your bank lending officer has a copy that he will let you borrow.

The dealer's mark-up

Of course, the manufacturer's price doesn't include any margin for dealer overhead or profit. Typically, the minimum dealer mark-up to cover these items is about $300. In some large cities where competition among car dealers is intense, however, you may be able to buy a new car for as little as $100 over the manufacturer's price. In rural areas, on the other hand, you may end up paying close to the sticker price.

WISEGUIDE

If you really want to pay rock-bottom price, you should wait for the right time of year to buy.

Late summer and early fall — just before the new models come out — is your best bet. Often, you can get a new car at a discount of 20 per cent or more from list price then. But you will truly save money only if you keep this car for at least three or four years, because it will suffer an immediate decline in value as soon as the new models are introduced. Additionally, you may not get as wide a choice of colors and options as you would earlier in the production year.

The next best time to buy is during the winter months — particularly from mid-December to late February. These usually are slow days in the new-car business, so that dealers are anxious to sell whatever they can, even if they have to give a better price than they really want.

Imported cars, by the way, don't usually show the same seasonal price patterns that domestic cars do, partly because year-to-year design changes are less drastic.

Tricks dealers play

New-car dealers have all sorts of tricks up their sleeves, and one of them is to try to tempt you to buy from them by offering a high trade-in price for your existing car. If you aren't careful, the dealer may simply jack up the price you are paying for the new car to offset the bonus he is giving you for your old car.

The dealer will actually know almost exactly what your old car is worth. To be in a position to bargain effectively, you should have this information at your fingertips too. You can either take the car around to a few used-car dealers to find out what they are willing to offer you, or you can look up the latest market value in the Red Book of Official Used Car Market Values. You can either order a copy from National Market Reports, 900 South Wabash Avenue, Chicago, Illinois 60605, or you can ask your bank lending officer for a look at his copy.

The dealer also might try to sucker you into a deal by making a **When is the deal final?** verbal offer that sounds fantastic, only to put something totally different into the written contract. It is important, therefore, that you get everything in writing before you agree to finalize the deal. You also should note that at many car dealerships no contract is final until it is signed by one of the dealership's owners. A salesman's signature may not be legally binding.

Another area where the dealer can boost his profits at your expense **WISEGUIDE** is through the sale of a large package of luxury options.

Profit margins on options tend to be higher than on the car itself, **Profit margins on** so that the dealer will undoubtedly try to get you to buy all the **options are high** options he can. This may prove a bit tricky for you, since if you want immediate delivery of a car from the dealer's inventory you will have to take whatever options are already installed regardless of whether you want them or not. If, on the other hand, you insist on specifying your options, you probably will have to wait two or three months for delivery from the factory.

Here are a few of the basic options that are available on most cars, **A listing of basic** along with their recent price range: **options**

• A V-8 engine costs anywhere from $90 to $400 more than a basic 6-cylinder engine. Also, it consumes more gas. It is worthwhile only if you haul large loads or drive long distances on the open highway.

• An automatic transmission costs about $225 more than a manual transmission. This may prove to be a valuable investment, however, since you may find it difficult to resell a car with a standard transmission.

• Power steering adds about $100 to the price. Again, as with automatic transmission, this adds to the resale value.

• Disc brakes, with power assist, cost about $60 to $80 extra. Although this may not add very much to the resale value, disc brakes are very worthwhile in the sense that they help prevent swerving during sudden stops.

• Air conditioning is one of the most expensive options, costing anywhere from $350 to $650. This makes sense only if you live where the temperature and humidity are high or if you do a lot of long-distance summer driving.

• Cost of a standard AM radio is approximately $60 to $90, and an AM/FM radio considerably more. You generally can recover the cost of an AM radio when you sell the car, but not of an FM radio.

WISEGUIDE

Besides adding to the initial price of the car, options tend to increase your operating costs.

Some examples

An example is that V-8 engine generally consumes about $25 to $50 more gas a year than a 6-cylinder engine and that it costs more to repair. Similarly, air conditioning can add $25 or more to your annual gasoline bill.

Special buying services

One last note about new-car buying: In recent years, special "buying services" have begun to spring up. These organizations promise large discounts off sticker prices by buying new cars in volume from certain dealers and then reselling them at mark-ups of only about $100 to $200. This can prove to be an excellent way for you to buy a new car at minimum price. But make sure that you know the name and location of the participating dealer. Is he near enough to make it easy for you to get the car serviced? Also, you should be aware that even if the dealer is nearby he may not be enthusiastic about giving you good service since he didn't make the sale to you himself.

WISEGUIDE

If buying a new car is tricky, then buying a used car can be nothing short of treacherous.

The dangers of used-car buying

The procedures here are much less formal and the level of bargaining can become much more intense. Furthermore, when buying from a new-car dealer you can always complain to the manufacturer if you feel cheated. There is no one to appeal to, however, if you feel that you have been taken advantage of by a used-car dealer.

This points up the need to be extremely careful when buying a used car and to do business only with dealers you have checked out in advance. Ask some friends whether they have ever bought a used car. If so, what do they think of the dealer? One possible approach is to buy only at the used-car department of a reputable new-car dealer.

By buying a used car you can avoid the high rate of depreciation associated with a new car. Conversely, however, you may find that your repair bills are much higher. To avoid being stuck with a lemon that will cost more to repair than it is worth, insist on a road test before you buy a used car. If the dealer refuses to allow this, you should regard it as a warning not to do business with him.

Low depreciation versus high repair costs

Along these same lines, it might be worth your while to have the car checked out by a good mechanic or an independent diagnostic center before you sign the purchase contract. The cost will be about $10 to $20. Names of local diagnostic centers can be found in the Yellow Pages under Automobile Diagnostic Services.

A car begins to lose value the moment you drive it out of the dealer's lot.

WISEGUIDE

That is simply an economic fact of car ownership. The rate of price depreciation is roughly 25 to 30 per cent of the original price the first year, 15 to 20 per cent of the original price the second year, 12 to 15 per cent the third year, 10 to 12 per cent the fourth year, 8 to 10 per cent the fifth year, and so on. Translated into dollars, a $3,500 new car would be worth about $2,500 after one year, about $1,800 after two years, about $1,300 after three years, about $950 after four years, and about $700 after five years.

Depreciation rates

Although age is the prime factor in determining a car's market value, the condition of the car also plays an important role. Therefore, it pays to keep your car in good mechanical shape — both as a safety factor and to maximize its eventual resale value.

Given decent care, the typical American-made car should go anywhere from 60,000 to 100,000 miles before maintenance costs get out of hand.

Ways to reduce your costs

• Your costs can be reduced by good driving. Forget about wheel-spinning starts, over-revving the engine and unnecessary slipping of the clutch. They all consume extra gas and add to wear and tear.

• Don't wait until something goes wrong before you get your car serviced. This is false economy. Regular servicing won't necessarily prevent a failure, but it can detect problems in their early stages and stave off more serious damage.

A money-saving tip is to experiment with various grades of gasoline to see which suits your car. Some government studies have found that the lowest grades of gasoline are adequate for all but a few high-powered cars. If your engine begins to knock, however, you should move up to a higher grade of gas.

It also is important to follow the servicing and maintenance procedures specified in the car warranty. If you don't, your warranty

New-car warranties

may be invalidated. The typical new-car warranty covers all defects and repairs for the first year or 12,000 miles, whichever comes first.

Used-car warranties

On the other hand, used-car warranties can be for as short a period as 24 hours. And even when they are longer, they don't necessarily give you full financial protection against break-downs and repairs. One reason is that a used-car warranty usually specifies that you will share all repair costs 50-50 with the dealer. It isn't all that uncommon for the dealer to simply jack up the repair bill to double his normal work rate, and then charge you half of the doubled amount. It's best to be cautious.

WISEGUIDE

Whatever type of car you buy, try to get to know the dealer's service manager.

Dealing with the service manager

When you bring in a car for repairs, give the service manager an itemized list of the things you want fixed. When you pick up the car, check the invoice against your copy of the list. If the car comes back unfixed — a distinct possibility — return it to the shop and politely ask the service manager to look into the problem. In the case of a new car, if the repair still isn't made to your satisfaction, call the factory zone service manager (zone offices are listed in your owner's manual) and ask for a joint meeting with him and the dealer. If you still aren't satisfied, contact the manufacturer directly in Detroit.

Renting and leasing a car

To avoid the headaches and high costs of car ownership, you might consider renting or leasing a car. But this is no real bargain either. In some major cities, it now costs a minimum of $17 a day plus 16 cents a mile to rent a full-sized car.

"Renting" refers to the short-term use of a car (a few days at most) while "leasing" usually involves a contract for a minimum of six months. Renting may make sense if you only need a car occasionally, but leasing really isn't that advantageous. If you do lease, chances are that you will end up paying more than if you had bought a car, since the leasing arrangement will always include a mark-up for the leasing company's profit.

Arranging an auto loan

Financing and insurance coverage also are major expenses of car ownership. In both cases, however, you often can save considerable money by shopping around for the best deal.

In the case of financing, the car dealer will usually offer to arrange a loan for you. But it is best to turn his offer down, since the interest cost will undoubtedly be quite high.

Should I borrow from the dealer?

Car dealers place their car loans with a bank or finance company, and you can probably go directly to the dealer's lender and get a lower rate on your own. This is because car dealers customarily get a rebate, or a "dealer's reserve" as it is called in the trade, for handling the financing. In fact, some dealers make more money on the financing than on the car itself.

Commercial banks and credit unions tend to be the least expensive sources of automobile loans.

How much interest will I have to pay?

Never take a loan from any other source until you have checked to see what kind of terms you can get from a bank or credit union. In general, you must be prepared to make a cash down payment of at least 25 per cent of the price of the car and to pay at least 10 to 12 per cent annual interest on the loan that you take out to finance the rest. Incidentally, the trade-in value of your old car generally can count toward the cash down payment.

Another point is that if anything goes wrong with the car you will still have to keep repaying your auto loan. As the law now stands in most states, the lender is merely a "holder in due course" of the loan who has no responsibility for the quality of the merchandise. In other words, if you have a gripe about the car you must take it to the dealer not the lender.

Automobile insurance: a major problem

Insurance can be one of the most frustrating aspects of car ownership. The cost is high, and if you do get into an accident it often is impossible to collect — even though you may be fully insured — unless you go to court and sue. Even then, it may take years to get your money. In addition, if you do file a claim, you run the risk that your insurance policy will be cancelled when it comes up for renewal.

The inefficiency of this system is illustrated by figures compiled by the Senate Antitrust Subcommittee. Of every $1 of automobile liability insurance premiums that Americans pay to insurance companies each year, only about 42 cents in actual insurance benefits is paid out, and of this only 14 cents goes to cover victims' out-of-pocket expenses. Of the 58 cents of overhead, 16 cents goes to lawyers, 14 cents for the costs on investigating and adjusting claims, and 28 cents for the expenses and profits of the insurance company.

"No-fault" auto insurance

One possible answer to this problem is so-called "no fault" automobile insurance, which already has been enacted in one form or another in about a dozen states and is being studied on the national level as well. Under this system, when an accident occurs each driver is paid by his own insurance company for his actual loss, regardless of who was at fault. The payments are made automatically, up to certain limits, without the need for court action.

In Massachusetts, where a strong no-fault law was enacted, premium rates for bodily injury coverage dropped 17 per cent in the first year.

The existing "fault" system

Under the "fault" system that still prevails in most states, on the other hand, an injured party must prove the other driver's guilt in

court. Then — and only then — will the guilty driver's insurance company pay damages.

Types of coverage: There are five main categories of automobile insurance coverage:

1. Liability ● Liability coverage is by far the most important, and is an area where you definitely should not skimp. The bodily injury part of your liability coverage pays for death, injury, sickness and disease resulting to others from an accident involving your car. The property damage part pays for damage to other people's property — their car, home, other buildings, etc.

2. Collision ● Collision coverage pays for damage to your own car in an accident. It is the most expensive type of auto insurance. The cost can easily run anywhere from $200 to $600 a year.

3. Comprehensive ● Comprehensive coverage reimburses you for damage to, or loss of, your car from ways other than collisions. Examples include theft, fire, wind damage and vandalism. By far the most common type of claim filed under this coverage is for shattered windshields.

4. Uninsured motorists ● Uninsured motorists coverage pays for injury to any member of your family caused by an uninsured or insufficiently-insured driver. This applies whether you are riding in a car or struck by a car while walking. Uninsured motorists coverage is very inexpensive — typically about $4 a year for $20,000 of insurance.

5. Medical ● Medical coverage pays for medical treatment for yourself or your passengers for injuries suffered in an auto accident, regardless of who is at fault. Payments are usually limited to those expenses incurred within one year of the accident. One quirk of this type of coverage is that in most cases the money will be paid even if you also collect for the same expenses from another insurance policy, such as a group medical policy at work.

WISEGUIDE

In other words, you can end up receiving double payment for medical expenses if you have automobile medical coverage. This is something your agent probably won't tell you about, but that you should look into if you have an accident.

Two types of package policies: In addition to offering these five basic types of coverage separately, most insurance companies also offer them in two basic package forms:

1. Family ● A family policy is, in all likelihood, the kind you currently have. It protects you against negligence claims whether you are driving your own car, somebody else's or even a rented vehicle. It also covers members of your household when they drive your car and other people when they drive it with your permission. It may even cover other members of your household when they drive someone else's car.

• A special policy usually is reserved for "prime risks" — people with good driving records who live in low-crime neighborhoods. Insurance agents don't like to sell this type of policy, because the premium usually is about 15 per cent lower than on a family policy and their commission is smaller. One basic difference between a family and special policy is that you cannot collect double payment for medical expenses when you hold a special policy.

2. Special

Automobiles can inflict spectacular damage. And unless you are adequately insured against such a possibility, you are running a big financial risk.

WISEGUIDE

Liability coverage usually is bought in a three-part series. A typical example would be a "50/100/10" policy. This simply means that the insurer's liability is limited to a maximum of $50,000 for injury to one person, $100,000 maximum for all people per accident, and $10,000 for property damage. Similarly, a 100/300/10 policy would insure you against a maximum of $100,000 for injury to one person, $300,000 total liability per accident, and $10,000 for property damage.

All 50 states require that car owners carry a specified minimum of liability coverage. In most states the minimum policy is 10/20/5. But this should be regarded as the barest essential.

Fortunately, it doesn't cost that much more to buy additional coverage. You should set your sights on coverage of 100/300/10 or even 300/500/10. The former will cost only about 30 per cent more a year than a 10/20/5 policy and the latter only about 40 per cent more. It is well worth the extra cost.

How much liability coverage do I need?

In determining how much to charge you for auto insurance, the insurance company will take a number of factors into consideration: age and marital status of the driver or drivers, use of the vehicle, distance driven to and from work, total annual mileage, driving record of all operators, type and age of automobile, limits of coverage, place of garaging, etc. You probably can get a lower rate by lying on your insurance application. For instance, you could understate the mileage driven. Is it worth the risk, though?

How much will insurance cost me?

If you are involved in a major accident and the insurer finds that your application contained misinformation, he may refuse to pay your claim.

WISEGUIDE

Studies have shown that the majority of Americans think that an auto insurance policy will cost exactly the same no matter which insurance company it is bought from. Nothing could be farther from the truth. Auto insurance rates vary significantly from company

The costs of insurance can vary widely

to company, and to find the best rate you are going to have to shop around.

A recent study by the Pennsylvania Insurance Department shows just how far apart prices can be. Here, for instance, are the prices that 12 large insurance companies would charge an adult driver in Philadelphia. The costs are based on purchase of a 10/20/5 policy that also includes uninsured motorists coverage, $500 of medical coverage, $50 deductible comprehensive coverage and $100 deductible collison coverage. The car involved in the example is a full-sized Chevrolet.

Insurance company	Annual cost of a policy in Philadelphia
Aetna Casualty & Surety	$529
Allstate Insurance Co.	468
Erie Insurance Exchange	397
Harleysville Mutual	504
Keystone Insurance	544
Nationwide Mutual	318
Pa. Manufacturers Assoc.	544
Pa. National Mutual Casualty	544
State Auto Insurance Assoc.	544
State Farm Mutual Auto.	382
Travelers Indemnity	412
U.S. Fidelity & Guaranty	544

Rates aren't the only factor

A comparison of rates alone is not a conclusive way to choose a company, however. There are other factors to consider. Are claims paid promptly and fairly? Is correspondence and billing handled efficiently? Is good insurance advice provided when needed?

Just as important is whether the company will refuse to renew your policy following a loss. Another danger point to watch out for is a provision that will allow the company to boost your premium sharply if you have an accident.

One way to assess these factors is to ask your friends how their insurance needs have been handled by their company. In addition, Consumers Union does an excellent survey of the quality of service provided by major auto insurance companies. Results of this survey can be found in the back of the Consumer Reports annual buying guide.

Ways to hold down your costs

There are a number of ways to hold down your insurance costs:

● Take collision and comprehensive coverage only if you really need them. These are the most expensive types of coverage. A basic rule of thumb is that if your car is worth less than $1,000 you are wasting money when you buy these kinds of coverage.

• If you do buy collision and comprehensive insurance, insist on a high "deductible" clause. With a $100 deductible clause, for instance, you will be liable for the first $100 of damage and the insurance company for anything above that. The higher the deductible, the lower the cost of the policy.

• Find out whether you qualify for any special rate discounts. Some of the discounts commonly available include safe-driver discounts, multi-car discounts, small-car discounts, etc.

1973

Year-by-year costs of car ownership

The first year in the life of a new car is far and away its most expensive — mainly because of the high rate of first-year price depreciation. After that, costs tend to level off. These are the estimated cost figures, from a U.S. Department of Transportation study, over the anticipated 10-year life of a new 1973 standard-sized car. One of the basic assumptions of the study is that the typical car is driven less and less each year as it gets older.

	Estimated annual mileage	Total cost	Per-mile cost
First year	14,500	$ 2,325.32	16.04 ¢
Second year	13,000	1,794.75	13.81
Third year	11,500	1,655.11	14.39
Fourth year	10,000	1,495.49	14.95
Fifth year	9,900	1,347.95	13.62
Sixth year	9,900	1,225.06	12.37
Seventh year	9,500	1,252.03	13.18
Eighth year	8,500	936.55	11.02
Ninth year	7,500	925.95	12.35
Tenth year	5,700	594.74	10.43
Total	**100,000**	13,552.95	**13.55**

Note that the figures in the government study are averages and are based on costs in the Baltimore area. Your own costs will be affected by numerous factors, including individual driving habits, climate, garage facilities, type of roads used and plain luck.

Year-by-year costs of running a car

93

Owning a car

One warning: under one commonly-used safe-driver plan, the premium automatically goes up 40 per cent if you are convicted of a traffic violation which results in the suspension of your driver's license.

Accidents also can boost your cost

Additional charges also are tacked onto the premium for an accident. In that case, a safe-driver discount may end up proving to be more expensive than a policy without such a plan.

What to do in case of an accident

What should you do in the event of an accident?

1) Call an ambulance for anyone who is seriously injured. Call the police, if necessary.
2) Secure names and addresses of all persons in the other car, descriptions of cars and license numbers.
3) Obtain names and addresses of all witnesses.
4) Measure any skid marks.
5) Do not under any circumstances admit responsibility and make no statement regarding the accident except to an authorized claims representative from your own insurance company.
6) Comply with state laws by filing required accident reports. Send a copy to your insurance company.
7) Do not disclose your policy limits to anyone.
8) Call your insurance company's nearest claims representative.

For most of us, driving a car is still worth the high cost. But it is your job to make sure you get the maximum amount of pleasure for the minimum expense. The best way to start is to *watch those costs.*

Per-mile costs of owning a car

The chart on page 93 shows the typical year-by-year costs of owning a standard-sized car. The figures below, taken from the same government study, compare per-mile costs of three different car sizes. These figures are based on owning each car 10 years and driving it a total of 100,000 miles over that period.

	Deprecia-tion	Mainte-nance	Gas and Oil	Garage, Parking and Tolls	Insurance	Taxes	Total
Standard Size	4.4¢	2.6¢	2.1¢	1.8¢	1.4¢	1.3¢	13.6¢
Compact Size	2.7	2.2	1.8	1.8	1.3	1.0	10.8
Subcompact Size	2.1	2.1	1.4	1.8	1.2	0.8	9.4

Chapter 9

Life insurance

Getting the Most for Your Money

How much life insurance do I need? What type? How much will it cost me? Those, in a nutshell, are the three main concerns of Americans when it comes to buying life insurance. **Three important questions**

Almost everybody recognizes the need for some sort of basic life insurance protection. In fact, studies show that 86 per cent of all male adults and 74 per cent of all female adults in this country are insured and that the average insured family carries a total of $25,700 in coverage.

Is $25,700 really adequate? Answering that question is what this chapter is all about.

Before the three basic points posed at the beginning of the chapter can be discussed, however, it is essential to describe the types of life insurance that are available and the advantages and disadvantages of each.

Every life insurance policy consists of a written contract between an insurance company and a customer specifying the amount of money that will be paid if the customer dies during the term of the contract. Also specified is the price, or premium, that the customer must pay for this benefit, as well as the name of the person to whom the death payment will be made. **What is life insurance?**

Life insurance serves two basic functions: **Two main functions**

● It protects your family against financial hardship if you die.

● Some types of life insurance also represent a limited form of savings account.

Insurance salesmen often make a big case about this two-fold benefit. In truth, however, insurance protection and savings are totally incompatible objectives over the long run.

Although many insurance policies provide you with both insurance and savings, you can only end up choosing one or the other. You cannot have your cake and eat it too. **WISEGUIDE**

Let's see why. If, on the one hand, you decide to keep the policy until the day you die so that your family can collect on the insurance, the underlying savings account (or "cash value," as it is called) becomes meaningless. It just disappears into the insurance company's coffers and does not represent money that you or your family will ever receive. **What happens to my "savings" if I die?**

If, on the other hand, you decide to cash in the policy and take out the savings during your own lifetime, the insurance protection will automatically be terminated.

Borrowing against the policy

In fact, the only way you can take any sort of advantage of *both* the insurance and savings aspects of a life insurance policy is to use the accumulated cash value as collateral to borrow from the insurance company. In that case, the insurance coverage will be continued, but in a reduced amount equal to the original coverage minus the loan.

Another drawback of combining insurance protection with savings is that the interest rate paid on the savings portion of a life insurance policy tends to be extremely low when compared with a savings account at a bank.

WISEGUIDE

Typical interest rate paid on the savings in an insurance policy is between 2½ and 3½ per cent — a point that most insurance salesmen manage to gloss over when making a sales pitch.

What should my primary insurance objective be?

This is not to say that you should never buy an insurance policy that combines insurance with savings. As you will see, this type of policy has definite advantages. But you shouldn't seek to save for your old age by loading up with life insurance. There are better ways to save. Your primary insurance objective should be to provide your family with adequate financial protection in the event of your death.

No tax benefits

A common misconception is that buying life insurance offers special tax advantages by enabling you to pass money on to your heirs tax free. This is not true. Like everything else you own, insurance proceeds are subject to estate taxes unless the policies have been irrevocably assigned to the beneficiary. This kind of assignation is tricky business, however, and should not be attempted without the help of a competent lawyer.

Three types of policies:

Every life insurance policy fits into one of three basic categories:

1. Term

"Term insurance" provides the most coverage at the lowest cost. You pay premiums for a fixed number of years, and the company pays a specified sum of money to your beneficiary (normally your spouse or children) if you die during the term. If, on the other hand, you live beyond the end of the term the company pays nothing; its obligation has ended. Term insurance is pure insurance with no frills.

2. Whole life

"Whole life," which is sometimes referred to as "cash value," "straight" or "permanent" life insurance, is the most popular type of coverage. Whole life combines insurance with a moderate amount of savings. Unlike term insurance, this type of policy never expires — except that if you live to the ripe old age of 100 the company will pay the death benefit to you rather than your beneficiary. You also are free to cash in the policy at any time up to age 100 and terminate the insurance coverage. In that case, however, you usually will receive less than the face value of the policy.

"Endowments" are the most expensive form of life insurance. Like whole life, they represent a combination of insurance and savings. The main difference is that the savings aspect is emphasized much more strongly in an endowment. An endowment matures after a specified number of years, at which point you receive a cash payment — representing your accumulated savings — in an amount equal to the death benefit. Typically, this payment is made either 20 years after you first sign up for the policy or when you reach age 65, depending on the individual policy.

3. Endowments

Endowments tend to be overly expensive if your primary concern is adequate insurance coverage. They are not a particularly good type of policy to buy.

WISEGUIDE

Furthermore, you may be surprised to learn that part of the proceeds from an endowment may be subject to income tax. Federal law specifies that if you cash in an insurance policy, instead of letting it run until your death, you must pay taxes on any net profit you make over the amount you originally paid in. This applies mainly to endowments, since gains are rare on other types of policies. The tax works this way: if you pay a total of $15,000 into an endowment over the years and receive back a lump sum of $20,000 when it matures, the extra $5,000 is taxable.

Endowments can be taxable

A fourth major type of insurance-related policy is called an "annuity." This is actually insurance in reverse. Instead of paying annual premiums and collecting a lump-sum insurance benefit on death, you pay a single chunk of money and collect a regular income for the rest of your life. Annuities often are bought with the cash proceeds from an endowment when it matures. *They are discussed in detail in Chapter 15.*

Annuities

Let's look at a specific example of how each of these three basic types of insurance works and how much each might cost:

John Smith is 30 years old, married, in good health and the father of two young children. He earns $12,500 a year and is insured for $10,000. One evening, John and wife sit down and decide it would be a good idea for John to take out another $20,000 of life insurance. They feel they can afford it, and with two young children there is a definite need for better insurance coverage. The next morning John visits his insurance agent and finds out that there are essentially three basic choices he can make:

How much a 30-year-old man might pay for $20,000 of insurance:

1. John can buy a $20,000, five-year term life insurance policy for $72.80 a year. After the five-year term is up, John will automatically be entitled to renew the policy for another five years, and so on to age 65. One hitch, however, is that each time he renews, the premium rate will go up. At the end of the first five years, for instance, the premium will go to $84.60, and after 10 years to

Term insurance — $72.80 a year

$113.20. And when he renews for the final time at age 60, the cost will be all the way up to $561.40 a year! So, he finds out, the low initial cost is only part of the story. Furthermore, at age 65 the policy will no longer be renewable. The insurance coverage will be ended, and if John is still alive he will have nothing to show for all the money he has shelled out to the insurance company except the fact that his family has been protected over the years.

Whole life — $320.00 a year

2. John can buy a $20,000 whole life policy for $320.00 a year. He will pay this amount for the rest of his life, and the insurance coverage will never expire. In addition, he will steadily build up a cash value in the policy that he can borrow against whenever he wants at low interest rates. And at age 65, if he wants to cash in the policy and terminate his insurance, he will receive a lump sum of $11,782 from the insurance company.

Paid-up whole life — $366.60 a year

Alternatively, John can buy a whole life policy that will be totally paid for at age 65. After that, the insurance coverage will continue but John will no longer have to make any payments. The cost, in this case, is $366.60 a year.

An endowment — $442.20 a year

3. Finally, John can buy a $20,000 endowment for $442.20 a year. He will pay that amount until he reaches age 65. If he dies before then, his family will receive $20,000. If, on the other hand, he lives to 65 the company will pay him the full $20,000 and terminate the insurance.

These examples actually represent only the most basic types of insurance protection.

WISEGUIDE

Insurance can be tailored in thousands of different ways to meet your specific objectives and needs.

Some ways to use insurance

For instance, you can:

● Provide your family with a single cash payment or, alternatively, with a regular income when you die.

● Arrange for your home mortgage or auto loan to be repaid automatically in the event of your untimely death.

● Provide money to care for your children and pay for their education.

● Arrange a regular pension for yourself and your wife after you reach retirement age.

● Buy an insurance policy on the life of your child that will automatically jump to five times the original coverage when he or she reaches age 21.

● Buy a package policy that covers everyone in the family.

In addition, you can custom design your policy through the inclusion of special clauses and provisions. Examples include a "waiver of premium" clause, under which premium payments are suspended if you become totally disabled for at least six months, and "double indemnity," which provides for double payment in case of accidental death (as opposed to death from illness). However, you usually must pay extra for such features.

Special clauses and provisions also can be included

Even where two different policies are essentially the same in all their clauses and provisions, different insurance companies may charge completely different rates.

How the price can vary

A Pennsylvania Insurance Department survey showed, for instance, that one large company charges a typical 35-year-old male $176.00 a year for a $10,000 whole life policy while another large company charges $248.10 a year for essentially the same protection.

WISEGUIDE

Unfortunately, however, you cannot necessarily tell which policy is the least expensive by looking at the premium cost alone. This is because some companies offer "participating" policies that rebate you an annual "dividend" out of the company's surplus cash. Furthermore, the cash value may build up more rapidly in one company's policy than in another's.

Determining the true cost of life insurance

In order to take such factors as dividends and cash values into account, most insurance experts measure the price of a policy on the basis of what is called the "interest-adjusted cost." This is arrived at by a complex formula, but you can save yourself the work of figuring out this cost by looking it up in Cost Facts on Life Insurance, published by the National Underwriter Co. in Cincinnati. This book, which should be available at your local library or from your insurance agent, lists interest-adjusted costs for all major U.S. insurance companies.

There is a second kind of price figure that is called "net cost." Many insurance salesmen include this figure in their sales pitch, but the experts warn that it is highly misleading in that it doesn't take into account the interest you can earn on your money if you don't spend it on life insurance.

A warning!

It is best to avoid pricing life insurance on the basis of "net cost." The most valid comparison is "interest-adjusted cost."

WISEGUIDE

Term insurance is a different matter. Price variations between companies tend to be much less than for whole life insurance, so it isn't nearly as important to shop around. Also, it is easier for the layman to compare cost differentials where they do exist, since term life has little or no cash value to cloud the true price picture.

How to price term insurance

In buying life insurance, you should consider finding a good agent or broker and relying heavily on his advice. One problem, however, is that the quality of people in this field ranges all the way from outstanding to terrible. To avoid being misled by a phony, it is best to know some basic facts about life insurance before you buy.

Where can I buy?

You actually can buy insurance from four main sources:

1. Insurance companies

• Some insurance companies sell directly to the public, with no middleman. This often is a relatively inexpensive way to buy, since there is no price mark-up for a salesman's commission. The disadvantage is that you don't have access to an agent's professional advice. One of the best life-insurance bargains of all is savings bank life insurance, available only at savings banks in three states — New York, Massachusetts and Connecticut. You must live or work in one of these states to qualify.

2. Agents

An insurance agent is a trained salesman who usually works for only one company. Agents are the most active sellers of life insurance to individuals.

3. Brokers

• An insurance broker sells insurance for a variety of different companies. Because of this, a good broker tends to be a better adviser than a good agent. In the final analysis, however, the quality of the individual counts far more than the technical difference between whether the salesman is an agent or broker.

4. Stockbrokers

• A fairly recent development is that stockbrokers are now allowed to sell life insurance. One potential disadvantage of buying from this source is that your stockbroker may not really know very much about how to tailor an insurance program to meet your needs.

How much insurance do I need?

The big question faced by most insurance buyers is, of course, how much coverage they actually need. A related question is what type of coverage it should be — term, whole life or endowment.

WISEGUIDE

A good agent or broker can provide valuable help when you review your insurance needs.

An agent profits from selling insurance, not from giving honest advice

But it should be remembered that an agent or broker will be operating from a position of conflicting interests — your desire for honest advice versus his own desire to make a handsome living. The more insurance he sells you, the bigger the commission he will earn. Furthermore, salesmen's commissions on term life insurance tend to be very low; as a result, most salesmen will argue against your buying very much of this type, even if it actually suits your needs.

The point is that, before visiting an agent or broker, you should have a basic idea as to how much insurance coverage is adequate in your situation.

Unfortunately, there aren't any simple formulas to determine just how much insurance you should buy. In addition, you must be realistic about the fact that it will be almost impossible to devise a life insurance program that will cover all of life's eventualities. And even if you could devise this kind of foolproof program, you probably wouldn't be able to afford it. **The amount of coverage is a matter of judgment**

You should focus instead on creating a program that will cover your most basic needs reasonably well and that is flexible enough so that it can be adjusted as your needs change. WISEGUIDE

An effective insurance program requires careful study and planning. Begin by listing all your existing life insurance policies, regardless of whether you hold them on an individual basis or as part of a group (through your employer, union, professional society or whatever). How much protection do these policies give you? Read the policies carefully so that you are aware of all the terms. If you have questions about a group policy, see the person in charge of the plan. **Start with an inventory of your existing policies**

Now you are ready to take a look at how much insurance you need versus how much you actually have. You must come to grips with two key questions: **Two key questions**

• First, if the family breadwinner were to die today, how much money would the family need to keep going?

• Second, where will that money come from?

If you do nothing else in your insurance program, it is important to insure against the untimely death of the family breadwinner. WISEGUIDE

It isn't easy to figure out just how much your family will need if you were to die. A number of factors must be taken into consideration. For instance, will your wife be able to earn some income by working? How much Social Security will she receive? Will she receive a pension from your employer? How will the children's education be paid for? Where will the money come from to support your wife in her old age? **Some factors to consider**

Let's take the case of Phil and Harriet Jackson — a young couple with three children age 10, 7 and 5. The family income is $11,000 a year, all from Phil's salary. The Jacksons own a $23,000 house, mortgaged for $19,000, and have $2,800 in a savings account. **A case in point — the Jackson family**

If Phil were to die, how much money would Harriet and the children need to keep going?

Four basic financial needs

First off, they would need emergency cash to pay for the funeral and other initial expenses and to tide the family over for the first few months after Phil's death. Second, they would need enough annual income to live on. Third, they would need enough money to pay for the children's college education. Fourth, it would be a good idea if they had enough money to pay off the mortgage so that there would be no need to worry about losing the house.

Phil and Harriet discuss the situation and decide that Harriet and the children could live comfortably on $9,000 a year if Phil were to die. Social Security, they find out from the Social Security Administration, would provide a little over $400 a month until the children reach maturity, of $4,800 out of the total $9,000 annually. Phil's company, however, wouldn't pay Harriet a pension, so they cannot look to this source for money. Furthermore, they decide that they would prefer that Harriet not have to draw money from the family savings account, since she would like to hold onto this cash as an emergency reserve.

Filling the gap with insurance

Insurance, then, will have to provide enough cash to give Harriet $4,200 a year — the difference between the $9,000 she would need and the $4,800 in Social Security.

How much insurance would be required to provide this kind of annual income? At 6 per cent annual interest, a lump sum of $70,000 would earn $4,200 a year forever. But $70,000 is a lot of life insurance — more than Phil and Harriet feel that they want or can afford.

So Phil and Harriet decide where they can cut back. For one thing, they realize, Harriet could take a full-time job once the children reach their late teens. So, as it turns out, insurance would have to provide Harriet with $4,200 a year for only about a dozen years, not the rest of her life. Hopefully, however, there would be enough money left over to serve as a small nestegg for her old age. In addition, Phil and Harriet decide to take out a low-cost "decreasing term" policy specifically to repay the mortgage if Phil should die. This way Harriet wouldn't have to worry about monthly mortgage payments and, as a result, could actually live on less than $9,000.

After talking it over with their agent, Phil and Harriet devise the following life insurance package:

Type of Policy	Annual Cost
A $3,000 whole-life policy earmarked for funeral expenses and initial emergency funds	$ 55.10
A $10,000 whole-life policy to provide money for Harriet to live on and, as a secondary objective, to provide potential funds for Phil's retirement should he live to 65	171.80
A $20,000 renewable term policy, also to provide money for Harriet to live on	72.80
A $19,000 "decreasing term" policy to repay the outstanding mortgage balance	55.00
Total annual cost	**$354.70**

Notice that, in the final analysis, the Jacksons' decisions were quite arbitrary. There is no way to formulize exactly what you should buy. Furthermore, insurance decisions must of necessity be based as much on what you can afford as on what you need.

A major consideration — what can I afford?

Unfortunately, most families need the greatest insurance protection in their early years when they can afford it least. That is where term life insurance proves to be particularly valuable since it provides maximum coverage at lowest cost.

It is impossible to say that either term or whole life is a better form of insurance protection. Generally, a combination of the two works best.

WISEGUIDE

Whole life, with its permanence and its emphasis on savings, can serve as the anchor of your insurance program. Term, on the other hand, can bolster the program at low cost.

Whole life plus term

Only when there is adequate insurance on the family wage-earner's life should you consider insurance on other members of the family. If you do decide to insure your spouse and children, a special "family plan" policy will probably be the most economical. Ask your agent about it.

If you have a tight budget, there are two basic ways to save on insurance costs without reducing your coverage:

Ways to save on costs

• Buy as much "group" life insurance as possible. This is a form of insurance (usually term insurance rather than whole life) available through your employer, union or other group. Premium costs can be as much as 25 per cent lower than on policies purchased individually.

• Arrange to pay your premiums annually rather than semi-annually, quarterly or monthly. You will receive a price discount of up to 8 per cent if you pay annually, in recognition of the fact that you are helping to reduce the insurance company's paperwork.

What happens if you stop paying for your life insurance policy? In the case of a term policy, the coverage simply ends and the policy is canceled. By law, however, you retain certain financial benefits if you stop paying on a whole-life policy or endowment. You can take these benefits in one of three ways: you can ask for a check equal to the latest cash value in the policy; you can arrange for a reduced amount of permanent insurance coverage with no further payments necessary; or you can convert the policy to a term policy with the same amount of coverage as your original policy for a limited period of time.

Can I just stop paying for a policy?

Sometimes, an unscrupulous insurance salesman will suggest that you terminate your existing policies and switch to something new.

Should I ever switch to a lower-cost policy?

Switching policies is an extremely unwise move, even if you can buy the new policy at a lower cost than your existing one.

Two drawbacks in switching

There are two main reasons to be cautious about switching. First, cash values build up more rapidly as the policy gets older; by switching you will have to start from scratch again. Second, after two years a policy becomes incontestable. This means that the insurance company must pay a death claim even if there were misrepresentations on your application or if you commit suicide. By switching, the two-year period will begin anew.

WISEGUIDE

If a salesman suggests that you discard your old policies in favor of new ones, insist that he put his proposal in writing. Then review it with an accountant, lawyer or other independent third party.

Combination plans — insurance plus mutual funds

One of the more intriguing new types of insurance plans combines term life insurance with a separate savings program — usually shares in a mutual fund. The insurance coverage starts out at a very high level — $50,000 for instance — and then slowly decreases each year as your savings program builds up. Part of each payment that you make is earmarked for insurance and part for savings.

This is similar to whole life insurance, except that in this case the insurance and savings are kept totally separate. The advantage is that combination plans offer you the potential chance to earn much higher savings returns than you would on a whole life policy.

Be careful before you sign up

Before you sign up for this type of plan, however, make sure you know exactly what you are getting into. And read Chapter 13, about mutual funds, so that you know how to find a good fund.

Keep your policy in a safe place

Once you do buy a life insurance policy, make sure you keep it in a safe place. If your policy is lost or destroyed it can be replaced, but not without some inconvenience and delay.

Chapter 10

Paying for medical care

The Facts

Medical expenses — particularly hospital costs — are the fastest-rising expense in the family budget.

Since 1967 the average cost of a stay in the hospital has risen approximately 70 per cent, to more than $700. During that same period the average doctor's fee has increased approximately 33 per cent. (Drug prices, the third major component in the family medical budget, have held fairly steady, however.)

What's gone wrong with our nation's medical system? Why are costs so sky-high? One factor, ironically, is that millions of families, taking advantage of new private and governmental health-insurance programs (particularly Medicare), are seeking more care.

Certainly this trend toward greater care is highly desirable. But the other side of the coin is that there has been little or no increase in medical facilities to handle the increased work load. As anybody who has ever taken high-school economics knows, an increase in demand for a product or service without a corresponding increase in supply is bound to lead to higher prices.

Family medical costs may prove difficult to control

To be realistic, you as an individual may find it extremely difficult to hold down your family medical costs in the face of the tremendous nationwide problems in health care. Medical expenses certainly are not as flexible an item as food or entertainment — areas where you can reduce your costs significantly if you really want.

It *is* possible, however, for you to cut corners here and there without sacrificing very much in the way of quality. It also is possible to avoid costly mistakes by arranging for medical services in an orderly and knowledgeable way, and to make sure that your health insurance program is in good shape to help you withstand the heavy financial burdens of a major illness or injury in the family.

What information is contained in this chapter?

This chapter is divided into two parts. The first part reviews ways to get good medical care at relatively reasonable cost. The second discusses the various types of health insurance plans that are available.

Almost 60 per cent of all hospitalizations could have been prevented if the condition had been promptly identified and treated.

WISEGUIDE

The value of regular check-ups

The starting point in holding down medical costs is to get a regular medical examination. An annual doctor's exam for every member of the family should be standard practice. This is an area where cutbacks are false economy — both because they can lead to higher bills later and because they can endanger your health.

Finding a family doctor

Unfortunately, finding a good family doctor is not always an easy matter. Several recent surveys have shown that the American public is extremely troubled by the breakdown in doctor-patient relationships in this country and by the gradual demise of the "general practitioner." One problem is that more and more doctors are becoming specialists rather than going into general practice.

If you already have a good family doctor, stick with him. If not, you should start looking around before illness strikes.

General practitioners versus specialists

It is important that you find a "family physician," not a specialist. If you have a pain in the chest, for instance, you can never be sure whether it is your heart, lungs, muscles or another cause. Instead of shopping from specialist to specialist trying to match the symptoms with a doctor, you should see a generalist who will diagnose the ailment and treat it himself or refer you to someone who can. This will save both time and money. Generalists' fees usually are much lower than those of specialists.

What is an internist?

Both "general practitioners" and "internists" can serve as family physicians. An internist is a physician with intensive postgraduate training in areas of medicine that are *not* involved with surgery, obstetrics, pediatrics, ophthalmology or other specialties. Increasingly, internists are taking over from general practitioners in the role of family physician.

Certification by the American Board of Internal Medicine is desirable but not essential. Many competent internists simply have not taken the Board's examinations.

Where to begin your search for a family doctor

Although you can ask your friends and relatives to recommend a doctor, these people aren't necessarily in a position to judge a physician's medical competence. A better approach would be to call your local medical society or a good local hospital. Ask the hospital for a list of internists who serve on its staff as attending physicians.

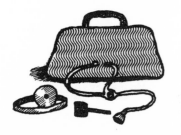

With a list of qualified candidates in hand, you can make the rounds to find one who personally suits your tastes and needs. Be candid with these doctors when you visit them. Tell them you are in the process of selecting a family physician, and feel free to ask each about his or her fees, willingness to make house calls, and hospital affiliations.

WISEGUIDE

Affiliation with a good hospital is generally regarded as the best sign of a doctor's competence.

To maintain his hospital affiliation, a doctor usually must meet specific standards, including refresher courses in the latest medical theories and techniques. No other organization or agency attests, in a way that the public can understand so easily, to a doctor's continuing competence.

Why is hospital affiliation important?

An alternative to finding a good doctor is to seek out a group medical practice. Group practices, in which several different specialists pool their talent and expensive office equipment, are a growing phenomenon. In most group practices, there should be physicians with the training and inclination to serve as family doctors.

Group practices

Check also to see whether there might be a pre-payment, comprehensive medical service plan in your area that would suit you better than a group practice or individual practitioner. Most of these plans are affiliated with the Group Health Association of America, 1321 14th Street N.W., Washington, D.C. 20005.

Pre-payment plans

If you need medical help in a hurry and your family doctor is unavailable, you can visit the hospital emergency room (in addition, many county medical societies operate a 24-hour-a-day telephone referral service so that you can get help at any time). But don't use the emergency room as a substitute for a doctor.

Emergency-room treatment can cost double or even triple a family doctor's fee for treatment of the same condition.

WISEGUIDE

Other hospital usage also should be avoided except where necessary. Hospital costs are extremely high, and it is financially foolish to go to a hospital for non-essential reasons.

When should I use a hospital?

- Don't stay overnight in a hospital for diagnostic tests that could be taken just as easily at a private clinic or on an outpatient basis.

- Where available, take advantage of pre-operation testing on an outpatient basis.

- Avoid being admitted on weekends if you have a choice. Most routine hospital services shut down on Friday afternoon, so you will have to wait until Monday for tests.

Finally, it is good practice to look over your hospital bill before you pay it. Ask for an itemization of charges. Did you really receive all the services for which you are being billed?

Your hospital bill

Mistakes in hospital bills are fairly common. Check to make sure you aren't being overcharged.

WISEGUIDE

Drug costs

Drug costs are an area of special interest when it comes to holding down medical expenses. Comparison shopping and "generic-name" buying can save considerable money.

Studies have shown that the price charged for exactly the same drug can vary widely among drugstores located within only a few blocks of each other. Retail druggists are usually free to charge whatever they want for a specific drug. Furthermore, druggists are prohibited in many states from advertising drug prices, so there is little competitive pressure to keep retail prices down.

How to comparison shop for drugs

It is a good idea to comparison shop among several different drug stores. You can try phoning around, but many druggists will refuse to disclose prices over the phone.

Some pharmacies, if they realize you are price shopping, will give you a low price on the first prescription only to jack it up on refills. If this happens, bring it to the druggist's attention or go elsewhere.

Generic versus brand-name drugs

Buying drugs by their "generic" rather than "brand" names also offers the potential for large savings. A brand-name drug usually is manufactured by the drug company that originally developed it. Once that company's patents expire, other drug companies are free to market the same product under its generic, or chemical, name.

Usually, the price is much higher for a brand-name drug because it includes an allowance for the developer's research costs. A generic-name marketer, on the other hand, has taken someone else's product rather than doing original research, so his costs and prices will often be lower even though he may be producing exactly the same product.

WISEGUIDE

To buy drugs generically, your doctor must specify the generic name in the prescription. Ask him to do so, and also emphasize to the pharmacist that you want a generic-name product.

Discount drug stores and mail-order purchases

For additional savings, you might consider shopping at discount drug stores or even ordering by mail. Mail order is perfectly legal for drug purchases, and a number of reputable firms market drugs this way — often at much lower prices than those charged at your neighborhood pharmacy.

You also should check your health insurance policies for possible reimbursement of drug costs. One estimate is that 35 per cent of the U.S. population has some form of out-of-hospital coverage for prescription medicines, mostly under major medical policies. But only a fraction of these people make use of this coverage, apparently because they are unaware that they can collect.

Health insurance

Insurance coverage is one of the most important aspects of medical care, since it provides the only method by which you can protect yourself against being devastated financially by a major illness or injury.

Whenever a person ends up in the hospital, one of his first reactions **Am I covered?**
— after the shock of being there in the first place — tends to be
concern over the cost. Am I covered?

Unfortunately, many Americans fail to go to the trouble of finding out what, if any, coverage they have until they are hospitalized. By then it may be too late, and they may have to carry the bulk of the financial burden themselves.

Although some form of across-the-board federal health insurance **WISEGUIDE** seems an eventual certainty, you should get the health insurance protection you need now.

A good program begins with careful planning. It also calls for a **Is my coverage adequate** review of your protections every year or two to make sure they **in view of today's high** have kept up with rising medical costs. Does your policy, for in- **medical costs?** stance, provide an allowance of only $20 or $30 per day for hospital room and board? If so, that may be grossly inadequate. In many cities, hospital costs are now close to $100 a day.

Read all your policies to find out exactly what kind of coverage they provide. Are there any major gaps? Also look for overlapping coverages, which increase your cost without giving you any additional protection.

Essentially, there are four basic types of health insurance policies: **Types of policies:**

- Hospitalization insurance is the most common type. Almost **1. Hospitalization** everybody needs this kind of coverage, and many employers provide it as a fringe benefit.

Blue Cross, the most popular hospitalization plan, commonly pays all or almost all hospital charges for a semi-private room for a specified number of days, plus half the cost for a specified number of additional days.

Hospitalization policies sold by private insurance companies may have similar benefits or, alternatively, may give you a fixed dollar amount for your hospital room each day, with an additional allowance for certain hospital services. At the very minimum, your policy should pay for hospitalization from the first day, after a $100 deductible that you pay yourself, for at least 21 days. In reality, the average coverage is for 60 days and many policies go to 120 and even 365 days.

- Coverage for "other basic medical expenses" applies to such **2. Other basic medical** in-hospital items as surgery, doctors' visits, diagnostic x-rays and **expenses** laboratory tests. Specific benefits vary from policy to policy and locality to locality, but the bare minimum should be 80 per cent of reasonable surgical services up to a maximum of $500, 80 per cent of the cost of anesthetic services, and 80 per cent of the cost of in-hospital medical services for at least 21 days. Many policies provide benefits that are much greater. Blue Shield is the most common plan.

3. Major medical

- Major medical policies are designed to protect you against the risk of truly catastrophic medical bills by taking over where basic plans run out. They cover almost every kind of medical treatment, both in and out of a hospital, and usually pay 75 to 80 per cent of medical bills not covered by other insurance. If, for instance, your bill comes to $1,000 and your hospitalization policy pays for half of this, major medical would pay for 75 or 80 per cent of the remainder, depending on the specific terms of the policy. Most major medical policies have a "deductible" clause, under which you pick up the first $100 or $500 or other specified amount of the tab. The larger the deductible, the lower the cost of the policy. On the whole, however, major medical coverage tends to be quite expensive. The bare minimum for a major medical policy should be that it pays 75 per cent of your otherwise-uninsured costs up to a total of $10,000 per illness.

4. Comprehensive

- Comprehensive policies combine most of the benefits of the other three policies in one plan. They are offered mainly by private insurance companies.

WISEGUIDE

cent of the U.S. population is, you probably have adequate basic health insurance. A major medical policy also might be advisable, however, to protect you against the cost of a major operation or prolonged illness.

Disability insurance

None of these four types of health insurance should be confused with disability insurance, which gives you money to live on should you be unable to work for a substantial period of time due to injury or illness.

How can I evaluate my policies?

Besides the length and amount of coverage, here are some specific points to check in your health insurance policies:

- Which members of your family are covered? A good policy should cover your spouse and children. However, most policies stop covering children somewhere between ages 18 and 23. The policy should provide grown children with an option to convert to a plan of their own.

- When do benefits start? Maternity, for instance, often is not covered until 10 months or a year has passed from the date you take out the policy. There also may be a waiting period for routine surgery, such as a tonsillectomy. For other medical services, however, the benefits should begin the first day of an illness or accident.

- Does the insurance apply outside the community where you live?

- Is the policy renewable and convertible? A good individual contract is guaranteed renewable until at least age 65 without change in premium or terms because of age. Your premiums will increase as general medical costs rise, of course, but should do so only in line with those of all policyholders in your "class." Also, a good

policy doesn't give the insurer the right to cancel the contract or raise your rates because you have needed a lot of hospital care or medical treatment. Your group contract at work should give you the right to convert to an individual policy if you leave your job.

● If you have a major medical policy, does its maximum limit apply to each separate illness or injury rather than representing a total lifetime maximum payout? A major medical contract that seems unusually inexpensive may simply be of the latter, less desirable variety.

● What are the "internal" limits in your major medical policy? This refers to the maximum payment for each day in the hospital, maximum payments for various types of surgery, etc. Some people take out a $25,000 major medical contract and assume they are fully protected. They neglect, however, to make sure the internal limits are high enough. A $25,000 policy that only pays $40 a day for hospital room and board is actually inadequate in light of today's high hospital costs. A $15,000 policy with an $80-a-day limit would provide better coverage.

● Are you getting the most for your money? Group plans are almost always less expensive and provide more total benefits than policies bought on an individual basis. But policies vary, so check specific prices and benefits before you sign up for a plan.

Price alone should not be your major consideration in choosing a health-insurance policy, since a low price may indicate that the policy has so many loopholes that it isn't worth buying.

WISEGUIDE

At age 65, almost all Americans become eligible for Medicare — the federal government's health insurance program for the elderly. (A recent law change also makes individuals collecting Social Security disability benefits eligible for Medicare, regardless of their age.) Medicare has two parts:

Medicare

● Part A is free and helps pay hospital bills, but you must sign up at your local Social Security office to gain coverage. Basically, Part A pays for the first 60 days of a hospital stay, less a $72 deductible, and offers partial coverage on additional days. Payments also are made for 80 per cent of specified in-hospital medical costs; you pay the other 20 per cent.

● Part B is a voluntary program that supplements Part A. For a premium of $6.30 a month, eligible persons can obtain insurance coverage that pays 80 per cent of "reasonable" doctors' bills, home health services, medical supplies, outpatient physical therapy services and other medical items. There is a $60 deductible clause.

Part B of Medicare provides excellent benefits for the cost and is well worth signing up for.

When am I eligible to enroll in Part B of Medicare?

There are only two periods of time, however, when you will be eligible to enroll in Part B. The initial period is a 7-month span that begins 3 months before and ends 3 months after the month in which you reach age 65. After that, you will be allowed to sign up only in an annual "general enrollment period." If you fail to sign up within three years of reaching 65, however, you forfeit your eligibility for Part B.

Medicaid

Medicaid is a seperate federal/state health insurance program for the poor (by contrast, *anybody over 65* — rich or poor — qualifies for Medicare). Among those potentially eligible for Medicaid are the aged, blind, disabled and members of families with dependent children. This insurance, like Medicare Part A, is free. For older people who qualify, Medicaid can fill many of the gaps in Medicare and will even provide you with the cash to pay for Medicare Part B. Details vary from state to state. Contact your local welfare office for information.

Supplemental health insurance for the elderly

Special policies also are available from private insurance companies to fill some of Medicare's gaps. A few of these "supplemental" policies, as they are called, may be worth the money. But the ones sold by mail — the most prominent type — generally end up delivering much less than promised.

Common traps in mail-order health insurance

Most mail-order insurance policies promise flat payments, averaging about $20 a day, for a policyholder's stay in a hospital. Premiums average about $70 a year. No physical examination is required. Will you really get your money's worth, though? Here are some common traps to watch out for if you buy supplemental health insurance by mail:

• Most policies don't cover, for the first two years, pre-existing physical conditions. This is a major loophole that often is used to reject policyholders' claims. According to one study, anywhere from 40 to 80 per cent of all claims filed during the first two years are turned down.

• Sometimes benefits don't start until the sixth day, which is beyond the five-day average hospital stay.

• Typical benefits of about $20 a day are well below the real cost of confinement in a hospital.

• Some companies try to lure customers by promising maximum payments of up to $25,000 or even $50,000 per illness. Rarely, however, does an individual ever run up that large a hospital bill. Elderly patients with lengthy illnesses generally are moved to nursing homes, and nursing home costs aren't covered by most mail-order policies.

Many mail-order health insurance policies provide little in the way of "real" benefits. Investigate before you buy.

WISEGUIDE

"First-dollar" insurance also is a highly questionable type of coverage. These policies, including a few of the mail-order variety cited above, promise to pay everything that isn't covered by other insurance, so that you don't have to pay a single penny yourself.

This is totally out of keeping with the basic concept of insurance, however. You should be prepared to absorb all small initial costs and count on your health insurance policy to protect yourself against major outlays.

"First-dollar" coverage

The high cost of "first dollar" insurance protection can in no way justify the benefits you receive in return.

WISEGUIDE

Educational expenses

The high cost of a college education

Financial planning for your children's college education should begin early. College will involve an extremely large expenditure on your part — perhaps more than you are aware.

Total cost of four years at an Ivy League school now runs to nearly $30,000, counting tuition, room, board, other fees and the student's personal expenses. On the other hand, scholarship grants tend to be plentiful at this kind of prestige school.

State universities cost considerably less — roughly $10,000 on average — but this still is quite a large sum of money. Furthermore, state and other publicly supported schools award the fewest and smallest scholarships. They consider their lower fees a form of aid.

An even less expensive alternative is a local community college. These colleges are well worth looking into if your resources are limited and you cannot get the financial aid you need at a larger school.

Of course, there are many different sizes and kinds of colleges to choose from besides the three types cited above. But this chapter will not attempt to tell you how to choose a college. It deals solely with the wide variety of methods that are available to finance today's high cost of a college degree once that choice has been made.

WISEGUIDE

College costs have approximately doubled during the past decade, and there is no end in sight to the rise.

How will I pay?

Unfortunately, many parents are totally unprepared. They think vaguely in terms of scholarships (only one student in five gets one) or some kind of help from the government (limited mainly to student loans). When the moment of truth arrives and they are forced to come up with the cash, they sadly borrow on their house or life insurance or sell off some of their stocks.

Two ways to deal with educational costs

Actually, there are two main ways to deal with paying for your children's education:

● You can save up the money in advance by starting an educational fund for each child within a few years of birth. For instance, a $30 monthly deposit in a savings account beginning in the month of the child's birth will give you a total of approximately $10,000, including interest, when the child reaches age 17.

● You can decide that you won't worry about the problem until your children are just about to enter college, in hopes that you will be able to tap whatever financial resources are available then.

A combination of the two probably is the best answer. You should try to save up something in advance, but the experts advise that there is no need to have every last penny stashed away. The important point is that you think out and plan for this heavy financial burden well ahead of time — preferably at least by the child's tenth birthday.

Advance planning is the key

Sit down and make a rough estimate of the total anticipated cost of a four-year education (you can obtain an excellent — and free — booklet on the cost at 1,200 different universities and colleges throughout the nation by writing to the Life Insurance Agency Management Association, 170 Sigourney Street, Hartford, Conn. 06105 or by asking your insurance agent to get you a copy). Then try to figure out in general terms where the money will come from. You probably can plan on allocating anywhere from $1,000 to $2,000 or more of your income toward educational expenses each year that your child is in college, depending on the size of your income and your other financial needs. Where will the rest come from?

How to figure where the money will come from

If you are rich, you probably will have little trouble coughing up enough cash on your own. If you are poor, you certainly won't find it easy to put your children through college, but there are numerous financial aid programs you can turn to for help. If, on the other hand, you are among the vast majority of Americans in the so-called "middle class," you may find yourself in a bind. Although there are many potential fund sources for you to tap, you will discover that parents are actually being called upon to put up more and more of the cash themselves.

Parents now contribute on average about 60 per cent of the cost of their children's college education, compared with about 40 per cent two decades ago.

WISEGUIDE

Large scholarships — once a primary source of college funds for the middle class — have, in particular, become difficult for many students to obtain. Colleges have made great efforts to spread their scholarship money around more widely to those in dire need, with the result that the average scholarship grant has become smaller. Furthermore, if you are counting on your son or daughter getting a scholarship purely on the basis of a superior academic record you may be in for a bad surprise. The primary determining factor at most colleges is now financial need, not academic standing.

Scholarships have become more difficult to get

Even when a scholarship is granted, it usually is done so as part of a package of financial benefits. The college might, for instance, grant a $600 scholarship together with another $300 in the form of a part-

Financial aid now comes mainly in package form

Educational expenses

time campus job and still another $300 in the form of a low-interest loan. The total aid package would come $1,200, but there would be strings attached to $600 of the amount.

Increasingly, loans are replacing scholarships as the major form of financial aid for college students in need.

The four main types of student loans:

This is a relatively recent development and is primarily an outgrowth of the 1965 Higher Education Act, which put the federal government into the student loan business in a big way for the first time. There are four basic types of student loans now available, although it is likely that the specific sources of, and rules for, these loans will change somewhat in coming months as new federal educational laws are enacted. You should check out details before you apply.

1. National Defense Student Loans

National Defense Student Loans are the least expensive type, but are only granted to needy students. Priority is given to students in the fields of mathematics, modern foreign languages, engineering and science.

Low interest

These loans are interest-free while the student is in school and after that carry an extremely low rate of interest — 3 per cent. Each loan is for 10 years, and repayments and interest start nine months after graduation.

Special cancellation provisions

There are special provisions, however, that may free the student from any need to repay. For example, if the student goes into teaching, 10 per cent of the loan is canceled each year he stays in that profession, up to a maximum of half the loan. And if he teaches in a designated low-income area elementary or secondary school or in a recognized school for the handicapped, the loan is automatically reduced by 15 per cent a year and can eventually be canceled in full. In addition, 12½ per cent of the loan is forgiven for each year in the armed forces, up to a maximum of half of the loan.

These loans are available in amounts up to $1,000 for each academic year, with a total maximum of $5,000 for undergraduate study. Separate low-cost federal loans also are available for graduate study in amounts up to $2,500 a year, provided that a student's total undergraduate and graduate borrowings don't exceed $10,000. National Defense loans are administered by each participating college, rather than by the federal government.

Each college decides on its own which of its students qualifies for a low-cost National Defense Student Loan. The place to apply is the financial aid office on campus.

A sampling of college costs around the nation
(annual costs)

College	Location	Undergraduate enrollment	Tuition	Fees	Room and board	Total
Albion	Michigan	1,755	$2,020	$ 31	$1,180	$3,231
Arizona*	Arizona	20,400	0	350	800	1,150
Auburn*	Alabama	13,800	450	0	820	1,270
Boston University	Massachusetts	14,800	2,490	116	1,356	3,962
Bowdoin	Maine	1,070	2,700	95	1,300	4,095
Brown	Rhode Island	3,200	3,050	0	1,400	4,450
Dartmouth	New Hampshire	3,360	3,060	0	1,460	4,520
Florida State*	Florida	19,000	0	570	1,000	1,570
Georgetown	Washington, D.C.	4,500	2,400	0	1,250	3,650
Georgia*	Georgia	16,000	480	81	1,650	2,211
Grinnell	Iowa	1,280	2,760	166	960	3,886
Harvard	Massachusetts	4,800	3,000	0	1,745	4,745
Hawaii*	Hawaii	17,500	170	63	822	1,055
Houston*	Texas	15,900	100	136	933	1,169
Johns Hopkins	Maryland	2,010	2,700	40	1,290	4,030
Kansas*	Kansas	15,000	466	0	950	1,416
Michigan State*	Michigan	33,900	630	0	1,143	1,773
Middlebury	Vermont	1,800	—	—	—	4,000
Nebraska*	Nebraska	16,000	535	0	940	1,475
New York University	New York	9,500	2,550	178	1,800	4,528
Northwestern	Illinois	6,580	3,000	0	1,250	4,250
Notre Dame	Indiana	6,620	2,300	50	1,000	3,350
Ohio State*	Ohio	33,700	720	0	1,245	1,965
Oregon State*	Oregon	13,500	510	0	960	1,470
Penn State*	Pennsylvania	35,600	780	0	1,065	1,845
Princeton	New Jersey	4,180	3,050	—	1,370	4,420
Stanford	California	6,500	2,850	0	1,360	4,210
Tulane	Louisiana	2,750	2,200	220	1,135	3,555
Tuskegee Institute	Alabama	3,000	1,075	0	725	1,800
Utah*	Utah	14,760	480	0	950	1,430
Vanderbilt	Tennessee	4,400	2,400	84	1,180	3,664
Wisconsin (Madison)*	Wisconsin	21,300	468	82	1,050	1,600
Yale	Connecticut	4,800	3,200	0	1,550	4,750

Not included: extra fees for specific courses, application fees, orientation-period fees, the cost of books, travel and personal expenditures.

*State-chartered universities that charge an additional fee (generally in the range of $200 to $1,600) to students from out of state.

Source:"1972-73 College Costs"
Life Insurance Agency Management Association

Educational expenses

2. Government guaranteed loans

A second important type of student loan involves a joint federal/ state program for guaranteeing repayment of loans made to students by banks, savings & loans, credit unions and other financial institutions. Interest rates are higher than on National Defense loans, but terms are still highly favorable. In most states, the maximum interest rate is 7 per cent a year, with the government paying all interest costs while the student is still in school and the student himself picking up the cost once he leaves college.

This program has had its ups and downs. Although it has been extremely popular with students, in the fall of 1972 massive bureaucratic snags resulted in lengthy delays in the processing of new loans. Hopefully, those problems have now been resolved once and for all.

The key provisions

● Maximum borrowing is $2,500 per year. Total maximum borrowing for all years of undergraduate and graduate study is $10,000.

● The student is given 10 years to repay. Although repayment can be delayed for time spent in the military, Peace Corps or VISTA, there is no "forgiveness" clause, as in National Defense loans.

● To be eligible, the student's family usually must have "adjusted gross income" of $15,000 or less a year. However, if your family earns more, you still may qualify for a guaranteed loan if the financial aid officer at your college attests that you have a real need.

WISEGUIDE

A key point is that your college financial aid officer is responsible for determining the maximum amount of your loan. But note that your loan application should be filed directly with a participating bank, credit union, savings & loan or other financial aid institution, not at a college aid office.

Can I borrow from more than one source?

A student can borrow under *both* the National Defense and guaranteed loan programs. Borrowing under one program in no way affects your eligibility for the other. Loans taken out by the student's parents under other lending programs — such as special tuition plans or medium-term bank borrowings — also have no effect on eligibility.

3. Bank loans

What happens if your family income is more than $15,000? In that case, a low-cost student loan may prove hard to find, although chances are that higher-cost borrowings will be readily available through normal commercial channels.

Your first stop might be a local bank, savings & loan or savings bank that participates in the guaranteed loan program. Such an institution may be willing to charge only 7 per cent interest even on a non-guaranteed loan. The hitch is that the student or his parents will have to pay all interest costs during his college years, rather than having the government pick up the tab.

High interest rates

It is likely, however, that the lender will want more than 7 per cent. Ten to 12 per cent or more is a realistic range at most banks.

Interest rates on special finance-company "tuition plans," on the other hand, may go as high as 20 per cent or more.

4. Other loans

A variety of other organizations also offer special student loans. Rates vary widely and should be checked out in advance before you sign up. Possible sources include the college itself and local civic and professional groups. Ask your high-school or college counselor about specific sources.

WISEGUIDE

Loans taken out under the two federally-sponsored programs generally are signed for by the student; he alone is responsible for repaying. Most types of commercial student loans must be signed for by a parent.

A student loan can affect a parent's tax bill

This can get tricky for tax purposes, and it might be worth your while as a parent to evaluate the best course of action in advance. This is because a working teenager or full-time student can earn as much as $2,050 tax free and the parents can still claim a dependency exemption of $750. There is an important "if," however: the parents must provide at least half of the child's financial support.

An example

One problem is in proving that the parents have actually provided their half. A student loan can wreak havoc in this area. Suppose, for instance, that your child wins a $1,200 scholarship and also earns $1,000 at a summer job and takes out a $1,500 loan. Under federal tax laws, the scholarship need not be included in the amount of support your child provides on his own. But these same laws specify that the summer earnings and loan must be included. If the student's total costs for the year come to $4,500 he will in this case have provided more than half (the $1,200 of earnings plus the $1,500 loan). You will lose your dependency exemption.

If, on the other hand, the father takes out the loan in his own name the situation will be reversed. The student will now be providing only $1,000 of his $4,500 in annual support, and the parents can take their $750 exemption.

WISEGUIDE

Tax situations vary from family to family, but they definitely should be given consideration when you take out a student loan.

The dangers of over-borrowing

Is a loan really the best way to finance an education? Many experts say yes, pointing out that you are merely borrowing against the child's future earning power. A college degree can add $200,000 or more to an individual's lifetime earnings, the argument goes, so why not borrow $5,000 or even $10,000 against this future income?

It is best, however, to exercise a degree of caution. There is a definite danger in saddling your child with a large debt that will take a fair part of his or her working life to pay off. The post-college years are usually the most difficult financially in an individual's life, and it certainly won't help if your child is faced with the burden of repaying a large loan.

Scholarships

Scholarships, on the other hand, need not be repaid. They may be available in amounts ranging anywhere from $100 to $4,500, depending on where you look and how much you need.

WISEGUIDE

Scholarships should be applied for mainly at your college's financial aid office. But don't overlook such sources as state agencies and civic and professional groups.

How are scholarships awarded?

Scholarships are distributed primarily on the basis of financial need. Most colleges, in evaluating need, resort to some type of standard financial analysis that compares a family's current income and assets with statistical data on "normal" family living expenses at various income levels.

For instance, on the basis of one widely-used system a family with two children and an annual income of $4,000 is expected to contribute $110 annually toward a child's college education. A family with two children and an annual income of $8,000 is expected to contribute $950. And a family with two children and income of $16,000 is expected to provide $2,520. (These figures are all based on family situations where there are no unusual financial problems.) The balance of the child's college costs will generally be covered by various forms of aid, including scholarships.

What is the College Scholarship Service?

More than half of all colleges rely on data supplied by the College Scholarship Service to rate a family's financial capacity. If your child applies for a scholarship, chances are that you will be required to fill out a standard CSS financial form. However, CSS doesn't actually determine whether a scholarship will be awarded. That is left to each college.

Increasingly, colleges also are requiring that parents submit a certified copy of their latest federal tax return in addition to the CSS financial sheet. This is because it has been found that some families cheat on their CSS forms in hopes that a larger scholarship will be awarded. One college has said its rule of thumb is that 10 to 15 per cent of all CSS forms are "at variance with the truth."

Will I have to sell my stocks?

College officials believe that this cheating stems largely from parents' fears that colleges will force them to sell all their stocks or other assets in order to pay tuition and other fees. Actually, colleges tend to be fairly lenient on this count and generally won't insist on a major liquidation of family assets or abrupt alteration of family lifestyle as a prerequisite for awarding a scholarship. Except in cases where family assets are unusually large, current family income is more important than assets in determining whether to award financial aid.

When applying for a scholarship:

- Apply for every award for which you might possibly qualify.
- Always apply for financial aid from a college at the same time you apply for admission.
- Be sure to obtain all necessary forms well ahead of time. Some colleges send out financial-aid application forms only on request.
- Pay close attention to deadlines.

A final point is that if your child's scholarship application is turned down and family circumstances change, you should feel free to reapply.

Some hints on applying for a scholarship

Most colleges reassess a student's financial needs each year and adjust their aid packages accordingly.

WISEGUIDE

On-campus jobs are another important aspect of the financial aid packages at most colleges. The largest program in this area is the federally-sponsored College Work-Study Program. Participating colleges are responsible for selecting the students who will receive jobs, but only full-time students who have substantial financial need and could not otherwise attend college are eligible. Each student normally works from five to 15 hours a week and receives from $200 to $600 per semester.

The College Work-Study Program

The federal government also sponsors Educational Opportunity Grants. Participating colleges select the students on the basis of exceptional financial need. These grants range from $200 to $1,000 per year and need not be repaid.

Educational Opportunity Grants

A variety of other special federal help is available to military veterans and to students qualifying under Social Security. You should look up the full details since they can be complex.

Other federal aid programs

- The Veterans Administration makes monthly payments to qualifying veterans who are college students. To be eligible, you must have served on active duty at least 181 days and must begin your schooling within eight years after your discharge. These benefits run for a maximum of 36 months. Educational assistance also is available to wives, widows and children of disabled or dead servicemen.

VA benefits

- Full-time students aged 18 through 21 are eligible for Social Security assistance if one of their parents is receiving Social Security disability or retirement payments or if a parent dies after having worked under Social Security long enough to be insured.

Social Security benefits

Finally, it is worth emphasizing that almost every college now has a financial aid office to help students line up funds for their education.

Educational expenses

A college financial aid counselor is the best source of information on student loans, scholarships and work programs. Don't be shy about consulting him. He is there to help you.

Chapter 12

The stock market

If you have provided for your family's basic financial security, it's **Am I ready to invest?** a good bet that you should be investing some of your money in the stock market.

Investing, once the exclusive province of the rich, is no longer so. More than 32 million Americans now own common stocks, and these investors live in all parts of the nation and come from all walks of life.

Before deciding whether the stock market is for you, you should **Two points to consider** ask yourself the following questions:
• Do you have enough savings to provide emergency cash? A minimum might be somewhere in the area of $2,000 to $4,000, depending on your specific situation and needs (see chapter 2).
• Do you have enough life insurance to protect your family adequately in case of your death? Just how much is the right amount for you is discussed in Chapter 9.

Do not invest until you have covered your basic financial commitments.

WISEGUIDE

One reason why you should exercise reasonable caution before **What is investment?** investing is that buying common stocks, unlike opening a savings account at the bank, can involve a high degree of risk.

Most forms of saving provide a fixed rate of return that you know in advance and can pretty much count on (for instance, the typical 5 or 6 per cent dividend rate at many banks). In addition, your initial capital is guaranteed — that is, you can always get back everything you put in, plus interest.

When you invest in stocks, on the other hand, you are never certain **You become part owner** just how big your ultimate profit or loss will be. This is because the **of the company** purchase of a stock gives you part ownership in that company, with all the inherent risks and potential rewards that ownership entails.

Investing is sometimes compared with gambling at the racetrack. **Not like gambling** But in reality a careful investor has very little in common with a gambler.

A careful investor studies each potential investment before buying (or relies on the advice of a good broker or investment adviser), spreads his risk among a number of different stocks rather than taking a chance on just one, and invests for the long-term rather than trying to make a quick killing.

The stock market

Careful research, diversification of investments and a long-term investment outlook are three hallmarks of a smart investor.

How investors make money

In deciding which stocks to buy, you should focus on companies with solid prospects for future earnings growth. If you choose wisely, you can expect to make money in two basic ways:

Dividends

● Many companies — particularly large, established ones — pay out a portion of their earnings to stockholders, usually once every three months, in the form of cash "dividends." The size of each dividend is determined by the company's board of directors. When profits go up, the directors often increase the dividend rate. (Conversely, when profits go down the dividend is sometimes reduced.)

Capital gains

● To some investors, however, it doesn't make much difference whether dividends are paid out to stockholders or kept by the company as "retained earnings" to be plowed back into the operation. Their main interest is in making money from "capital gains" — that is, profits from the eventual sale of the stock for a higher price than was initially paid. The company itself has no control over the price of its stock. The price level is determined by what investors are willing to pay for the shares at any given moment in the public trading market, such as on the New York Stock Exchange. This in turn is generally based on the company's earnings — especially on anticipated future earnings. Each investor's hope is that he will be a bit smarter than the next fellow and only pick shares that go up in price.

WISEGUIDE

Investors with little need for current income from their investments often don't care whether a company pays dividends. If no dividends are paid, in most cases it simply means the company is retaining the money to expand its business and thus increase the underlying value of a share of its stock.

A 9.3 per cent annual return

Despite the risks of investing, then, there's also an excellent chance for making money, particularly if you buy shares of companies with solid financial growth and then stick with these stocks for the long haul. A classic study in this area, conducted by the University of Chicago, found that over a 40-year period stocks listed on the New York Stock Exchange gained an average of 9.3 per cent a year, lumping the good years together with the bad. What makes this figure particularly impressive is that the 40-year period included the Depression, when stock prices were in a state of total collapse.

Facing is the Dow Jones Industrial Average, a compilation based on the prices of 30 well-known common stocks, such as General Motors and Sears Roebuck. It is Wall Street's most popular measure

The Dow Jones Industrials

of how the stock market is performing, and will give you an idea of the general upward trend of stock prices since the end of World War II.

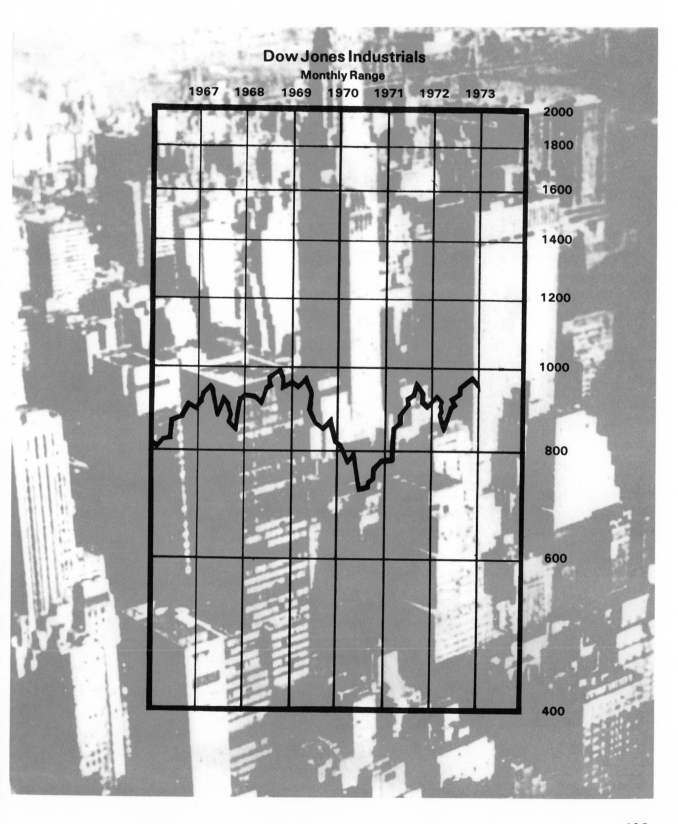

125

The stock market

The need for good investment advice

Unless you take the time and trouble to study investment in depth, you must seek advice before plunging into the stock market. You need guidance on what shares to buy and on the timing of your purchases.

This is a point that cannot be emphasized too much. For without good investment information, your chances of success in the stock market are slim. "Hot tips" from friends and purchases of stocks on hunches simply won't do, and if that's the way you intend to invest your interests would be better served by leaving your money in the bank.

WISEGUIDE

Good information is the key to successful investing.

Finding a stockbroker

Finding a competent stockbroker is the first step in investing, and perhaps the most important step of all.

Stockbrokers are the people who handle orders to buy and sell stocks and who, in most cases, dispense advice to their customers on which stocks might offer the best opportunity for profit.

Narrowing your search

In the first area — the handling of buy and sell orders — most major brokerage houses stand on roughly equal ground. It's in the second area — the dispensing of investment advice — that you should concentrate your search.

Unfortunately, stockbrokers tend to promise better advice than they actually provide, and often they aren't really interested in servicing an account of less than $10,000 (even though nearly two-thirds of all American investors fall into the under-$10,000 category).

WISEGUIDE

It can be hard for a small investor to find an astute broker. You may have to do some searching. But this is time well spent if you hope to be successful in the stock market.

The Stock Exchange's referral service

To help investors with small amounts of cash find a stockbroker, the New York Stock Exchange provides a free referral service. You can receive a list of brokers willing to take on your account, no matter what the size, by writing to Directory, Post Office Box 1971, Radio City Station, New York, N.Y. 10019.

With a little hunting about, however, you should be able to find a stockbroker on your own. Most of the very large firms — such as Merrill Lynch, Pierce, Fenner & Smith; Bache & Co.; and Paine, Webber, Jackson & Curtis — will take an account of just about any size. You can either arrange an appointment in advance or just walk in off the street. Even better, a friend or business associate might be able to recommend a competent broker with whom he's dealt.

First off, you'll want to do business only with a brokerage house that can display this shield:

Your account should be insured by SIPC....

This means the firm is a member of the government-sponsored Securities Investor Protection Corporation, and that your account is automatically insured for up to $50,000 (including a maximum $20,000 cash balance) in the event the broker goes out of business.

You should be careful to note, however, that you are in no way insured by SIPC against losses in the stock market itself. You are insured only against the broker's inability to return the cash and securities he owes you if his firm goes on the rocks.

...but you aren't insured against market losses

Some investors leave their stock certificates with their broker as a convenience. You should never leave more than $50,000 worth, however, since that's the maximum insurance coverage.

WISEGUIDE

Other important considerations

Beyond doing business only with an SIPC-member broker, you should take these factors into consideration:

Profitable?

● Is the firm profitable? Some brokerage firms will give you their latest profit-and-loss statement, others won't. But you should satisfy yourself that the firm is doing well earnings-wise and isn't heading for financial trouble that could leave you stranded. Recent experience has showed that brokers, just like other businessmen, aren't immune to bankruptcy.

Successful recommendations?

● How good have the firm's past recommendations been? It's doubtful that any firm will give you a complete rundown, since they aren't required by law to do so. But you might ask for some old research reports and check the price of each stock then versus now. If you find only one or two winners, it's a tip-off that the firm's recommendations probably aren't that good. Or perhaps a friend who does business with the firm can tell you in general terms how successful his broker's advice has been.

The account executive?

● What do you think of the individual salesman (usually called an account executive or registered representative) who will handle your account? He will be your sole contact at the firm, and if you don't feel comfortable about dealing with him you should look elsewhere for a broker.

WISEGUIDE

As with retaining a lawyer, the individual account executive is as important as the brokerage firm itself.

Other sources of advice

Although brokers are the main source of investment advice, they aren't the only one.

Advisory services

Several hundred organizations publish stock market advisory services, ranging from mimeographed newsletters to detailed weekly market reports, to help investors choose which issues to buy. Their quality varies widely. A subscription to one or two of the better services might prove helpful if you invest mainly on your own, rather than relying on your broker's advice. Names and addresses of specific services can be tracked down in the financial sections of major daily newspapers, particularly The New York Times. The best approach would be to start with an inexpensive three-month trial offer, so you can decide for yourself whether the service is worthwhile before committing to a full one-year subscription.

Investment managers

Some organizations, such as bank trust departments and investment management firms, will take over full management of your investments, saving you the headaches and fuss. It can be tricky business choosing a good firm, for two main reasons: you are never quite sure how effective a job they'll do, and, for the most part, these firms only take on large accounts. Small investors tend to be left out in the cold when it comes to this kind of total management. Retention of an investment manager isn't a very realistic alternative, then, for investors with only $5,000 or $10,000.

Investing on your own

If, on the other hand, you are sufficiently enthusiastic to manage your own investments without any professional advice at all, you can start with one of the books on investment which have been published in recent years. The financial columns of the press are useful sources of everyday company news and of background material. In addition, you can obtain any company's latest annual and quarterly financial reports — even if you aren't a stockholder in that company — by writing to the company's corporate secretary.

Your stockbroker also might be of some help when you have questions, but don't expect him to be equipped to educate a beginner in investments. If you only have a small amount to invest, he cannot afford to spend too much time on your affairs.

The more knowledge the better

The more you can learn about companies the better. For example, it would pay to have a basic knowledge of profit-and-loss statements and balance sheets. The main thing is to acquire sufficient background to understand the workings of the market and be able to fathom the financial prospects for individual companies.

It can be great fun to follow the stock market and keep track of your own investment performance. But experience, as in so many other matters, can only come with time. If it becomes a strain rather than a pleasure, the simple answer is to invest in mutual funds (which are discussed in Chapter 13).

WISEGUIDE

A little knowledge is a dangerous thing. You cannot learn too much about your investments.

Different kinds of investments

A variety of choices

Americans have an astonishing array of investment vehicles and techniques to choose from. It's a confusing assortment, and professional advice is a must for any investor who isn't quite sure whether he should be putting his money into common stocks or buying municipal bonds or investing in a convertible debenture or whatever.

Brokers, lawyers, accountants and bankers all are equipped either to give broad advice on choice of investments or steer you to someone who does know. Beware, however, of the investment salesman coming to you unsolicited with hot deal in hand, because he probably is trying to sell you whatever earns him the biggest commission, regardless of your actual needs.

The pros and cons of investing

Advantages:

As the nation prospers and business profits increase, stock prices can be expected to rise also. In this way investing offers individuals from all walks of life a chance to participate in the economic growth of America.

Ownership of common stocks, like ownership of other forms of pro perty, can provide a hedge against inflation, because stock prices often rise during periods of mild to moderate inflation, helping to offset the erosion in the real value of money.

Tax advantages can be gained from long-term investing. In particular, your profit on any stock that you hold at least six months before selling, is subject to only half the rate of federal income tax that is applied to most other types of income.

The mechanics of investing are relatively simple. Unlike most other forms of property, shares of stock can be bought and sold easily. Also, prices can be checked daily in the newspaper or by calling your stockbroker.

Disadvantages:

The most obvious is the risk. While in past years stock prices have tended to rise, you never can be sure about the future.

Even if the market as a whole does go up, your own stocks might go down. To spread the risk, you should purchase a number of quality issues — three of four at minimum — rather than shooting all your money on one.

If you suddenly need to sell your stocks to raise cash, you may be forced to do so at a time when prices are low. It's important, therefore, to set emergency cash aside in a savings account before you invest.

It can be difficult for the small investor to obtain sound investment advice. Wall Street tends to reserve its best advice for big investors, and this can put the small stockholder at a competitive disadvantage in the market.

How to read a stock table in the newspaper

The highest and lowest prices, in dollars per share, that this particular stock has been traded for during the current year

Name of the stock (unless otherwise specified, this the the company's common stock; preferred stock is denoted by "pfd," warrants by "wt")

Annual cash dividend currently being paid on this stock; if there is no dividend indicated, then probably none is being paid

The day's trading volume in this stock in hundreds of shares (42 equals 4,200 shares, for instance)

The change in closing price from the previous day's closing price

The last — or "closing" — price at which the stock was traded during the day

The day's lowest price

The highest price at which the stock was traded during the day

The price-earnings ratio for this stock (the previous day's closing price divided by the latest 12-month, per-share earnings for the company); Wall Street uses price-earnings ratios to measure relative values among different stocks

— 1972 —				Sales	P-E				Net
High	Low	Stocks	Div.	100s	Ratio	High	Low	Close	Chg.
39¾	29¾	Dillon	.80b	24	19	31	30⅝	30⅝	− ⅞
201¾	132¾	Disney	.20b	68	70	181	179¼	180¼	+ ¼
26	17⅜	Disston	.03e	54	17	19¾	19½	19½	
42	33⅜	DistSeag	.70	8	21	38⅜	38⅛	38⅜	− ½
9⅞	3	Diversfd Ind		45		3⅛	3	3	− ⅛
30	25⅛	DivMge	2.73e	62	10	26⅞	26½	26⅞	+ ⅜
54⅞	36¾	DrPepper	.43	20	61	49½	49⅛	49½	+ ½
80	54	DomeMns	.80	9	32	67⅞	67½	67½	+ ¼
9½	8	DomkFd	.63e	18		8¾	8⅜	8¾	+ ¼
13¾	9⅜	DonLJen	.10e	9	12	9¾	9⅝	9¾	
28	18½	Donnelley	.44	43	16	21⅜	21¼	21¼	+ ⅛
39¼	19⅝	Doric Cp	.32	8	12	28	27⅝	27⅝	− ⅛
26½	13	Dorr Oliver		17	140	18¼	18¼	18¼	
17⅞	12⅞	Dorsey	.10	17	8	13	12⅝	12⅝	− ⅜
58½	51⅛	Dover Cp	.78	2	18	54	54	54	− ⅜
98¾	78	DowChm	1.80	55	25	95⅞	95⅜	95⅜	
13⅜	4⅝	DPF Inc		24		5½	5⅛	5⅛	− ½
36⅜	26½	DravoCp	1.40	9	11	29	28⅝	29	+ ½
44⅛	30¾	DressInd	1.40	102	16	42⅜	41⅝	42	− ⅜
47½	36¾	Dress pf	2.20	25	...	44⅜	43¾	44	− ¾
42	33¾	Dressr pfB	2	19	...	39¼	38⅞	39	....

131

The stock market

With so many different types of investments available, it can be hard to choose what's right for your individual needs. Professional advice is in order, particularly if you venture outside the stock market.

A. A closer look at common stocks

As we've discussed, common stocks are the most important type of investment. They are sometimes referred to as "equities," since they give you rights of ownership in the company.

Some stocks are "listed" on a stock exchange, others are traded "over the counter." This can be an important distinction.

Listed stocks

Listed stocks tend to be those of the larger, more stable companies (although there are many exceptions to this rule). Price movements, in turn, tend to be less erratic in these stocks. Also, more information about daily trading activity is available.

There are 13 different stock exchanges spread across the nation, the two largest being the New York and American stock exchanges, both located in New York.

What is a stock exchange?

An exchange is just what the term implies. It's a central marketplace where stockbrokers get together to buy and sell shares. The advantage is that all orders in a particular stock will be channeled to a single spot on the trading floor, providing greater control over the ebb and flow in each issue.

Each exchange is an independent organization, operating under government supervision, that sets its own standards for the types of stocks it will allow to be traded at its facilities. For instance, the New York Stock Exchange, by far the biggest of all, requires that a company earn at least $2.5 million annually before taxes and have at least 2,000 stockholders before its shares can be admitted to trading. Thus, a listing there is a sign that the company is well established.

Even though purchase of a listed stock often involves less risk, this doesn't absolve you of the need to investigate carefully before you buy.

The OTC market

Stocks of companies that don't qualify for listing on an exchange are traded over the counter. (In addition, a few major corporations, such as American Express, Anheuser-Busch and Bank of America, have chosen for various reasons not to seek a stock exchange listing even though they are fully qualified. Their shares also are traded "OTC.")

How it works

Over the counter simply means that there is no central spot where the shares are traded. A variety of individual OTC dealers across the nation, working out of their own offices, each buys and sells the stock. These dealers communicate with each other by telephone and electronically through a special computer system called NASDAQ, rather than meeting physically on a trading floor to buy and sell. Since OTC is an informal network rather than a formal organization with specific listing standards, any stock can be traded there, no matter how big or small. The only requirement is that someone wants to buy or sell the shares.

In past years the OTC market, because of its lack of structure, has tended toward shoddiness in the way it operates. But tremendous strides have been made, and the disadvantages of buying OTC stocks — namely a lack of trading information and a tendency for prices to collapse in times of stress — are no longer the major deterrents they once were.

The need for caution

Investors should, nonetheless, be a bit more cautious about dealing in OTC stocks than in listed ones. OTC stocks are generally more speculative in nature than listed securities. If you are able to pick a fast-growing young OTC company that hasn't yet qualified for listing on a stock exchange, you could make a lot of money. But for every big OTC winner there are probably an equal number of big losers. Investigate before you invest.

WISEGUIDE

The OTC market is the proving ground for young companies not yet qualified for a stock exchange listing. As such, the potential risks and potential rewards both tend to be greater for investors.

B. Preferred stock

Some companies, in addition to raising capital through the sale of common stock, issue "preferred" stock.

Holders of a company's preferred shares stand one position in line ahead of holders of the common stock, particularly in terms of their rights to collect dividends.

Rights to collect arrears

If earnings are poor and the dividend has to be cut, the dividend on the common stock goes first. If there still isn't enough money for dividends, only then does the preferred dividend go. Even if that does happen, however, preferred stockholders generally have rights to collect "arrears" — that is, if and when profits go back up again they receive all their overdue dividends before a dividend can be paid on the common stock.

Sound good? It is if all you want from your investment is a steady annual cash income. The problem is that the dividend rate on preferred stock never changes. No matter how much the company's earnings rise, there is no increase in the preferred dividend rate.

WISEGUIDE

Preferred stockholders receive a steady cash income. But since they don't share in the company's profits, there's little chance for making capital gains on this type of stock.

C. Bonds and debentures

At the front of the line, when it comes to claims against the company, are the holders of its debt securities.

The two main types are bonds, which represent a lien against a specific piece of the company's property, and debentures, which represent a more general claim against the company's property as a whole. The claims of bondholders have preference over those of debentureholders if the company goes bankrupt and has to be liquidated.

Debt securities are issued for a specified period of time, often 30 or 40 years, and at a specific rate of interest. When the term of issuance expires, the bond is said to "mature" and the holder receives his money back in full. In effect, the holder has made a loan to the corporation for that period.

Safety plus high yields

High quality corporate bonds are an extremely safe investment that have recently provided annual yields in the range of 8 to 9 per cent.

Drawbacks

But there are three major drawbacks to investing in bonds:

● Minimum purchase generally is $1,000, and even that is low. Many dealers won't handle orders of less than $10,000.

● Bond prices fluctuate in the open market, in response to changes in interest rates. If prices decline, you may not be able to get all your money back unless you wait to maturity.

● By owning bonds you have no protection against the effects of inflation. During inflationary periods the price of a common stock can rise substantially, helping to offset the erosion in the purchasing value of your dollars. Bonds, on the other hand, provide no such hedge.

WISEGUIDE

Corporate bonds are the most secure type of corporate investment, followed by debentures, preferred shares and common shares.

D. Convertible securities

Convertible securities, a relatively new type of investment, have become quite popular in recent years with both the corporations that issue them and the investors who buy them. They come in two basic forms — convertible debentures and convertible preferred stock.

The best of two worlds?

Convertible securities represent an imaginative attempt to provide investors with the best of two worlds. The dividend or interest rate is predetermined, just as with any other debt security. In addition, the securities can be converted into the company's common stock at a specified ratio of exchange.

It is this "conversion feature" that provides investors with leverage for profits. If the price of the company's common stock rises, the value of the convertible securities also will rise since there's more value to the shares for which the securities can be swapped. Meanwhile, the holder of the convertible securities has the protection of a fixed interest or dividend rate (although this rate is usually quite a bit lower than on non-convertible debt securities).

WISEGUIDE

The purchase of convertible securities is an intriguing new area of investment. To get into this field, however, you will need professional advice, since conversion ratios, market values and rates of return can be extremely complex.

E. Warrants

A somewhat related, although much riskier, form of investment is the purchase of warrants.

If you hold a company's warrants — and only a few dozen companies have actually issued these hybrid securities — you have the right to purchase a specified number of the company's common shares for a specified price until a given date. This is different from a convertible security in two ways: there is no underlying market value to the warrant itself, and when you use a warrant to acquire stock you have to pay cash (whereas conversion of a convertible security into stock doesn't involve any cash outlay; the only cash you have paid is to acquire the convertible security itself).

An example will illustrate how warrants work:

An example

Gulf + Western Industries, the big conglomerate, is one of the companies that has issued warrants. Each G+W warrant automatically entitles the holder to buy 1.027 G+W common shares from the company for $55 whenever he wants, up to an expiration date of January 31, 1978. After adjusting this total price to the basis of a single share of stock, the equivalent purchase rate is about $53.55 a share. In other words, if the market price of G+W common stock is greater than $53.55, the warrant has some value since it would enable you to buy stock at that price and immediately resell for the higher market price. If the warrant expires without G+W stock ever reaching that level, however, you lose whatever you paid to buy the warrant.

WISEGUIDE

Warrants are a highly speculative form of investment and are not recommended for the beginning investor.

F. Buying on margin

Purchasing securities on "margin" is a method of investment rather than a type of security.

To use margin is to buy securities with borrowed money. This is particularly relevant to the purchase of common stocks. The Federal Reserve Board regulates the amount of cash you have to put up (currently 65 per cent of the total price of the stock). You can borrow the rest, or the other 35 per cent, from your broker or bank.

How you can profit

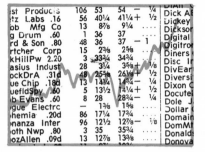

What this does is give you leverage to make more money than you could from a straight cash purchase. A simple example will illustrate:

You buy 100 shares of stock X for $50 a share, or a $5,000 total price. You decide it would be appropriate to do so "on margin," and so you put up the required minimum of $3,250 in cash ($5,000 x 65%) and instruct your broker to lend you the other $1,750. Then, much to your delight, everything works out according to plan. The price of the stock rises to $100 a share, or a total value of $10,000, and you sell. After deducting the $1,750 loan from the $10,000 sale price, you've come out with $8,250 in cash for yourself. Not bad, considering that you have nearly tripled your initial $3,250 investment. If you had bought totally on cash, you would have doubled your investment, since the price of the stock itself exactly doubled.

How you can lose

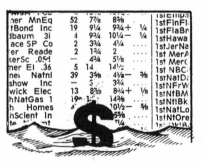

But let's look at the same transaction another way. Suppose the price of the stock had declined to $17.50 a share (or a total market value of $1,750) instead of rising. What would that leave for you? Exactly nothing. The $1,750 market value, you will note, is equal to the loan, which still has to be repaid. Your $3,250 investment has been wiped out.

The advantage of buying on margin, then, is that whatever you make on the borrowed money is yours to keep. You only have to repay the loan with interest, not give the lender a share of your profits.

The danger is that you could easily lose everything you put in, because the loan has to be repaid before you can collect any cash for yourself from the ultimate sale of the shares.

WISEGUIDE

Margin purchases give you extra leverage to make lots of money or lose it all.

G. Municipal bonds

No discussion of investment opportunities would be complete without mention of tax-exempt municipal bonds and of U.S. Treasury securities.

From the standpoint of the individual investor, municipals are the more important of the two. They are debt securities issued by the thousands of state and local governments throughout the nation — your own town, for instance, or the local school district — to raise money for new facilities.

Tax-free interest

These bonds offer the special feature of tax-free income. The interest you receive is free and clear of federal income taxes. You don't even have to report it on your tax return!

This is particularly valuable to well-to-do investors in the higher tax brackets. For example, a 4 per cent interest rate on a municipal bond would, for an investor in the 50 per cent tax bracket, provide an "equivalent taxable yield" of 8 per cent. This is because half of the 8 per cent he earned on a taxable investment would simply end up going to Uncle Sam anyway.

Here are some other "equivalent yields," by income bracket, based on 1972 tax rates for couples filing joint returns:

Some typical equivalent yields

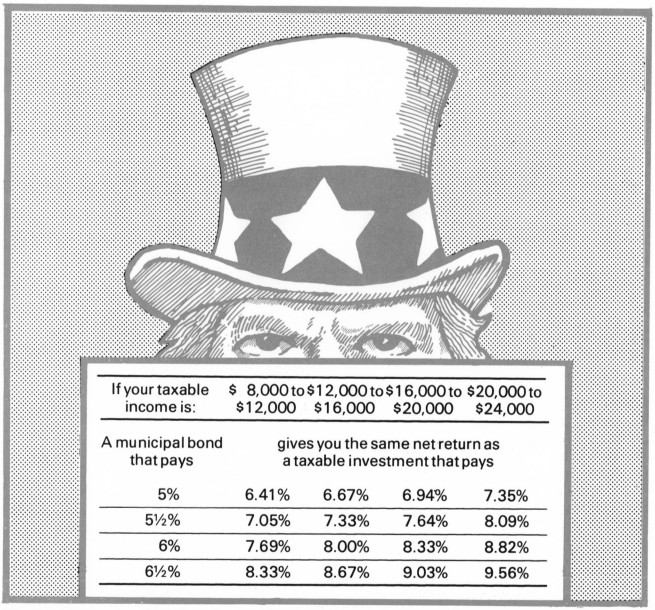

If your taxable income is:	$ 8,000 to $12,000	$12,000 to $16,000	$16,000 to $20,000	$20,000 to $24,000
A municipal bond that pays	gives you the same net return as a taxable investment that pays			
5%	6.41%	6.67%	6.94%	7.35%
5½%	7.05%	7.33%	7.64%	8.09%
6%	7.69%	8.00%	8.33%	8.82%
6½%	8.33%	8.67%	9.03%	9.56%

In recent years a number of brokerage firms have started promoting the sale of municipal bonds to the average investor. Unless you want a quarterly cash income from your investment (rather than long-term capital gains) and are in a high tax bracket, however, buying municipals probably would be a mistake. The stock market is still a better place to make substantial amounts of money over a long period of time.

Who should buy municipals?

The stock market

H. U.S. Government securities

The federal government, through the U.S. Treasury, issues a variety of different debt securities. These are the most secure investments available, since they are guaranteed from default (but not from price declines) by the U.S. government itself. Because of their safety, they tend to carry lower interest rates than comparable corporate bonds.

Among the specific types of government securities are long-term bonds, medium-term notes and short-term Treasury bills.

Treasury bills

Of the three, Treasury bills are of the most potential interest to the average investor, especially during periods of instability in the stock market. These short-term securities are a safe place to put your money temporarily, often at an attractive yield, if you think it's a bad time to own stocks. Treasury bills are sold in denominations of $100,000 and up.

The mechanics of investing

A simple process

Once you have opened a brokerage account, the mechanics of investing are relatively simple.

You phone in any order to your account executive, and the firm then buys or sells the common shares or other security as you have directed. A bill confirming all the details is mailed to you, and you are given five business days from the date of the transaction to pay for the purchase. Conversely, the broker is allowed to wait five business days before crediting your account with cash proceeds from a sale.

What a quotation is

It is a good idea to ask your broker for a "quotation" before actually placing an order, however. After checking out the market for that particular stock, he should respond with a "bid" price and an "asked" (or in the case of a listed stock he may simply tell you the latest price at which the shares have actually been traded). The "bid" might be, say, $29 a share, meaning that some other investor or dealer is willing to buy your shares for that price. The "asked" might be $29.50, which means that the shares are available for purchase in the open market for that much. This gives you an advance indication of how much you can expect to receive or pay, depending on whether you want to sell or buy.

Are you satisfied with the quotation price? Perhaps not. Maybe **Open orders**
you are disappointed that you cannot get more money for your
shares or that you cannot buy the stock for less. If so, you may want
to hold out for a better price. In this case you can specify to your
broker that you will only sell for X dollars or more a share or buy
for a certain amount or less. This is called placing an "open order,"
and your broker is automatically obligated to purchase or sell the
securities if and when the price reaches the level you have specified.

Besides the cost of the stock itself, you have to pay a fee, or **What it costs to invest**
"commission," to your broker for each transaction he handles for
you. Commissions average about 2 per cent of the total price,
although on transactions of less than $200 they can range as high
as 6 per cent. As you can see, buying small amounts of shares is
expensive.
   Commissions are calculated on the basis of a sliding scale. The
following rates are typical of those charged by brokerage houses to
buy or sell shares on the New York Stock Exchange. If you buy,
the commission is added to the price. If you sell, it is deducted from
the cash you receive.

	$5 Stock	$20 Stock	$50 Stock
50 Shares	$9.40	$23.00	$42.50
100 Shares	$16.40	$38.00	$65.00
200 Shares	$32.80	$70.00	$124.00
300 Shares	$49.20	$94.00	$175.00

   In addition to paying a commission, on small orders — generally **The "odd-lot differential"**
those of less than 100 shares — transacted on a stock exchange you
also will be charged an "odd-lot differential." This is simply an
extra charge that is tacked on, on top of the commission. On the
New York Stock Exchange, the rate is one-eighth of a dollar
(or 12½ cents) per share. In other words, if you buy 50 shares of a
stock selling for $20 a share, you actually will be charged $20⅛. If
you sell 50 shares of a stock with a market price of $20, you will
actually receive only $19⅞. Sound like the odds are stacked against
the small investor? You are right. Whenever possible, then, you
should deal only in blocks of 100 or more shares and avoid paying
an odd-lot differential.

One way to avoid excessively high commissions if you only have a **Monthly Investment Plan**
small amount to invest is to sign up through your broker for the
New York Stock Exchange's Monthly Investment Plan. This program enables you to make monthly purchases of a NYSE-listed
stock at special commission rates. However, some brokerage houses
won't open an MIP account for you.

Payroll deduction plans

A better possibility is that your employer may offer a payroll-deduction MIP program that enables you to buy his stock. Several hundred major corporations do so, and they pay the brokerage commissions for employees as an added incentive for them to invest in the company. An employee who owns a piece of the business, the theory goes, will tend to take his work more seriously.

Dollar cost averaging

Besides the savings on commissions, MIP enables you to "dollar cost average" your purchases. In other words, rather than trying to guess whether a particular moment is a good time to buy stocks, you are buying regularly each month on the assumption that your average purchase price will work out to a reasonable level and that you will make a profit by holding onto the shares for the long haul.

Some final words of advice

Which gets us back to the most important point in this chapter. As a small investor, you have little hope of outsmarting the professionals who trade in and out of the market each day. You can't expect to beat them at their own game. If you do decide to invest, then, make sure you investigate carefully before you buy, make sure you buy several different quality issues in order to spread your risk, and make sure you don't lose sight of your long-term investment objectives in a vain attempt to make a quick killing.

A profile of America's 32 million stockholders

Average age is 48

Median income is $13,500

Nearly two-thirds own less than $10,000 of stock

People owning more than $50,000 of stocks, on the other hand, make up less than 10 per cent of the shareholder population

Women don't really control the nation's wealth after all! Barely over half of all adult stockholders are men, barely under half women

Among minors, the male lead is bigger. Boy stockholders outnumber girls by three to two

Housewives and retired persons are the leading occupational group

More than three-quarters live in metropolitan areas

Less than one per cent are farmers

More than half have attended college

More than 10 per cent, however, didn't even complete high school

They must be rich in Vermont! That state leads the nation, with nearly a third of its residents owning stock

In absolute terms, though, California is the leader, with 1.3 million resident shareholders

Chapter 13

Mutual funds

If you have read Chapter 12, you may be interested in investing in the stock market but still may have reservations about it. Do any of these descriptions apply to you?

Are mutual funds for me?

- You would like to invest, but know very little about stocks.

- You are prepared to take some risk, but would like to minimize it as much as possible.

- After providing for your essential savings, life insurance and so on, you only have a small amount left over for investing.

- You have little spare time and cannot afford to devote it to keeping up on the stock market.

If any of these descriptions fits, you may find that investing through a mutual fund is the answer to your needs.

A mutual fund is an organization through which a large number of investors pool their money and put the combined sum under the care of a professional investment manager.

What a mutual fund is

The key point to keep in mind is that when you buy shares in a mutual fund you are in effect becoming part owner of the common stocks held by that fund and you make or lose money according to how well those stocks do in the market.

Some financial counselors believe that the stock market has become too treacherous for small investors who want to buy and sell stocks on their own. They suggest that buying shares in a good "no-load" mutual fund — one that doesn't add a sales charge onto the price of its stock — has become the best course of action for most small investors.

WISEGUIDE

Is it the best course for you, though? This chapter deals with that and other questions about mutual funds.

Should I buy a "no-load" fund?

Who actually buys mutual-fund shares? Although fund shareholders come from all walks of life and live in all 50 states, the heaviest concentration is among the well-educated and among families in the upper income brackets. For example, 30 per cent of all American families with incomes of $25,000 or more a year own fund shares compared with only 2.4 per cent among families earning less than $8,000. The "average" mutual-fund owner is in his mid-40's, has some college education and earns $13,000 to $14,000 annually.

The "average" mutual-fund owner

Mutual funds

Altogether, about 8.5 million Americans own mutual-fund shares. Many of them invest directly in the stock market as well and use fund shares to supplement their overall investment program.

WISEGUIDE

Far and away the most common objective of those who buy mutual-fund shares is to build up a substantial nestegg for retirement.

Advantages: Investing through a mutual fund offers these advantages:

Diversification
- Diversification of risk. Most funds buy 100 or more different stocks, so that there is little danger that your assets will be appreciably affected by a sharp price decline in any one or two.

Professional management
- Professional management of your investments. The person in charge of a fund's investment portfolio usually is an individual of considerable experience and training. You probably would find it impossible to afford to retain such an individual on your own.

Convenience
- Convenience and simplicity. As you will see, it is an easy matter to buy a fund's shares and, subsequently, to sell them back to the fund if and when you want your original cash plus your profits — or minus your losses, if the fund hasn't done well.

Disadvantages: There are two main disadvantages:

Inconsistent results
- Not all mutual funds are equally successful. There are many good funds, but many mediocre and downright bad ones as well. You must be careful, therefore, to check out a fund's investment record before you buy. Even if you do pick a fund with a good record, however, you cannot be absolutely sure; the fund's manager might lose his touch and you would be stuck with a second-rate investment.

Limited profit potential
- You are unlikely to get rich buying fund shares, and you will miss out on the fun and excitement of managing your own investments.

WISEGUIDE

If you invest on your own, you might possibly make a killing by putting all your money into one stock that goes through the roof. But the diversified portfolio of a mutual fund reduces your chance for huge profits — just as it reduces your risk of big losses.

Mutual-fund investors can do well
Nonetheless, many mutual-fund investors have done quite well over the years. A recent study gave these figures:

1) If you had made a $10,000 deposit in a savings account at the beginning of 1950 and left it there untouched at 5 per cent interest

"No Load" versus "Load" Funds

How far ahead are you by investing in a no-load mutual fund (one *without* a sales charge) instead of in a load fund (one *with* a sales charge tacked onto the price of its shares)?

One large mutual fund that recently dropped its 8½ per cent sales fee and switched over to no-load status is Financial Industrial Income Fund. In doing so, that fund decided to go back and calculate how an investor would have fared over the years if the fund had sold its shares on a no-load basis all along.

The initial investment cited in this theoretical example is $10,000, made on February 1, 1960. On a load basis, the value of this investment would have immediately been reduced to $9,150 after deduction of an $850 sales fee. On a no-load basis, by contrast, the $10,000 would have retained its full value.

As you can see, that $850 initial difference turns into $3,231 over a period of 12 years.

We want to emphasize, however, that a no-load fund that performs poorly is no bargain. In that case you are better off paying a sales fee and investing in a load fund that does well.

Year ended December 31	Value of "load" investment	Value of "no-load" investment	Difference
Initial investment	$ 9,150	$10,000	$ 850
1960	11,133	12,170	1,037
1961	12,860	14,062	1,202
1962	12,562	13,727	1,165
1963	15,226	16,643	1,417
1964	17,721	19,370	1,649
1965	20,863	22,804	1,941
1966	19,711	21,550	1,839
1967	27,193	29,697	2,534
1968	37,588	41,095	3,507
1969	31,407	34,339	2,932
1970	29,657	32,424	2,767
1971	34,631	37,862	3,231

(compounded annually) until the end of 1971, you would have ended up with a total of $29,256.

2) If, on the other hand, you had used that same $10,000 to buy shares in the typical mutual fund, you would have ended up with $94,008.

Sound good? It is. But you should keep in mind that the 1950-71 period was one of the best ever in the stock market. Prices rose in 16 of those 22 years. There is no assurance that prices will continue to rise nearly as sharply in coming years.

**Prices can go down
as well as up**

In other words, there is a degree of risk no matter how you invest in the stock market.

WISEGUIDE

If you are not prepared to risk your money, don't invest — not even through a mutual fund.

How a mutual fund works

How does a mutual fund operate? In simple terms, the basic concept goes like this:

A group of investors gets together and decides that each, on his own, cannot do very well in the stock market. So they pool their investment funds and hire a professional investment manager to take charge. The investment manager makes all decisions on which stocks to buy and sell. He also takes care of all administrative details, and every three months he sends each of the fund members a written report on how well the fund is doing.

In return, he takes for himself an annual fee equal to approximately ½ of 1 per cent of the dollar amount of assets (stocks plus cash and other assets) in the fund; this fee is deducted from the dividend income earned by the fund or, if necessary, from the fund itself.

**Buying into the fund
and getting back out**

Sound simple? So far it is. But what happens if one of the fund members decides that he wants to take out some or all of his money because he needs it to buy a house or send his son through college? Or what happens if a friend of one of the original members hears about the fund and decides that he would like to join in?

Obviously there has to be some way to decide the exact amount of money that will be given back to the original investor who wants to get out and the price that the new investor must pay to get in. Why not base both amounts, you might ask, on the current market

value of the stocks and other assets in the fund? Just total up the value of everything in the fund and divide by the number of people participating. Well, in essence that is exactly what is done.

Once a day, each mutual fund calculates its "net asset value per share" — an amount equal to the total assets of the fund divided by the number of shares in the fund that are owned by investors. This figure fluctuates from minute to minute, of course, in line with changes in the market value of the stocks owned by the fund.

What is the "per-share net asset value"?

When you buy or sell shares in a mutual fund, the price is based on the latest day's net asset value per share.

WISEGUIDE

There is one hitch, however. Although almost all funds buy back their shares at the exact net asset value (a few buy back at net asset value less 1 or 2 per cent), the vast majority of mutual funds tack on a fee of around 8½ per cent when they sell you their shares. To see how this works, look at some typical price quotations taken from the standard table of mutual fund prices in the morning newspaper.

The high cost of sales fees

	Bid price	Asked price
Affiliated Fund	$ 7.07	$ 7.65
Dreyfus Fund	12.59	13.80
Fidelity Fund	17.31	18.92
Investment Company of America	14.73	16.10
Investors Mutual	10.73	11.67
Massachusetts Investors Trust	12.79	13.98
Wellington Fund	12.10	13.22

In each case, the "bid" price equals the net asset value per share. This is the amount of money you will receive if you own shares in the fund and decide to turn them back in for cash.

The bid price

The "asked" price, on the other hand, is the amount you will have to pay if you want to buy shares in the fund. It includes a mark-up for a sales fee.

The asked price

Mutual funds

You will receive nothing in return for this sales fee. It simply covers the fund's costs of paying the broker or salesman who sold you the shares and the costs of advertising and other marketing expenses.

What is a "load" fund?

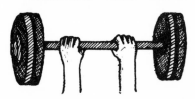

Funds that charge a sales fee are sometimes referred to as "load" funds. There are approximately 500 such funds in existence in this country. Many load funds have done an outstanding job of investing their shareholders' money over the years, but you nonetheless start out 8½ per cent behind when you buy shares in one of these funds. The per-share asset value will have to rise that much ju ʋ for you to break even; only after that can you make a profit.

Stockbrokers and other financial salesmen are paid big commissions for selling the shares of "load" funds — which is a major reason why they push them so hard.

Will a salesman really recommend the best fund?

This is a point you must watch out for. Don't buy a particular fund just because a salesman tells you to. His main interest could be to line his own pocket.

"Net redemptions"

Partly because of the high sales fees, many investors have turned sour on mutual funds in the last few years. This is reflected in a recent surge in "net redemptions" — an excess of shares being cashed in over new shares being bought by investors. Before mid-1971, the mutual fund industry had *never* experienced a single month when redemptions were bigger than sales. Now that kind of month is routine. Increasingly, investors have been getting out of mutual funds and putting the money into savings accounts.

No-load funds

There is an alternative, however, to buying a load fund. This is to buy shares in a "no-load" fund — one that doesn't charge any sales fees. You can purchase shares in a no-load fund one day and, if the asset value doesn't change, turn around and sell them right back to the fund the next day at the same price. There are nearly 200 no-load funds to choose from, and the number is growing every month.

Most brokers won't tell you how to find a good no-load fund, since there is no sales commission in it for them.

Finding a no-load fund

But you can track down specific funds by looking for the small advertisements they often run in the financial sections of major newspapers or you can obtain a list of members in the No-Load Mutual Fund Association by writing to the Association at 475 Park Avenue South, New York, N.Y. 10016.

A good no-load fund is probably your best bet, then. But how do **How to choose a**
you go about choosing one? Here are the steps: **specific fund**

1) What are your basic investment objectives? You should decide **Investment objectives**
before you invest. If you are young and willing to take a greater-
than-average risk, you probably will want a "growth" fund that
tries to build up its assets by buying stocks with superior performance potential. If you are retired, on the other hand, you might
want to look at "income" funds — ones that emphasize dividend
and interest income more than growth.

There are five basic categories of funds to choose from, listed here **WISEGUIDE**
in order from least to most conservative: capital gains funds,
long-term growth funds, funds that emphasize a combination of
growth and current dividend income, balanced funds, and income
funds.

---

2) Look into the 10-year performance records of the funds in the **How well have the fund's**
category you have chosen. Forbes magazine runs an excellent **investments performed?**
annual survey of fund performance. There also are a number of
specialized publications that provide data in this area; often, they
advertise in major newspapers. Or perhaps your local library has a
copy of Investment Companies, a book published annually by
Arthur Wiesenberger & Co.; this is *the* definitive publication in
rating fund results.

Short-term investment performance — one or two years, for in- **WISEGUIDE**
stance — is relatively meaningless. You want to know how well a
fund has done year in and year out, in bad markets as well as good.

---

3) Once you have focused on three or four funds with superior **Send for a free**
records, write to each for a copy of its prospectus. This is a detailed **prospectus**
document that must, by law, be given to you before you buy any
shares. Read it over:

• Check whether the fund might possibly be in hot water with the
Securities & Exchange Commission, the government agency that
keeps watch over mutual funds.

• Does the fund's performance stack up the way you thought?

• Is the fund so large that it might have difficulty keeping up its
investment record? Any fund with more than $1 billion in assets
begins to become clumsy to manage. It's best to keep away from
funds this big if you are looking for truly outstanding performance.

• Are the fund's latest redemptions greater than its sales of new
shares? This is a key point to look for, because if the fund is suffering from a consistent net outflow of cash the fund manager may
have to be more concerned with how to sell off stocks in order to

raise this cash, than with achieving good performance. You can find this bit of information in the fund's "statement of changes in net assets" toward the back of the prospectus. Look in this table for the specific number of shares sold versus number redeemed, and then calculate whether the latter exceeds the former.

* Are management fees reasonable — less than ½ of 1 per cent of the fund's net assets each year?

4) Choose a fund.

5) Once you have bought, keep track of the fund's record.

WISEGUIDE

If, after you have bought into a fund, it has two or three bad years in a row you should consider looking elsewhere. One disadvantage of a load fund, however, is that it will prove costly to switch because you will have to pay a new sales fee.

"Open-end" funds
Mutual funds are sometimes referred to as "open-end" investment companies, because there is no limit to the number of shares they can sell to the public.

"Closed-end" funds
A "closed-end" investment company operates a bit differently. It sells a predetermined number of shares onto the open market, and then lets investors trade them back and forth. The fund itself will neither issue new shares nor buy back existing ones.

If you want to buy into a closed-end fund, you will have to deal through a broker just as you would with any industrial stock. There are approximately 40 large closed-end funds in existence.

WISEGUIDE

For most investors, open-end funds are a better investment vehicle than closed-end funds.

Other types of investment funds
The mutual fund concept also has been applied to a variety of other types of investment funds. They include:

* bond funds

* real estate funds

* cattle funds

* oil drilling funds

Should I buy one of these funds?
Unfortunately, in many cases these funds merely serve as a way for the promoter to rake a little cash off the public. Costs sometimes are high and rates of return low, although this is buried deep in the fine print. You should seek professional advice before buying. Furthermore, these funds often promise special tax benefits to buyers. But will the tax savings really be worthwhile to someone in your bracket?

A possible exception might be some of the bond funds. These have **Bond funds**
mushroomed in recent months, and the better ones offer extremely
attractive yields — sometimes as high as 8 per cent a year.

A reputable bond fund might be the perfect answer for an investor
looking for a relatively safe investment with a high yield.

WISEGUIDE

Chapter 14

Women and their money

Are women discriminated against in finance?

Women occupy a special position — but not necessarily an enviable one — in American society when it comes to money.

Most men find it fairly easy to obtain bank loans, open charge accounts, deal in such speculative investments as real estate and commodities, and otherwise venture into the world of finance.

For women, however, the rules of the game often are more restrictive. Loans, in particular, can be hard to obtain. And some brokerage houses actively discourage women from opening their own accounts or from trading in highly-speculative commodity contracts.

Ironically, this type of economic discrimination occurs despite the fact that women control a huge portion of the nation's personal wealth — mainly in the form of real estate and securities owned in the wife's name for estate and tax purposes. (But do they control more than half, as is commonly believed? Probably not. Although figures in this area are sketchy — partly because so much wealth is owned jointly by husbands and wives — the best available statistics seem to suggest that women's share of the wealth is only about 40 per cent).

What this chapter contains

This Chapter discusses the problems that you as a woman may encounter in obtaining credit and what you can do about them. Also discussed are some of the financial complexities faced by families with working wives and some of the basic financial implications for both parties — husband and wife — in a divorce. (Tax laws that affect working wives are reviewed in Chapter 17.)

WISEGUIDE

Economic discrimination against women has become a matter of increasing public concern in the U.S.

Why so much concern?

Two factors, in particular, have accounted for this concern. First, as more women take full-time jobs and earn an independent income they are demanding the full economic benefits that should go with being members of the commercial work force. Second, the women's liberationist movement has forced a hard look at women's overall standing in society.

Some specific examples

Recent hearings by the National Commission on Consumer Finance found that financial discrimination against women existed in all stages of life — whether single, married, separated, divorced or widowed; with or without children; rich or poor; young or old.

- A regularly-employed woman in her early thirties couldn't get a loan to purchase a vacation home although she had enough cash to make a substantial down payment. Her fiancé, who had been through bankruptcy, easily obtained a loan to purchase the same property with a smaller down payment.

- A woman widowed for six years found it easier to open charge accounts in her dead husband's name than in her own.

- A 25-year-old working wife — supporting her husband in college — was unable to obtain a bank loan to buy a used car even though she had a good financial record and substantial salary.

- A young researcher and her husband looked around for a home mortgage, but found that since she was less than 29 years old most lenders would not count her salary in figuring the amount of mortgage money that would be lent to the couple. She discovered that if she had been in the 30-to-38 age bracket, half her salary would have been counted. Only if she had been over 38 would the lenders have taken her full salary into account.

- A woman in her forties who, as head of her household, wanted to buy a house for herself and her children couldn't get a mortgage without the signature of her 70-year-old father, who was living on a pension.

WISEGUIDE

Any woman who is married or has been married will find that credit depends almost exclusively on the financial standing of her husband. Similarly, when a single woman with a good credit rating of her own finally marries she will usually find that her old rating is wiped off the books and replaced by her spouse's.

This is because the laws in most states make a husband responsible for his wife's debts, but not vice versa. Furthermore, some lenders say they are reluctant to lend money to younger women for fear that they will become pregnant and quit their jobs.

A husband is responsible for his wife's debts

The St. Paul (Minnesota) Department of Human Rights sent a man and woman separately to 23 different banks to borrow $600 for a used car. Each was earning $12,000 a year, was the sole support of a family and had almost identical financial and personal qualifications.

A case in point

About half the banks applied more stringent standards to the woman than to the man. A frequent approach was to refuse to lend the woman money without her husband's co-signature while waiving the co-signature requirement for the man.

Women and their money

What can I do?

What can you as a woman do if you are concerned about unequal treatment?

Write your Congressman

● First, you can write to your representatives in the state legislature and in Congress. New laws will have to be enacted.

Complain to lenders

● Second, if you are turned down for credit on what you think is the basis of sexual discrimination, you can demand to know why. Many retail stores and some banks will buckle under pressure and issue you the credit you want. This is becoming increasingly true. Call the store's credit manager and put up a fuss.

Refuse to shop where credit is denied

● Finally, if you really feel strongly, you can refuse to do business with institutions that discriminate against women in the granting of credit, and you can let them know you are doing so.

Working wives

The special financial problems of working wives represent another area of interest to many women.

Who should own what?

This often raises some basic questions that can in turn promote a degree of family tension. Should the wife have a separate checking account? Who should own the house? Who should own the car? How much income is the wife actually contributing to the family?

A working wife's actual income may be quite low

A number of studies have shown that, after deducting income taxes, baby-sitting and transportation expenses and the like, only about a quarter to a third of the typical working wife's gross salary actually is available for family use.

Should I work anyway?

You may feel it is worth working anyway because of the sense of satisfaction and feeling of independence it gives you. But you should nonetheless be aware of just how much money you actually are contributing to the family from your job.

Sit down some evening and figure out your income versus the actual expenses that are created by your job. Among the expenses you should take into account are the cost of your car, baby-sitting costs, housekeeping help, clothing for the job, income taxes, the added expense of eating out at lunchtime, etc.

Three ways to manage the family finances:

Financial experts point out that there are three basic ways to handle family finances when the wife works:

How women view money

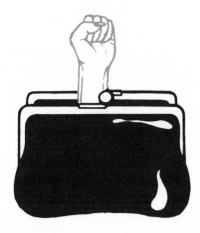

Economic power
Only two out of five believe that women play a "major" role in the economic life of the nation — as consumers, borrowers, savers, investors and voters.

More than half feel that this role is "about right." On the other hand, 27 per cent would like to have greater economic power.

Taxes
Nearly three out of four believe that tax rates are "unreasonable"

Those who feel hardest hit are divorced and separated women and middle-income wives.

Budgeting
Half say they keep a budget.

But only two out of five of these budget-keepers report that they keep successfully within the spending limits of their plan.

For a majority, there is no money left for "saving, investing and other such things" after essential bills are paid.

Most women worry that the problem will get worse. Three out of four don't believe that their family income will keep pace with the rising cost of living the next few years.

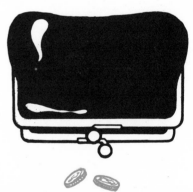

Investing
Just over half feel that the stock market is "as risky as gambling". Yet two out of five believe that investing in the market "is a good way to share in America's growth and prosperity"

Four out of five say they would rather keep money in a savings bank than play the market.

Financial decision-making
Four out of five own their savings and investments — except life insurance — jointly with their husbands.

Only 14 per cent of women stockholders decide by themselves which stocks or mutual funds to buy, and 42 per cent say their husbands alone decide.

Borrowing
Two out of three feel that borrowing is a "perfectly normal part of using money intelligently". They reject the idea that borrowing indicates a failure to live within one's means.

Yet three out of four believe that borrowing is "a bad practice to fall into".

Most debts incurred by married women are loans made jointly with their husbands. The notable exception is credit purchases at department stores, where women sometimes assume full responsibility for repayment themselves.

Source: Virginia Slims American Women's Opinion Poll, 1972

153

Women and their money

1. Joint accounts

● You can pool all income and outgo, with you and your husband maintaining joint checking and savings accounts. This often works well for couples with relatively limited income, and it offers the advantages of greater simplicity and a sense of sharing. It's best, by the way, to have a single master checkbook; separate books that draw against the same account can lead to chaos.

2. Half and half

● You can go half-and-half, consolidating part of your incomes to cover basic expenses but leaving each partner free to open a separate account for savings and for luxury spending. You also can keep a third, joint savings account for such long-range goals as an expensive vacation or the children's education.

3. Separate accounts

● You can each open totally separate checking and savings accounts and divide up the family expenses. It is important to specify in advance exactly what each partner will be responsible for paying. The husband, for instance, might pay the mortgage and utility bills, among others. The wife might be responsible for food, telephone and entertainment. Some families even maintain three checking accounts, one of them jointly for routine monthly expenses.

WISEGUIDE

You should choose the family financial-management system that best suits your financial circumstances, personalities and way of life.

Property ownership

Forms of property ownership can become tricky matters in any marriage, regardless of whether the wife works or not.

How should we own our home?

● Most couples own their homes jointly. This generally is O.K., except that the lawyers often draw the line against this arrangement when family net worth exceeds $120,000. This is because assets above that value are subject to estate taxes, and under some forms of joint ownership the full value of the house, not just half, will have to be included in the estate of whichever partner dies first.

How should we own our car?

● Single ownership of a car usually is recommended. If the car is jointly owned, there is the possibility that both husband and wife can be sued in the event of an accident involving one or the other. Another danger is that the wife may not be able to recover damages for her injuries if the car is owned jointly.

How should we own stocks and bonds?

● Although many couples hold common stocks and bonds jointly, some lawyers suggest that separate ownership often is best to avoid tax and legal complications — particularly for couples in higher income brackets.

WISEGUIDE

In all these matters of property ownership, you should consult a competent lawyer before taking any action.

Property ownership can become particularly troublesome in the event of divorce — which may be a major argument *against* joint ownership. The divorce rate is rising rapidly in this country. It has gotten to the point where there are now one-third as many divorces and annulments each year as marriages. You may be confident that your own marriage will last, but at least you should be aware of the financial implications if it doesn't.

The effects of a divorce

Insurance arrangements are an area where special care should be exercised in a divorce proceeding. It is important to review your insurance situation *before* separation or divorce papers are signed.

What happens to our insurance?

Your health, life, automobile and homeowners policies all are likely to need changing if your marriage ever breaks up.

WISEGUIDE

A husband's family health policy, for instance, will continue to cover the children as long as they remain the husband's legal dependents. But the ex-wife will no longer be covered and she generally cannot convert her portion of the policy either. Unemployed divorcees with past medical troubles often find it next to impossible to get good-sized individual health policies.

Health insurance

In some cases the husband's life insurance policies are included in the divorce settlement to his ex-wife. But the husband should keep in mind that, in this event, he won't be able to borrow against the policies or change their provisions in any way.

Life insurance

If the wife wants to continue living in the couple's former house or apartment, insurance on the home and furnishings is her responsibility unless specified otherwise in the divorce settlement. But the husband, if he leaves any personal possessions in the house, must take out a separate policy.

Homeowners insurance

155

Chapter 15

Retirement

Planning for retirement involves three basic considerations:

- Where will you live?
- What will you do with your time?
- Where will your money come from?

None of these questions can be answered quickly. And why should they be? They involve important decisions that you should work out over a period of years rather than in a few minutes or hours.

Where will my retirement income come from?

This chapter discusses the third question — your retirement income.

Thanks to the wonders of modern medicine, the lifespan of Americans is increasing. At the turn of the century, the average life expectancy in this country was 47 years. Today it is more than 70. Coupled with a trend toward earlier retirement, this means more years of leisure for the elderly. Unfortunately, however, that is only part of the story.

WISEGUIDE

Retirement entails a major adjustment in life that few Americans know how to make.

Learning to live on half as much

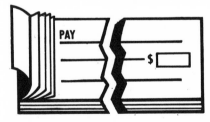

The financial adjustment is only part of the problem, but it is nonetheless a big part. The average individual's income is cut in half when he or she retires. Despite the wide variety of financial resources (including Social Security) that are now available to ease the financial strain of retirement, the Department of Health, Education and Welfare says that a quarter of the nation's elderly live in poverty.

How large will your own retirement income be? Many people, if asked that question, don't have the foggiest notion what the answer is. They put off thoughts of retirement until it is just around the corner. But a happy and financially secure retirement doesn't just happen. It requires planning. And good planning takes time.

WISEGUIDE

There is no specific age to begin planning for retirement. Give some thought to it now, whatever your age and regardless of how distant retirement may seem in your future.

When to begin planning for retirement

You may find if difficult to think about retirement if you are in your twenties or thirties. But you should at least have an idea of how you will prepare for retirement and when you will start.

If, on the other hand, you are in your fifties or early sixties you already should have a specific financial plan in mind. You don't? Then get to work on one now.

Remember that many preparations for retirement must be made while you are still working.

WISEGUIDE

To help you, a typical "intermediate" budget for a retired couple in mid-1972 is shown at the right. Compare it with the working-family budget shown on page 17 and you will discover some important differences. For instance, housing costs (as a percentage of total expenses) usually are much higher in retirement. Food and medical costs also tend to eat up more of your retirement dollars. Taxes, on the other hand, usually are much lower. Clothing costs also are somewhat less.

The above retirement budget, prepared by the Bureau of Labor Statistics, is based on several assumptions: the couple has no dependent children, they live in their own home (on which the mortgage has been paid) and they enjoy good health. No allowance has been made for future price inflation, but you can get a rough idea of how much the same intermediate budget might cost in the years ahead by increasing it 4 per cent a year.

The Bureau says that a "lower-level" budget for the same couple would be about $3,200 and a "higher-level" budget about $7,400.

Intermediate budget for a retired couple		
Food	$1,255	26.3%
Housing	1,673	35.0
Transportation	438	9.2
Clothing and personal items	429	9.0
Medical care	427	8.9
Other consumption	262	5.5
Other items	287	6.0
Income taxes	5	0.1
Total	**$4,776**	**100.0%**

Is this enough? Only you can tell. If you don't own a mortgage-free home or if you anticipate high medical bills, your retirement costs could be considerably more. The same holds true if you plan to travel a great deal once you are retired.

Will my own expenses be higher?

If you are 60 or older, you already should be well down the road toward adjusting your spending habits in order to bring them in line with the reduced income that comes with retirement. Begin by forecasting your probable income and expenses. Some work-related expenses like clothing, lunches and union dues will be eliminated. A two-car family can save $1,000 to $1,500 a year by selling one of them. Some communities reduce their property tax rates for homeowners over 65.

Keep a detailed list of expenses for a few months to see where your money goes now and where costs can be cut back. You might even try living for a month on the amount of money you will have after retirement.

WISEGUIDE

An example Let's look at the theoretical case of George Porter. George, an office manager for a pharmaceuticals company, is 54 years old and plans to retire at age 65. After reviewing the situation in detail, he decides that he can count on retirement income from the following sources:

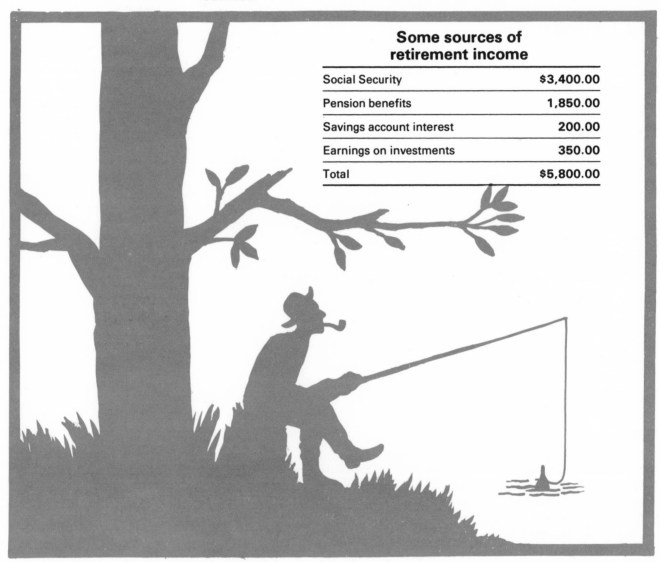

Some sources of retirement income

Social Security	$3,400.00
Pension benefits	1,850.00
Savings account interest	200.00
Earnings on investments	350.00
Total	$5,800.00

Comparing income with expenses George estimates that he and his wife will need approximately $8,000 a year to live comfortably in retirement, and he decides that there are two ways he can make up the $2,200 deficit. First, he checks with his insurance agent and finds that his life insurance policies will have a cash value of approximately $20,000 when he reaches 65. The policies can be converted at that point into an annuity that will pay George and his wife nearly $2,000 a year as long as either one is still alive. The drawback is that the insurance coverage will be terminated when the policies are converted. But this will be a small price to pay, since life insurance coverage will be less important to the Porters in retirement than during George's working years.

The second possible course of action is for George to continue **A part-time job?**
working part time. This will have the dual advantages of helping
George keep active and easing the emotional strain of an otherwise-
abrupt change in life-style. One danger is that his earnings may
become so large that he will forfeit all or part of his Social Security
benefits. Under current law, you can only earn up to $2,100 a year
without surrendering part of your benefits (more on that later in
this chapter).

In the final analysis, George decides to keep both courses of action
open and make up his mind later. There is no reason to rush into a
decision. The important point is that he has thought through his
plans and knows that acceptable alternatives are available.

If, on the other hand, George had discovered that he simply wouldn't **A crash savings**
have enough money for a comfortable retirement he could have **program?**
chosen to cut back immediately on his current expenditures and
begin a crash savings program.

Many people actually prefer to lower their standard of living during **WISEGUIDE**
their later working years — when their children have grown up and
no longer represent a financial drain — in order to save for a
retirement budget.

Where will your own retirement income come from? As a bench-
mark to guide you, the table at right breaks down total retirement
income in this country by sources.

Work, while representing the largest single source of income for
elderly Americans, is in some ways the least productive. Federal
regulations discriminate against on-the-job earnings by requiring
that in certain cases they be offset against Social Security benefits.
In general terms, the rules work this way:

Under age 72, you are allowed to earn up to $2,100 a year without
forfeiting any of your Social Security income. For every $2 earned
above that, you forfeit $1 in Social Security. Regardless of your
total earnings, however, you are entitled to Social Security payments during any month in which you earn less than $175 and are
not active in self-employment. To cite an extreme example, if you
earn $5,000 a year and somehow manage to lump it all into one
month you can still collect full Social Security benefits in each of
the other 11 months.

When you reach 72, you can earn as much as you like from a job
without any reduction in Social Security benefits.

Sources of income for Americans over 65	
Earnings from work	30%
Income from savings and investments	25
Social Security	26
Other public pensions	6
Private pensions	5
Veterans benefits	3
Public assistance	3
Other sources	2
Total	**100%**

Source: Social Security Administration

Social Security benefits will *not* be reduced for non-work sources **WISEGUIDE**
of income, such as pension benefits, investment earnings and
savings-account interest. Only on-the-job earnings (from employment or self-employment) count against Social Security.

Will I have to take a job?

Despite this disadvantage, for many individuals over 65 income from a job is the only way to meet rising costs and achieve even a modest standard of living. Most other sources of retirement income, such as savings interest, pension benefits and annuities, provide fixed payments that will not keep up with inflation. (Social Security will soon be a notable exception. Beginning in 1975, boosts in Social Security benefits for inflation will be automatic. The increases will be based on any increases in the government's cost-of-living index.)

What kind of job?

You should be realistic about the type of work you can find and the amount of money you can earn. Although job discrimination based on age is illegal in the case of workers under 65, there is no such legal protection for older workers.

Where to get help

This doesn't mean, however, that you won't be able to find a full or part-time job that gives you decent money together with a sense of satisfaction. If you do have difficulty finding acceptable work, look into retraining programs that are available to the elderly. Your state employment office also can provide you with valuable help. Or write for information to the Manpower Administration at the U.S. Department of Labor, Washington, D.C. 20210.

WISEGUIDE

Are you thinking about setting up a small business of your own when you retire? This may be the best approach of all, but some caution is in order.

Are there any legal problems?

For one thing, there may be legal implications in the type of work you want to do. Are there any zoning ordinances that prohibit or restrict your right to carry on certain types of business in your house? If you rent, are there any restrictions in your lease?

You also should find out whether there are any state or local regulations covering the kind of work you want to do. Possibilities include health, welfare or safety regulations in connection with preparing food for sale, taking care of children or renting out rooms.

Don't be the victim of an unscrupulous scheme

Finally, you should be aware that retirees who are looking to go into business for themselves are prime targets for unscrupulous promoters. Government officials warn that you should be particularly careful of any "business opportunity" which requires the use of expensive equipment. Some advertisers and salesmen hold out the hope — or even the promise — that you can earn extra money by purchasing, renting or making "free" use of some expensive piece of equipment to make products or provide a service; many of these schemes go under the guise of legitimate "franchising" operations. Be careful! If you don't pay close attention, you may end up with a big hole in your savings account, a useless piece of machinery and no extra income to justify your "investment."

If you do want to go into business for yourself, it is wise to talk it over with the Small Business Administration.

The Small Business Administration

The SBA is a government agency that offers free and valuable guidance, even on part-time ventures. The address of the nearest SBA office can be found in the phone book or by writing to the SBA, Washington, D.C. 20416.

Social Security

Many retired workers and their widows rely totally on Social Security for their support. How much can you expect to receive when you retire? Specific monthly payments are based on a complex formula that takes into account your average earnings under Social Security over a period of years. But regardless of how little you have earned, the minimum you will receive in Social Security benefits (based on 1973 rate schedules) is $170 a month if you retire at age 65.

Do I qualify for the $170 monthly minimum?

There is one important qualification, however. To be eligible for this $170 minimum, you must work at least 30 years under Social Security before you retire. If you work fewer years, minimum benefits are reduced by $8.50 a month for each year less than 30, down to an absolute minimum of $84.50 on retirement at age 65.

Average benefits — $160 for individuals $270 for couples

Actually, the *average* payment to individual retirees across the nation is about $160 a month. For couples, the average payment is about $270.

Is that enough? Probably not. If you sit down and figure it out, you will realize, for instance, that the average payment to couples comes to $3,120 a year — not even enough to meet the absolute minimum retirement budget cited by the Bureau of Labor Statistics!

Despite a recent series of large increases in Social Security benefits, you shouldn't rely on Social Security alone for your retirement income.

Other points about Social Security

Besides the basic $170-a-month minimum, there are a number of other important points you should know about Social Security:

● If you choose to retire at age 62 instead of 65, you will receive monthly payments equal to 80 per cent of the amount you would be entitled to at 65.

● Conversely, if you decide to keep working beyond 65 and forego your Social Security benefits right away, you will receive a 1 per cent increase in benefits for each year you do so between ages 65 and 72.

Retirement

• Widows' benefits used to be less than those of retired workers, but a recent law change has corrected that problem. A widow who waits until age 65 to begin collecting Social Security now gets an amount fully equal to the amount her husband would have received at 65. If she decides to begin collecting at age 60, however, she only receives 71.5 per cent of his benefits.

• One major advantage of Social Security income, by the way, is that it is tax free.

Determining your own Social Security benefits

How do you find out how large your own Social Security benefits will be on retirement? There are two steps:

1) Drop by your nearest Social Security office and pick up a copy of the form entitled "Request for Statement of Earnings." Complete this form and mail it to Social Security headquarters at P.O. Box 57, Baltimore, Md. 21203.

2) When the Statement of Earnings comes back, take it to your nearest Social Security office and ask that your benefits be calculated. If you are unable to find the office address in your phone book, ask for the address at your post office.

If you are already close to retirement, the Social Security Administration puts out a special leaflet, "Estimating Your Social Security Retirement Check," that will give you further information on your benefits.

Private pensions

Company and union-sponsored pensions are designed to supplement Social Security. Most companies use intricate formulas to determine precise benefits, with the formulas generally taking into account your length of service and amount of earnings.

WISEGUIDE

The typical annual pension for someone who has been with his company at least 35 years would be about half the amount of his peak earnings minus half the amount of his Social Security benefits.

Am I entitled to a pension?

Unfortunately, most pension plans are geared to the needs of middle and upper-income employees rather than to the lower-income workers who need the money most.

Are you entitled to a pension? Even if you think you are, it is best to check out the details to make sure you know exactly what you will be getting and what you need to do to qualify. Corporate pension plans are notorious for their loopholes, and it is better to find out about them early in your working career than too late.

"Vestment" of pension rights

The most notable loophole involves the question of "vestment." This term refers to whether you have full rights to the money credited to your pension account even if you quit work or are fired or laid off well in advance of age 65. If your pension benefits become fully vested after a specified number of years on the job, it means that you are thereafter entitled to the money in your account no matter what happens.

162

Most pension plans do *not* carry full vestment rights in the early years of your employment. Often, you must work for the company at least 20 years *and* reach age 55 before you are given any right to collect anything on retirement. If you are laid off after working 19 years, in many cases you are simply out of luck.

According to some estimates, only half of all workers covered by pension plans ever end up receiving actual benefits. And many of those who do get pensions collect less than $1,000 a year.

WISEGUIDE

What can you do? Not much. There is the possibility of eventual Congressional action to correct this situation, but meanwhile about the only thing you can do is check into your own benefits so that you at least know where you stand. It is particularly important that you clearly understand your vestment rights if you are over 40 and thinking of changing jobs. Will your old employer pay you a pension when you reach age 65? Will your new one pay? If switching jobs means that you cannot collect a pension from either, it may be best to stay put.

Make sure you understand how your employer's pension plan works

Annuities are another potential source of retirement income. As mentioned in Chapter 9, annuities are a form of life insurance in reverse. You pay a specified sum to an insurance company, and in return the company guarantees you a pre-determined cash income for the rest of your life.

Annuities

Annuities are sold two ways:

Two kinds of annuities

● You buy a "deferred" annuity on the installment plan. This involves regular payments — $200 every six months, for instance — on your part into the annuity over a period of years. When your payments are completed — typically at age 60 or 65 — the tables turn and the insurance company begins paying you. Deferred annuities often are sold in combination with life insurance, in a package called a "retirement-income" policy.

● You pay a lump sum of cash — $10,000, for instance — and begin collecting your annuity income immediately. This is called, naturally enough, an "immediate" annuity. This kind of annuity often is bought with the proceeds from an ordinary life insurance policy or endowment when it matures.

It is almost always less expensive to convert an existing insurance policy or endowment into an annuity than to buy an annuity with cash. Conversion eliminates the salesman's commission.

WISEGUIDE

Should I buy an annuity? Are annuities really worth buying? It depends what you are looking for.

For The advantage of an annuity is this:

● You will receive a guaranteed income for the rest of your life. Regardless of what happens, you can count on that check arriving in the mail every month. And if you live to be 110, you will make out like a bandit by collecting far more money than you ever put in. This is because payout schedules are based on the *average* anticipated remaining life span for your age. Those annuity buyers who live less than the average lose out, those who live longer win.

Against This is the disadvantage:

● In return for this lifetime guarantee, you forfeit a high rate of interest. Annuity payments generally are calculated on the basis of an underlying interest rate somewhere in the range of 2½ to 4 per cent — much lower than you could earn elsewhere. In addition, your income from most types of annuities will never increase. You are stuck with the same monthly income no matter how badly inflation erodes the value of your dollars. And if you buy an annuity at age 65 only to die at 66, under some forms of annuities the insurance company will simply pocket the huge difference between what you paid in and what they had to pay out during that one year.

WISEGUIDE Annuities are best as a supplement to other sources of retirement income. You will have to trade off low interest in return for a guaranteed lifetime income.

Types of annuities There actually are a variety of different types of annuities. Some are called "straight" annuities and specify that payments will cease when you die. Others are called "certain" annuities and guarantee that the payments will continue for a specified number of years — usually 10 or 20 — even if you die before that time is up; any remaining payment will go to a beneficiary of your choice. (Of course, if you live longer than the specified time the payments will continue until you die.) Still others are called "refund" annuities and guarantee that even if you die quickly payments will continue until your full original payment price is refunded.

Straight annuities offer the highest payouts For the most part, straight annuities offer the highest payouts since there is no provision for continued payouts after your death.

The table on page 165 shows the amount of lifetime monthly income you would receive at various age levels for buying a $10,000 straight annuity. This table is based on one insurance company's actual rates. Note that other companies may give you more (or less) for your money and that it is worth shopping around for the best terms.

How much lifetime monthly income will $10,000 buy?

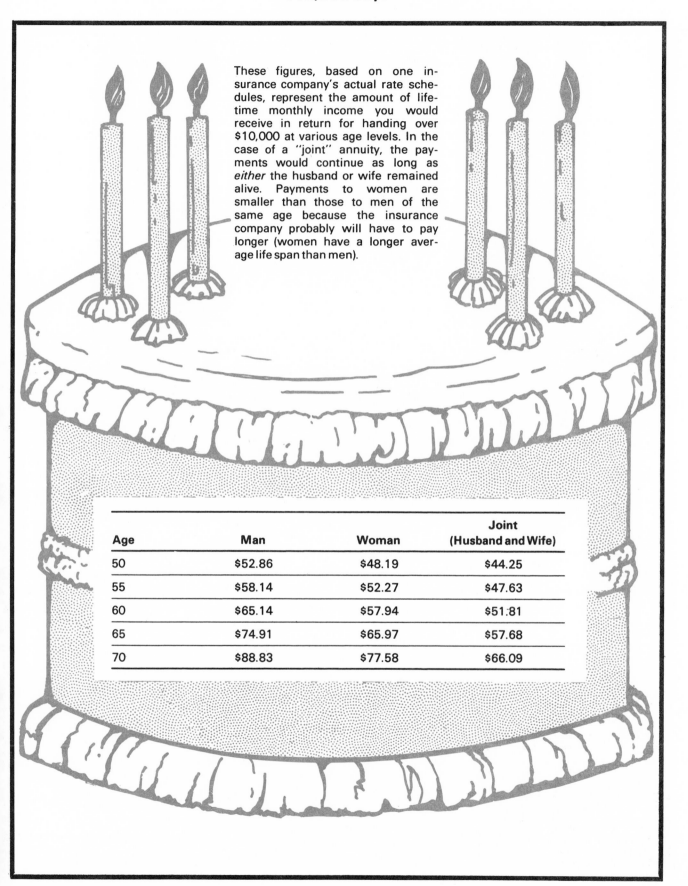

These figures, based on one insurance company's actual rate schedules, represent the amount of lifetime monthly income you would receive in return for handing over $10,000 at various age levels. In the case of a "joint" annuity, the payments would continue as long as *either* the husband or wife remained alive. Payments to women are smaller than those to men of the same age because the insurance company probably will have to pay longer (women have a longer average life span than men).

Age	Man	Woman	Joint (Husband and Wife)
50	$52.86	$48.19	$44.25
55	$58.14	$52.27	$47.63
60	$65.14	$57.94	$51.81
65	$74.91	$65.97	$57.68
70	$88.83	$77.58	$66.09

Retirement

Variable annuities

Another possible approach is to buy a "variable" annuity — one where the payments fluctuate in line with the performance of the underlying investments. Generally, there is a guaranteed minimum payout (lower than that on a straight annuity) with the potential for making more if the investments do well.

Taxes on annuity income

For tax purposes, your monthly income from an annuity will represent a combination of partial repayment of your initial purchase price and payment of interest on your money. The repayment is not subject to income taxes, but the interest is. Typically, if you buy an annuity at age 65, about 30 per cent of each monthly payment will represent taxable interest. Check this out carefully before you buy.

If you don't like the low returns on annuities, there are other approaches to consider:

Mutual fund withdrawal plans

● Many mutual funds, if you own at least $10,000 worth of their shares, will arrange a special plan to sell off a small part of your holdings each month and send you a check. This is called a "withdrawal plan." If stock prices do well, you may be able to continue withdrawals indefinitely this way. This is because in most withdrawal plans the underlying value of the fund shares has traditionally increased more rapidly than the amount being taken out. For instance, if you take out $100 a month and the value of your remaining shares increases by an average of $150 a month you will be coming out ahead. Be sure, however, to read Chapter 13 on mutual funds before selecting a fund for this kind of program. And don't ever put all your retirement assets into a withdrawal plan. Despite the excellent results in the past, these plans are still risky business.

Savings withdrawals

● You can set up a savings account at a bank and withdraw in a similar way on your own. The advantage: interest rates are higher than on most annuities. The disadvantage: your money may eventually run out and you will find that you have "outlived" your account.

U.S. Savings Bonds

Are Series E Savings Bonds a good way to save for retirement? The government says so, promoting sale of the bonds on the basis that you don't have to pay tax on the interest from the bonds until you cash them in. If you have retired by then, you presumably will save by being in a lower tax bracket. (On most types of bank savings accounts, by contrast, you are taxed on the interest as it is credited to your account each year.) Although the tax deferral provision of savings bonds is something of an advantage, in dollar terms your tax savings probably will be small.

WISEGUIDE

Buying Series E Savings Bonds may be an acceptable way for you to save for retirement, but don't make up your mind to do so solely on the basis of the small tax savings you might obtain in return.

Keogh plans

An area where your tax savings can be quite substantial involves so-called "Keogh plans" — named after the congressman who sponsored the original legislation. Keogh plans are a device through which self-employed individuals, such as doctors, consultants, owners of small stores, artists and the like, can set aside a tax-free retirement fund, contributing up to 10 per cent of their net income each year into the fund, up to a maximum contribution of $2,500 a year.

How a Keogh plan can reduce your tax bill

The tax advantage of a Keogh plan is two-fold:

• First, you can deduct each year's contribution from your taxable income.

• Second, you need not pay any taxes on the profits earned on the assets within your Keogh plan until you begin to make withdrawals after retirement. You own mutual fund shares in a regular account? Then you must pay taxes on each year's income. You own these shares through a Keogh plan? Then each year's income stays in the account tax-free. As you might guess untaxed assets grow more quickly than ones diminished by taxes.

The drawback

There is one major drawback in establishing a Keogh plan: your savings are frozen until you are at least 59½ years old. You must pay a penalty for withdrawing anything before then, except in case of total disability.

How to establish a Keogh plan

By far the easiest way to set up a Keogh plan is through a bank, insurance company or mutual fund that offers a "master" Keogh plan that has been approved by the Internal Revenue Service. Otherwise, you might have to go through the red tape of getting the IRS to approve your own individual plan. It's best to consult a lawyer before committing yourself in this area.

WISEGUIDE

Just about any income from self employment qualifies for a tax-sheltered Keogh plan.

Do I qualify?

Self employment need not be your primary source of income. You can work days at a regular job and serve as a self-employed consultant at night, and your nighttime earnings will qualify. Your wife works part time running her own little nursery school? Those earnings may qualify as well.

Should I sell the house when I retire? Almost all the types of retirement programs we have discussed so far require that you put up a fairly large amount of cash. Many couples, however, enter retirement with almost all their savings tied up in their home. Should they sell it and invest the cash elsewhere?

This is a difficult question to answer. Individual circumstances vary, and your own financial situation and needs must be analyzed carefully.

WISEGUIDE As a general rule, however, if you own a mortgage-free home it probably will prove to be the least expensive place for you to live. An apartment will almost certainly cost more.

Caution — don't sell before you reach 65! If you do decide to sell, you should hold off until you are at least 65. Your house may be worth more than you think, and if you sell you may end up with a big taxable profit. Individuals 65 and older get special tax breaks that should make it more than worth your while to wait.

Retirement communities Where will you live if you do sell your house? Special "retirement communities" won't suit everybody, but they do have some important pluses. One is the lower cost of living — an important consideration once you are on a fixed income.

Many churches, labor unions and fraternal organizations build retirement homes and villages, usually moderately priced. However, the waiting lists often are very long. If you want to live in one of these facilities, be sure to get your name on the waiting list well before you retire.

Other important retirement decisions There also are a number of other important decisions you will have to make as retirement begins to approach:

● Do you want to retire before 65 at reduced benefits or wait and receive more?

● You may have to choose between dropping a group life insurance policy or keeping it in effect at a much higher premium.

● You may have to decide whether to take your pension benefits in a lump sum immediately, in the form of a monthly income for a limited number of years, or in the form of a smaller monthly income guaranteed for life.

Choices of the latter two types often must be made within 30 days of retirement and, once made, usually cannot be changed.

WISEGUIDE There are many complex financial decisions involved with retirement. Think them through well ahead of time so that you won't have to make up your mind under last-minute pressure.

Chapter 16

Making a will

This chapter deals with three of the most misunderstood and neglected areas of personal finance:

* Making a will.

* Forms of property ownership — individual ownership, joint ownership and trusts.

* Estate and gift taxes.

"Why should I be bothered with such matters?" you might ask. "Only the rich need to worry about wills and the like." Think again.

Do you want to protect your loved ones from lengthy, costly and unnecessary aggravation (and perhaps from outright financial hardship) when you die? If so, you must take the time to put your financial affairs in order now, regardless of how little or how much you are worth. And you must update your estate plans regularly to make sure they continue to serve your needs.

This may seem like morbid business. But many people don't think about the financial implications of their death until old age makes it even more difficult to think about   or an accident or unexpected death makes it too late.

Protecting your loved ones when you die

It is far more sensible to review your financial preparations for death when you are young. Death will be a remote prospect then, and it will be easier to deal with these matters openly and calmly.

WISEGUIDE

Once you have gotten over the psychological hurdle of facing up to the problem for the first time, it becomes easier to reconsider as life goes on and your needs and wishes change.

Unfortunately, many people do nothing either out of inertia or because they are simply unaware of the special problems created by death and of the advance decisions that must be made to minimize the delay, frustration and costs to their heirs. They assume that everything will work out all right on its own.

Getting over the psychological hurdle

Nothing could be farther from the truth. Estate plans must be organized properly (with the help of a competent lawyer, if at all possible) if your property is to pass on to your heirs in the way you want and at the lowest cost.

The starting point is the making of a will — a written document that specifies exactly how your property should be distributed when you die.

Estate plans don't just happen by themselves

Making a will

Who should have a will? Just about everybody, whether rich or poor or in-between. Both the husband *and* the wife? Yes.

Why make a will? Dying "intestate" (without a will) is inefficient and irresponsible. Even where the rules for the distribution of your property will be essentially the same whether you make a will or not (and chances are they won't be), there are excellent reasons for making one anyway.

For
- Failure to make a will may cause inconvenience and delays for your survivors — particularly in terms of lengthy probate court proceedings.

- Settling your estate probably will be more complicated and costly if there is no will.

- Use of a will is the only way you can personally select those who will administer your estate as executors. Otherwise, the selection will be up to the court.

- Without a will you lose the privilege, available in most states, of naming a guardian for your minor children.

- Without a will your knowledge of your property and your advice as to its use and disposition cannot be passed on. It dies with you.

- Finally, the process of making a will provides an opportunity — in fact, it puts pressure on you — to consider your affairs from the viewpoint of provision for your dependents, estate taxes and even provision for your own lifetime.

Against Nothing.

Do not put off making a will. It is crucial to the financial peace of mind of your loved ones when you die, and procrastination is unfair to them.

How to make a will How do you go about making a will? There are two ways:

Do it yourself? 1) You can read a book on wills and then write your own. This method, however, is extremely risky. To stand up in court, a will must contain all the proper legal language. In addition, all the details — including the witnessing of your signature — must be handled in exactly the right way. Some of the requirements may seem downright silly at times, but they must nonetheless be complied with.

Hire a lawyer? 2) You can hire a lawyer to help you write your will. Unless your

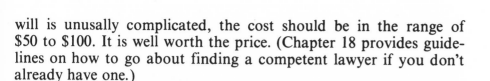

will is unusally complicated, the cost should be in the range of $50 to $100. It is well worth the price. (Chapter 18 provides guidelines on how to go about finding a competent lawyer if you don't already have one.)

What a will contains

What kind of information goes into a will? There are essentially five types:

- Who should get your money and other property when you die.

- In what amounts.

- When they should get it.

- How it should be safeguarded.

- Who should administer the distribution.

Property not subject to the workings of your will

Not all your property comes under the domain of your will, however. Certain types — particularly life insurance proceeds, pension benefits, U.S. savings bonds and property held in joint tenancy with another person — pass directly to the designated beneficiary or co-owner outside the operation of a will.

What happens if I don't have a will?

Despite these exclusions, most of us own considerable property that is subject to a will. And where no will exists, this property is distributed in accordance with state-regulated "lines of succession."

In most states, the surviving spouse gets one-third of an estate and the remainder is split among the children unless there is a will specifying otherwise. If you have no children, your spouse may have to share your estate with your parents, brothers, sisters, nephews, nieces and other relatives.

An example

Take the case of Frank Renquist, a 38-year-old salesman. Frank is married, has two minor children and helps support his widowed mother by providing her with $100 a month. If Frank were to die without a will, one-third of his belongings would automatically go to his wife, two-thirds to his children, and his mother would get nothing. That is simply the law in most states, and there is no way around it without a will.

Frank would actually prefer that his children only get a nominal amount, that his mother inherit a small sum and that his wife get the rest. There is no reason, as he sees it, for his children to receive two-thirds of his estate, since his wife would continue to support them. So he consults a lawyer and draws up a will to carry out his wishes in the event of his untimely death.

Making a will

Lawyers usually charge for their services by the hour, so it is important to work efficiently with your lawyer if you want to keep the cost down.

How to work with your lawyer on a will

Begin by drawing up a detailed list of *all* your assets — real estate, automobiles, savings accounts, checking accounts, investments, furniture, life insurance policies, etc. Indicate next to each the estimated value of the property and the way in which it is owned (individually or jointly, for instance). Policy and serial numbers also should be listed, where appropriate. Even though life insurance and certain other types of property probably won't be included in your will, it is important that your lawyer know about them so that he can understand your needs and can help you minimize estate taxes.

Who do I want to name as beneficiaries?

Send this list to your lawyer, with a summary of how you would like your property distributed when you die. Be sure of the full names, Social Security numbers and addresses of beneficiaries. If you wish to exclude a son or daughter, be certain to state so. (A wife's dower rights, however, prevent her from being disinherited by her husband.)

If you are rewriting an existing will, be sure to send a copy of the old one (and be sure to destroy the original copy of the old will as soon as the new will is signed and witnessed). If you have only minor revisions to make, your lawyer may advise that a "codicil," or supplement, can simply be added to your existing will.

WISEGUIDE

It is important that you be candid with your lawyer. Let him know about *all* your assets and their estimated value.

Choosing an executor

Besides deciding how your property should be distributed, you must choose an executor. This decision should not be taken lightly, since the executor will play a central role in the supervision of your estate after you die. His duties include taking an inventory of your assets, paying all valid claims, paying all the expenses of distributing your estate, paying federal estate taxes and state inheritance taxes, transferring ownership of your property to your heirs, and making a final accounting to the court. Obviously, this is not an easy job and should not be left to someone incompetent in these matters.

There are two basic possibilities in selecting an executor, each with its own advantages and disadvantages:

A relative or friend?

● You can choose a relative or family friend — your spouse or a son or daughter, for instance. The advantage is that the supervision of your estate is kept within the family. Also, costs may be lower this way. If, on the other hand, yours is a large or complex estate

a friend or relative may lack the knowledge to cope with the situation.

● You can choose someone who is in the business of serving as executor — most notably a bank trust department. This may cost more, but in return you will gain an expert's knowledge. In addition, such an organization will always be there; it will not die before you do, as an individual might.

A bank trust department?

It is common courtesy (and good business practice) to ask the person or organization in advance whether they are willing to serve as your executor.

WISEGUIDE

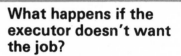

If you don't ask and it turns out that they don't want the job, they can simply refuse to serve when you die. The court will then appoint an administrator, just as if you didn't have a will at all.

What happens if the executor doesn't want the job?

Are wills ever declared invalid by the court? The answer is yes. According to some estimates, more than a third of all wills end up being thrown out.

A challenger need not prove anything as spectacular as mental incompetence or fraud to have your will declared invalid. Simple pencil notations on the will, erasures, or unsigned or unwitnessed amendments may be enough.

When wills are not valid

Another reason for challenge may be that the will is out of date. When is updating necessary? You should consult your lawyer for details, but here are some common events that might indicate a need to revise your will:

When is it necessary to update my will?

● Moving to a different state (inheritance and property-ownership laws, as we have mentioned, vary from state to state, and a will that is valid in one may not be in another).

● Birth of a child.

● Divorce or remarriage.

● Death of a beneficiary.

● Death of a witness, executor, guardian or trustee.

● Acquisition of a major new asset — such as the purchase of a new house or receipt of a sizable inheritance.

● Sale or other disposal of property mentioned in your will.

You can draw up a new will as often as you wish — reflecting changes in your assets, changes in your desires, changes in your family situation, etc.

WISEGUIDE

Making a will

Where to keep your will

Your will is not recorded anywhere (until you die, of course), so there is no need to file notice of a new one. It *is* important, however, to keep the original copy of your most recent will in a safe place. The best choice may be to leave it with your lawyer. A safe deposit box is not so good, since your executor may have difficulty getting into your deposit box right away.

The original copy of your will, it should be noted, is the *only* copy that counts. Photocopies and carbons generally will not stand up in court.

What is a "letter of last instructions"?

Besides drawing up a will, you should write a separate "letter of last instructions." This is addressed to your executor, to be opened on your death, and should contain the following types of information not suitable to the will itself:

- Where your will may be found.

- Where other important documents — insurance policies, deed to your house, marriage certificate, stocks and bonds, etc. — may be found.

- A list of your checking and savings accounts.

- A list of any special benefits — veterans' benefits, pension payments, fraternal benefits, etc. — payable upon your death.

- Funeral and burial instructions.

- The location of your safe deposit box and where the key may be found.

- A statement of reasons for unusual actions taken in your will, such as disinheritances.

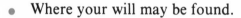

WISEGUIDE

One advantage of a separate letter of last instructions is that it can be revised as necessary without any need to change the will itself.

Probate court

When you die, your will is filed in a local probate court. Now the real agony begins for your heirs. Probate courts are notorious for their sense of caution and lack of speed. Processing of your estate can take anywhere from one to four years or more, and only then will your beneficiaries actually lay their hands on their inheritance.

Avoiding probate

Certain types of property, however, need not go through probate court. These are the same types we mentioned earlier as being excludable from your will — life insurance proceeds and jointly-owned assets, in particular. They go directly to the designated beneficiaries or co-owners outside of probate; the court simply has no jurisdiction.

What is "the poor man's will"?

In fact, "joint tenancy" — a special form of property ownership — is sometimes referred to as "the poor man's will" since the property

will automatically pass to the co-owner upon your death regardless of whether or not there is a formal will specifying so.

WISEGUIDE

Almost all your property can be held in some form of joint ownership that avoids the need for a will and probate court. But holding property jointly for that reason alone can be foolish.

Probate versus estate taxes — don't get confused

An important distinction should be noted here. Jointly-held property, just because it avoids probate court (and therefore also escapes probate fees), isn't exempt from estate taxes. What is subject to probate proceedings and what is subject to estate taxes are two entirely separate matters. (More on this important distinction later in this chapter.)

Five types of property ownership:

There are actually five basic forms of property ownership that you might use. Although the technicalities of each vary somewhat from state to state, in broad terms they are:

1. Sole tenancy

● Sole tenancy. You and you alone own the property. You must provide for the disposition of this property in your will if you want to make sure it goes to the person of your choice.

2. Tenancy in common

● Tenancy in common. In most circumstances, this is not a particularly good form of ownership. You own a particular share of the property (the rest is owned by another individual or individuals), and when you die the distribution of your share must go through probate. You should, of course, specify this distribution in your will.

3. Joint tenancy

● Joint tenancy. This is the most popular form of joint ownership. It is characterized by the kind of legal gobbledegook that says that *each* of the tenants owns *all* of the property. In practical terms, this means that full ownership goes to the surviving tenant or tenants on the death of one. Your will has nothing to say about the disposition of the property, nor does the probate court get involved if you die without a will. Transference to the other tenant or tenants is automatic. Note: the standard legal phrase to indicate joint tenancy is "John Doe and Mary Doe, joint tenants with right of survivorship, and not as tenants in common." The full phrase generally is advisable to make sure that joint tenancy has actually been established in the eyes of the law.

4. Tenancy by the entirety

● Tenancy by the entirety. As with joint tenancy, full ownership of the property passes automatically to the surviving tenant outside of the purview of the probate court. Tenancy by the entirety is available only to married couples. And there is a special twist: neither party can sell or dispose of his or her interest without the consent of the other. In other words, come hell or high water you are locked in. Tenancy by the entirety is not allowed in some states, and in others its use is restricted.

5. Trusts, etc.

• Trusts, custodial accounts and beneficial accounts. These range all the way from incredibly complex tax-saving devices for the rich to simple bank trust savings accounts, with one individual holding sole control during his lifetime and the account proceeds passing directly to the designated beneficiary upon that individual's death.

WISEGUIDE

Property ownership can become extremely complicated. Good legal advice is called for, particularly if there is a chance that your estate will exceed $60,000 when you die.

How estate taxes can affect property ownership

That figure — $60,000 — is the level at which federal estate taxes begin to be levied. Careful consideration must be given to types of property ownership if this tax bite is to be minimized.

The disadvantages of joint tenancy

Below the $60,000 level, joint tenancy with your spouse may be a perfectly acceptable way to own your house and other family possessions. But even then there are serious drawbacks to joint tenancy:

• You can become overly complacent about estate planning. A common mistake is to think that there is no need to have a will since everything is held jointly and will go to the surviving spouse anyway. The problem is that after one spouse dies the other, entrenched in bad habits, may fail to make a will even though it has suddenly become essential. And, of course, there is always the danger that the husband and wife will be killed *together* without a will, and a court will have to determine disposition of their jointly-owned property according to state law.

• Family squabbles can develop over jointly-held property. A divorce, in particular, can become a mess.

• The property is fully subject to any liability of either owner. If the husband is a general partner in a business that goes broke, for instance, all of the couple's jointly-owned property may be sold off to satisfy the claims of creditors. Property held solely in the wife's name usually is shielded from such claims.

• On the death of one of the joint tenants, cash accounts and other assets probably won't be released to the survivor until federal estate taxes and state inheritance taxes have been paid.

• Contrary to popular opinion, joint ownership isn't a device for saving on estate taxes. The *full* value of the property is included in the deceased person's estate, not just half.

WISEGUIDE

Estate taxes are an area of concern primarily to individuals and couples with the prospect for owning more than $60,000 of property when they die.

In general, estate-tax rules work like this:

● All of the following assets must be included in the estate for tax purposes, regardless of whether they are processed through probate court or not: real estate, cash, stocks and bonds, annuities, life insurance proceeds, business interests, personal possessions, etc.

● Deductions are allowed for the following items: funeral expenses, executor's and lawyer's fees, state inheritance taxes, debts, etc.

● In addition, a special "marital deduction" allows a surviving spouse to exempt half of his or her partner's estate from taxes. On a $200,000 estate, for instance, only $100,000 would be taxable. To qualify for the marital deduction, however, certain conditions must be met, including: the surviving spouse must be entitled to lifetime income from the property; this income must be payable at least annually; the surviving spouse must have the unqualified right to, in turn, leave the estate to anyone he or she wishes.

● Once the taxable value of the estate is determined, a rising scale of tax rates is applied. The first $60,000 is tax free, the next $5,000 is subject to a 3 per cent tax and so on up to a 77 per cent tax on anything over $10 million.

Keeping estate taxes to a minimum

Minimizing estate taxes is one of the most complicated areas of estate planning. In general, however, if your estate is large enough to be subject to taxation there are two main ways to arrange your financial affairs during your lifetime in order to reduce estate taxes on your property when you die:

● Judicious use of trusts.

● Judicious use of tax-free gifts.

These are matters where a lawyer's guidance is essential, but in brief:

The use of trusts

Trusts are created mainly because the property owner doesn't want his estate to be inherited immediately by his heirs. Sometimes this is a device for saving taxes. At other times the property owner simply doesn't believe that his heirs are capable of managing the property on their own.

WISEGUIDE

In a trust, title to the property passes to a trustee — often a professional — who then administers the assets for the designated beneficiary.

An example

In its simplest form, a trust might be established by a husband for the benefit of his wife for the remainder of her lifetime. She would receive all income from the trust, and on her death the trust might be dissolved and the assets passed on to the children for use as they

see fit. This is a common tax-saving device among the well-to-do.

Tax-free gifts

Owners of large estates also might consider giving away some of their assets to the intended beneficiary in order to reduce the ultimate tax bill when they die. One drawback: once the property has been given away, you lose all control over it. If you need it later, you are out of luck — unless, of course, the recipient is willing to give it back.

How gifts are taxed

Federal tax rules are quite specific as far as gifts are concerned. These rules provide that you may give $3,000 tax-free each year to any individual or individuals of your choice. You could even go so far as to give $3,000 to each of 100 or more different people and not have to pay any taxes.

Furthermore, you are allowed a $30,000 lifetime exemption in gifts to each individual. This is on top of the $3,000 annual exemption. In other words, you could give $33,000 the first year and $3,000 a year thereafter without having to pay any taxes. Taxes on amounts above that range anywhere from 2¼ per cent up to 57¾ per cent, depending on the size of the gift.

WISEGUIDE

If the gifts are given jointly by a husband and wife, the limits are doubled — $6,000 a year to each individual and a $60,000 lifetime exemption.

State-imposed gift taxes

These, it should be noted, are the basic *federal* gift tax rules. The states impose gift taxes of their own, and in many cases a $30,000 lifetime exemption is not allowed.

The advantage of gifts

Why make gifts? Perhaps your son stands to inherit $150,000 from you when you die. By giving it to him piecemeal in the form of tax-free gifts, you might be able to avoid all estate taxes.

WISEGUIDE

One warning: if you die within three years of making a gift, the courts may rule that your gift was made "in contemplation of death" and require that full estate taxes be paid on the amount regardless of the fact that it has been given away.

Talk to a lawyer before making major gifts

These are merely rudimentary guidelines, and any decision to try to reduce your taxable estate through tax-free gifts should be discussed thoroughly with a competent lawyer.

Figuring Federal Estate Taxes

George Andrews, married and the father of two sons, dies one cold September morning. His estate, left entirely to his wife, consists of:

Life insurance benefits	$100,000
The family house (owned jointly with his wife)	45,000
Investments	53,000
Savings	8,200
Checking account	700
The family car	3,200
Personal possessions (furniture, clothing, jewelry, etc.)	7,800
Gross estate	**217,900**

The following deductions are allowed for estate tax purposes:

Funeral and burial costs	2,500
Debts	3,100
Probate costs, executors' fees, lawyers' fees and other expenses	7,500
Total deductions	-13,100
	204,800

Subtract the tax-free marital deduction equal to one-half of net estate	-102,400
	102,400

Subtract another $60,000 for the standard deduction	-60,000
Net taxable estate	**42,400**

Federal estate taxes due on $42,400 (including credit for state inheritance taxes)	**$5,308**

Note: Estate taxes and probate costs could have been reduced through the proper use of trusts and/or tax-free gifts. Consult a qualified lawyer.

Chapter 17

Taxation

This chapter offers common-sense advice for saving on your federal tax bill.

Each year, around the 15th of April, we all grit our teeth and face up to the unavoidable: the filing of another annual income-tax return.

However, the aggravation goes beyond the simple act of filing. Many Americans have a deep-seated distrust of the nation's tax-collection mechanism, and they believe that they aren't getting anything close to a fair shake.

Do our tax laws cater to the rich? One recent survey showed, for instance, that more than two-thirds of all Americans believe that the federal tax laws are structured for the benefit of the rich and not for the average man.

Are they? Probably yes. But it will take sweeping federal legislation to correct that problem.

What you can do Meanwhile, all that you can do as an individual taxpayer is seek to minimize your own income-tax bill within the limits of existing law.

WISEGUIDE

There is nothing in the law that says you have to pay more than the minimum, and if you do so it will either be out of ignorance or laziness. In short, it will be your own fault.

Will my return be among those audited? One of the most striking features of the American tax system is that each individual is left to calculate his own taxes, rather than having them calculated by the government. Just to keep everybody relatively honest, however, about 5 per cent of all tax returns are audited each year by the Internal Revenue Service. And *100 per cent* are screened for mathematical accuracy.

Minimizing taxes versus evading them Federal tax laws are complex and at times ambiguous, and as a result there sometimes is a fine line between legitimately *minimizing* your taxes and illegally *evading* them. The latter can lead to stiff fines and even prison sentences (although prison terms are rare, except in the case of blatant fraud).

Should I use a tax consultant? Partly because of the increasing intricacies of our nation's tax laws, a growing number of Americans are seeking the help of so-called tax consultants. These range all the way from store-front operators who lock the door and disappear quietly into the early morning darkness of April 16 to highly-skilled tax lawyers and accountants who deal exclusively with corporations and the rich.

It might be worth your while to go to a tax-preparation firm or, better yet, an accountant or tax lawyer for help if you are intent on minimizing your federal tax bill. Such a professional adviser may be able to point out perfectly legitimate tax-saving tips that you are simply unaware of.

But beware of the individual or firm that promises huge tax savings! Use of a professional tax adviser is no shield against personal liability. If you underpay your taxes and the IRS finds out, you are fully liable even though your return may have been prepared and co-signed by your adviser. You cannot go crying to the IRS with the excuse that the firm misled you into illegally taking this deduction or that.

A warning — you are fully liable for the information in your tax return

Penalties for failure to pay your full taxes on time total 6 per cent annual interest on the unpaid amount plus a 6 per cent late payment penalty for a total of 12 per cent. (The second 6 per cent need not be paid, however, if you can prove to the IRS's satisfaction that failure to pay on time was due to a "reasonable" cause.) Furthermore, the IRS can tack on a penalty of 50 per cent if it can show that you cheated with forethought, as opposed to merely making a mistake out of ignorance or negligence.

How much is the penalty for underpaying?

How, then, can you legitimately reduce your tax bill and not have to fear the wrath of the federal tax collector? There is a way:

Ways to reduce your tax bill

Most legitimate tax-reducing points relate to deductions, exemptions and exclusions — sums that you are allowed to subtract from your taxable income.

WISEGUIDE

Deductions, in particular, are the name of the game when it comes to keeping your taxes under control. Knowing *which ones* to claim is essential. Knowing *how* to claim them also helps. The relatively small savings add up — if you know what they are. And, of course, the large deductions stand on their own as big money-savers.

Knowing which deductions you can take

It should be emphasized, however, that calculating your annual tax bill is not an exact science. With the vagaries inherent in certain types of deductions, two perfectly intelligent people can take the same set of basic figures and come up with two somewhat different bottom-line totals for the amount of tax due.

But regardless of the exact bottom-line total you arrive at yourself, it is extremely important that you keep careful documentation of what you have done and the deductions, exemptions and exclusions you have taken. This documentation will be essential if you are called in by the IRS for an audit.

The need for careful documentation

The IRS examiner will want proof of all the claims you have made on your tax return, and the burden of this proof will rest on you and not on the IRS.

WISEGUIDE

What kind of records should I keep?

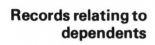

Among the types of documents and papers you should keep on file are:

- Receipts for contributions.
- Property-tax records.
- Sales receipts relating to large sales-tax deductions claimed on your return.
- Canceled checks.
- Brokerage-account records.
- Records of unreimbursed business expenses.

In addition, you should file away the note paper on which you have made all your mathematical calculations used in filling out your return. This will enable you to reconstruct your calculations in the event of a dispute.

Records relating to dependents

You also should keep detailed records establishing the amount of support that you have provided to individuals you claim as dependents. This generally isn't necessary for minor children who live at home, but can become important in the case of children away at college or dependent parents.

WISEGUIDE

You must keep all this documentation for at least three years. The IRS is free to audit your return at any time during that period, and a claim on your part that you have thrown your documentation away will get you nowhere.

Home-improvement records

Another important kind of record-keeping (and an area where millions of taxpayers fall down) involves home improvements. Profits from the sale of a house generally are taxable, although the tax can be deferred indefinitely as long as you buy a new, more expensive house within a year of selling the old one. Such a profit is defined as the difference between the price you originally paid for the house and the price you eventually sold it for. The cost of improvements made in the interim can be added to the purchase price, however, thereby reducing your ultimate tax liability.

An example: You buy a house for $20,000 and sell it five years later for $25,000. During that period you made improvements worth $2,000. If you have kept the proper documentation (and *only* if you have kept it) to back up your improvement costs, your taxable gain will be reduced to $3,000 ($5,000 less the $2,000 in improvement expenses). Improvements, it should be noted, generally are limited to items that add value to the house. This is opposed to maintenance and repair costs, which generally cannot be used as an offset against your profit. Consult the IRS or a tax adviser for details. And be sure to keep these records indefinitely, since they will be a necessary part of your files as long as you keep deferring your tax liability.

Who must file a federal income tax return? Just about everybody with substantial income from any source. You may not have to file, however, if your income falls below these minimums in the diagram.

Do I have to file a tax return?

Single (under 65)	Single (over 65)	Married (both spouses filing separate returns)
$2,050	$2,800	$750

Married (both spouses under 65)	Married (one over 65)	Married (both over 65)
$2,800	$3,550	$4,300

In filling out your tax return, the basic initial decision that you must grapple with is whether to accept the standard deduction that the IRS allows or whether to itemize your deductions. This is an area where many taxpayers lose out. They could save money by itemizing but don't do so — mainly because they don't realize that it would be worth their while. Some others who do itemize overlook certain deductions that they are unaware of.

Standard deduction versus itemizing

If you choose to take the easy route and file your tax return on the so-called "short form" — IRS form 1040A — you will have no choice but to take the standard deduction. Itemization requires use of the "long form" (1040). Use of the short form will make your job of filing much more simple, but note that you are not allowed to use this form if your dividend or interest income totals more than $200 during the year. (Continued on page 186.)

Should I use the "short form"?

Taxation

Avoiding Common Errors

1. Start working on your return early. Don't wait until the last minute.

2. Take the time to decide whether it is less expensive to itemize your deductions or use the standard deduction. Don't be lazy about this!

3. Double-check your arithmetic. Make sure that all figures are recorded accurately and that your tax is computed correctly.

4. Round off all figures to the nearest dollar.

5. Write your Social Security number on the check for your tax due. Also make sure it is included on all forms and schedules. Tax returns are processed by Social Security number, not by name.

6. Attach your W-2 forms.

7. Sign the return. If a joint return, both husband and wife must sign.

8. Attach the required statements or schedules.

9. Use the right tax table, line or column.

10. Keep a copy of the return and all statements and schedules for your own files.

What's Deductible
A checklist of major items:

Contributions	**Cash gifts**	All donations to qualifying non-profit organizations — charities, schools, museums, churches, etc.
	Gifts of used clothing and other property	You must get a written receipt from the charity
	Gifts of securities	Securities in which you have "long-term capital gains" are best from a tax viewpoint.
	Travel expenses for charity	Six cents per mile, plus tolls and parking
Taxes	**Real estate taxes**	On a home, cooperative apartment, condominium, etc.
	Sales taxes	Look up the basic allowable amount for your income level in the IRS table, then add any sales tax for large purchases made during the year
	Income taxes	All state and local income taxes are deductible on your federal return
Medical expenses	**Doctors' fees, hospital costs (including meals), psychiatric fees, dental expenses, etc.**	Deductible only to the extent that the year's total exceeds 3 per cent of your adjusted gross income; expenses reimbursed by insurance payments are *not* deductible
	Medicines	Deductible only to the extent that the total exceeds 1 per cent of your adjusted gross income; anything above that is then lumped in with other medical expenses that are subject to the 3 per cent exclusion
	Travel	Six cents per mile, plus parking and tolls, for the round trip to see a doctor
	Health-insurance premiums	Half of your total premium payment is deductible, up to a maximum of $150 a year; the other half can be lumped in with those general medical expenses that are subject to a 3 per cent exclusion
	Medicare	The $6.30 monthly fee for supplemental coverage is deductible as a health insurance premium
Interest	**Mortgage costs**	The interest portion of each mortgage payment is fully deductible
	"Points"	Points paid to obtain a mortgage are deductible; they are *not* deductible, however, if paid to obtain a specific service
	Personal loans, auto loans, charge accounts, credit cards, etc.	The interest is deductible
Miscellaneous deductions	**Alimony**	Deductible, except that court-ordered payments for "child support" are not deductible

Moving costs	Deductible, up to a maximum of $2,500, if you move to another job location at least 50 miles further from your existing home than your old job; the deduction includes such indirect moving expenses as new-house hunting and real estate agents' fees	
Casualty losses	Uninsured property damage or loss resulting from a storm, accident or theft generally is deductible to the extent it exceeds $100; you must have proof, however, that you actually sustained a loss	
Political contributions	Up to a maximum of $100 on a joint return, up to $50 on an individual return; must be made to a candidate who has announced his intention to run for a specific office	
Child-care costs	Deductible up to $400 a month, if you meet certain qualifications:	

1. both parents must work full-time

2. the child must be under 15 years old

3. the family's income cannot exceed $18,000; above that, your deduction is reduced by $1 for every $2 you earn

Investment expenses	You can deduct travel costs to your broker's office, rental of a safe deposit box to keep securities, subscriptions to investment publications, etc.
Home-office expenses	If you maintain an office at home, you may qualify to deduct the room's share of rent or depreciation, utilities, insurance and cleaning; an employer requirement is not necessary to qualify

What Isn't Deductible
A checklist of major items:

Personal expenses		
Food	Not deductible, except for unreimbursed meals away from home on business or charity	
Housing	Not deductible, except to the extent you claim your home is used for business purposes	
Travel	Not deductible, except when related to business, medical or charitable purposes	
Personal care	Toothpaste, toiletries, cosmetics, vitamins, bottled water, etc. — usually not deductible	
Clothing	Not deductible, except in the case of the unreimbursed cost of uniforms and work clothes required by your employer and which you cannot adapt for general wear	
Educational costs	Not deductible, except where required to maintain or improve your skills for your present job (see page 189)	
Gifts	Not deductible, except when made to qualified nonprofit organizations	

Taxes		
Federal income taxes	Not deductible on your federal tax return	
Social Security taxes	Not deductible	
Fines	Not deductible	
Fees	Driver's licenses, auto inspection fees, dog licenses, hunting licenses, marriage licenses, bridge tolls, water bills, etc. — all not deductible	
Other taxes	Excise taxes, customs duties, federal estate and gift taxes, cigarette and liquor taxes — all not deductible	

Interest	Municipal bonds	Interest on debt used to purchase tax-free bonds is not deductible
	Another person's loan	Interest you pay on behalf of someone else is not deductible, unless you are legally responsible for making payment
Medical costs	Illegal operations	Not deductible
	Funeral and burial expenses	Not deductible
	Maternity clothes	Not deductible
	Child-care costs	Not deductible, except for true medical expenses or where both parents work full time
	Other medical costs	Not deductible if reimbursed by insurance
Insurance	Life insurance	Premiums are not deductible
	Home insurance	Premiums are not deductible, except to the extent you claim your home is used for business purposes
Miscellaneous	Legal fees	Generally not deductible unless related to a business or investment purpose; some examples: defense of a breach of promise suit, property settlement in a divorce, defense of civil or criminal charges resulting from a personal relationship, preparation of a will — legal fees in each case are not deductible
	Gambling losses	Not deductible, except that they may be offset against your gambling winnings
	Lottery tickets	Not deductible
	Benefit tickets	The cost of tickets to charity bills, shows and other charitable events is deductible only to the extent that the price exceeds the normal cost of attending such an event
	Bribes and other illegal payments	Not deductible

WISEGUIDE

If you are unsure whether it is less expensive to itemize your deductions or not, do a rough calculation of your tax bill each way and then decide.

How much is the "standard" deduction?

Remember that if you decide not to itemize, you can take a flat deduction of 15 per cent of your adjusted gross income, up to a maximum standard deduction of $2,000. The minimum standard deduction, on the other hand, is $1,300. No matter how small your income, you probably will be entitled to a deduction at least that large.

This may sound like a lot, but almost everybody who owns a house with a large mortgage will do better by itemizing. This is because both the mortgage interest costs and the property taxes on your house are deductible on your federal tax return, and in all likelihood they will exceed the standard deduction.

Some advice from the IRS

The IRS offers this specific advice on itemization versus use of the standard deduction: you will save money by itemizing if your "adjusted gross income" (line 14 on the short form and line 17 on the long form) is less than $8,667 with itemized deductions of more than $1,300. If your adjusted gross income is between $8,667 and $13,333, you will save money by itemizing if your deductions total more than 15 per cent of income. Above $13,333, you will save money by itemizing if your deductions total more than $2,000. Otherwise, you are better off taking a standard deduction.

Adjusted Gross Income	less than $8,667	$8,667 - $13,333	over $13,333
Itemized Deductions	more than $1,300	more than 15% of income	more than $2,000
Use	1040	1040	1040

In general, deductions break down into seven major areas of concern to the average taxpayer:

Kinds of deductions:

● Interest costs — whether on your mortgage, car loan, personal loan, charge account, brokerage account or whatever. The loan need not be taken out for business purposes to qualify. Almost any legitimate interest cost is deductible. One major exception: interest on loans used to buy tax-free municipal bonds.

1. Interest

● Contributions. They qualify for tax deductibility when made to almost any nonprofit organization — churches, charities, educational organizations, scientific organizations, cultural organizations. Cash, property and securities all count. Note: a common charitable deduction that is often overlooked is 6 cents a mile when driving your car in service to charity.

2. Contributions

Furthermore, donations to the campaigns of political candidates also qualify, although only to a limited degree. You can choose one of two methods for taking political deductions. You can take a direct credit against your tax bill for half the amount of your contributions in any single year, up to a maximum contribution of $50 if you are married and filing a joint return and up to $25 if single. Thus, the maximum permissable tax credit on a joint return would be $25 (half of $50) and on an individual return $12.50. Alternatively, you can claim an itemized deduction from taxable income, as with most other types of deductions, of up to $100 on a joint return and $50 if you are single. Which approach is better? Here's the answer:

Political donations

If your tax bracket is below 50 per cent, you generally are better off taking a direct tax credit for political contributions. If it is above 50 per cent, a deduction from taxable income usually saves more.

WISEGUIDE

● State and local taxes. Almost all kinds qualify — property taxes, school taxes, sales taxes, income taxes, gasoline taxes, etc. (Those that *don't* qualify include liquor and cigarette taxes and fees for such items as a driver's license or fishing license.)

3. Taxes

State income taxes

Don't overlook the important fact that you should deduct all state and local income taxes that you *actually paid* during 1973 (or whatever taxable year is involved). An example: If you paid $200 on January 15, 1973, as the final installment on your 1972 state income tax bill you should deduct that amount on your 1973 federal tax return, not your 1972 return.

WISEGUIDE

Your actual cash outlay for state income taxes (including amounts withheld from your salary) during the 12 months of 1973 is the amount you should claim as a deduction, not the bottom-line tax liability listed on your latest state tax return.

How large can my sales-tax deduction be?

Another hint: consult the IRS tables in the instructions that come with your tax return for the standard sales-tax deduction allowed in your state for someone with your level of income. This should be viewed as the *minimum* sales tax deduction. You can add to this figure the sales tax you paid on any major purchases made during the year — a television, refrigerator, car, boat, sofa, expensive jewelry, etc. (Be sure to keep the sales receipts to document your claim.) Also, don't forget to add your city sales tax, if applicable.

4. Medical expenses

• Medical expenses. These become deductible when the year's total exceeds 3 per cent of your adjusted gross income. Lots of things besides doctors' bills count. If, for instance, your doctor tells you to go south to protect your heart in winter the cost of transportation is a deductible medical expense (your meals and lodging are not, however). The IRS even goes so far as to give this offbeat example: your doctor has prescribed that you take two ounces of whisky twice a day for relief of angina pain resulting from coronary disease. You guessed it. The cost of the whisky is deductible! Almost all doctor-prescribed activities and purchases for the treatment or relief of a specific medical condition are deductible, but expenses related to the general improvement of your health usually are not (even if they are doctor-prescribed).

Some examples

If your child's summer camp or private school makes a separate charge for medical care, it is deductible. So are transportation expenses for visits to the doctor. Other deductible medical items include eyeglasses, false teeth, artificial limbs, crutches, wheelchairs and seeing-eye dogs.

Health-insurance premiums

In addition, the premiums you pay for health insurance are deductible. There is a slight hitch, though. You must separate these premiums, for tax purposes, into two equal halves. The first half is fully deductible on its own, up to a maximum of $150. The second half must be lumped in with all other medical expenses that are subject to the 3 per cent limitation.

Are medical expenses that have been paid or reimbursed through your health insurance deductible for tax purposes? The answer is no.

5. Business expenses

• Certain out-of-pocket business expenses. This is an extremely tricky area. If you do claim any deductions, be sure you can back them up. This type of deduction often is a red flag to the IRS and greatly increases your chances for an audit.

An office at home

A common example of this type of deduction: if you use a portion of your home or apartment as an office for free-lance business activities, you clearly are entitled to a deduction. The situation gets a bit more muddled, however, if you have a full-time job and maintain an office at home related to that job. Although the IRS used to insist that no deduction be allowed unless the employer required a home office, recent court decisions have had a liberalizing effect. All that is now vital is that the use of a portion of your residence as an office be directly related to your business. How large a deduction can you take? Generally, you can deduct a proportionate share of total rent or depreciation costs, utilities, insurance and cleaning bills. For instance, you could take one fifth of these costs if you set aside one room in a five-room house or apartment as an office.

Are subscriptions to professional journals related to your job deductible? The answer is yes, as long as the cost isn't reimbursed by your employer. The same holds true for membership dues in professional societies, for union dues, and for service charges equal to union dues required to be paid to a union by a non-member as a condition of employment.

Union dues and membership fees in professional societies

What about job-related educational expenses? If the courses meet specific legal or employer requirements for keeping your salary, status or employment — or if they help you maintain or improve your skills for your present job — the cost is deductible. If, on the other hand, the courses are designed to help you move up to a better job or are necessary to meet the minimum requirements of a job you already hold, no deduction is allowed.

Educational expenses

Fees paid to an employment agency to help you find a new job are deductible.

Employment-agency fees

Entertainment and other job-related expenses incurred on behalf of your employer also are deductible. Be sure to keep careful records, since deductions of this type are likely to be challenged by the IRS.

Entertainment costs

Certain household moving costs related to your job also are deductible, up to a limit of $2,500.

Moving expenses

The catch is that your new job must be at least 50 miles farther from your existing home than your old job. If, for instance, your old job was 14 miles from home via the shortest widely-traveled route, your new job must be at least 64 miles from that home to qualify for a tax deduction in the event you move.

A special word of advice about business expenses

Note: Moving costs and employee business expenses are not technically "deductions." They are listed instead on the Adjustments to Income section of your return and can be claimed regardless of whether you itemize deductions or not. Conversely, any reimbursements you receive from your employer for movings costs or other expenses must be listed as taxable income on Part II of your return (Income other than Wages, Dividends, and Interest).

If you do move, it would be wise to hire a tax specialist to prepare your return for that year. Filing may be tricky, and he should be able to save you considerable aggravation and money.

Daily travel costs

Finally, daily travel expenses between home and work *are not deductible.* But if you hold two jobs, travel expenses between job # 1 and job # 2 *are* deductible (12 cents for the first 15,000 miles and 9 cents for each succeeding mile, plus tolls).

6. Investment expenses

● Expenses incurred in connection with investments. If, for instance, you invest in the stock market you may be entitled to a variety of deductions, including the cost of any market-related publications you buy and the cost of your safe deposit box (only, however, if you leave a stock or bond certificates inside).

Investment-counsel fees

Are investment counsel and bank custodial fees deductible? Yes. What happens, on the other hand, if you attend the annual stockholders' meeting of a company whose shares you own. Is the cost deductible? No. The IRS considers this a nondeductible personal expense.

Rental property

Rental property may qualify for certain deductions, although the IRS and courts have tightened up in recent years in an attempt to curb widespread abuse. A common example is a vacation home that you personally use a few weeks or months of the year and rent out the remainder of the time. You may be entitled to deduct a portion of the maintenance, utilities, depreciation, etc. But this is a complex area, and it is best to seek the advice of an expert.

● Expenses for the care of dependents. A recent series of tax-law changes allow, under certain circumstances, large deductions for child-care expenses where both parents work full time. Also covered by the law are situations where a surviving parent is raising the children alone or where a dependent relative — husband, wife, parent, grandparent, adult child, etc. — is physically or mentally incapable of self-care.

7. Dependent care costs

To be specific, the following child-care costs may qualify for deductions:

Which specific child-care costs can I deduct?

● Baby-sitting expenses when both parents are away at work (but not while they are out socializing).

● Household cleaning costs if both parents work full time.

● Fees for sending a child to a day-care center, nursery school or private kindergarten (but not to first grade and above).

● In summer months, the cost of day camp.

The rules are complex, but in general they state that the child must be under 15 years old and that the deductions can be claimed only if they enable the taxpayer to take or keep a paying job.

How old can the child be?

Don't overlook the fact that you need not be married to qualify for these deductions. The crucial questions are whether the expenses are necessary to help you care for a dependent and whether they enable you to be gainfully employed.

WISEGUIDE

Maximum deduction is $400 a month, so long as the family income is $18,000 or less. Above $18,000, however, your annual deduction is reduced by $1 for every $2 you earn. The practical effect of this rule is that no deductions are allowed for individuals or couples earning more than $27,600 a year.

Maximum deduction — $400 a month

In the case of deductions for the care of incapacitated adults, the rules specify that the dependent must be mentally or physically incapable of caring for himself and must live with you in your home. There are certain limitations to your deductions if the individual has his or her own income (even though it may be in the form of nontaxable disability payments). Check with an expert for details.

Deductions for incapacitated adults

Sound like there are a lot of potential types of deductions available to the average taxpayer? There are. But the IRS isn't going to point them out if you fail to take advantage of them yourself. You must either search them out on your own or hire a tax expert to help.

It's up to you to find your own deductions

Deductibility rules are in a constant state of flux — due to court decisions, a steady outpouring of new IRS rulings and occasional changes in federal tax laws.

Have you a question? Check it with the IRS

One of the best ways to keep up to date is to spend 75 cents each year (tax deductible, by the way) for the IRS's annual booklet, Your Federal Income Tax. Or you can call or visit your local IRS office to clear up any questions you might have about the deductibility of specific items. This is a free service provided by the IRS.

WISEGUIDE

If you do have questions, don't wait until the last minute to ask! Minimizing your tax bill is done best with advance planning and care — and free from the last-minute pressures of having to meet the April 15 filing deadline.

Exclusions from taxable income

Not all the items that can reduce your tax bill are deductions. Another section of your return is headed "Adjustments to Income," and these adjustments — or exclusions, as they are sometimes called — offer the possibility for important savings since they represent income that you don't have to count in figuring your taxes.

WISEGUIDE

One of the most important exclusions is "sick pay."

Sick pay

The rules regarding the exclusion of sick pay from your taxable income are quite specific. To start, your employer must have a regular policy of continuing to pay employees who are out of work due to illness or injury (the illness or injury need not be job related). The policy doesn't have to be a written one. It can be informal; the key point is that it must be followed consistently.

Three rules to keep in mind

Your employer does have such a policy? Then there are three additional rules to keep in mind:

● If your sick pay is more than 75 per cent of your regular pay, you must wait 30 calendar days from the original date of illness or injury before beginning to exclude the money from your taxable income.

● If your sick pay is less than 75 per cent of your regular pay, the waiting period is seven days.

• Finally, if your sick pay is less than 75 per cent of your regular pay *and* you are hospitalized for at least one day during your absence from work, there is no waiting period at all.

A disability pension also may qualify as excludable sick pay. In addition, an exclusion is granted for damages received for injury or illness and income from workmen's compensation.

WISEGUIDE

Other types of tax-free income

Other types of income that generally are exempt from federal income taxes include:

• Interest on tax-exempt state and municipal bonds (you may have to pay state income taxes on this interest, though).

• Scholarships.

• Social Security benefits.

• Welfare payments.

• Life insurance proceeds (note, however, that they are subject to estate taxes).

Tax credits

Direct tax credits represent still another form of potential tax savings.

Credits versus deductions

The difference between a tax "credit" and a tax "deduction" is a highly significant one. A credit is deducted dollar-for-dollar directly from your actual tax bill. An example: if your tax bill (before credits) comes to $1,000 and you are entitled to a credit of $50, you would end up paying $950 in taxes. If, on the other hand, you were entitled to a $50 deduction, the savings wouldn't be nearly as great. This is because deductions are made from income subject to taxes, not from taxes themselves.

The "retirement income credit" — a special bonus for retired people to help them keep their tax bills down — is a key federal tax credit.

WISEGUIDE

Retirement income credit

This credit equals 15 per cent of such types of income as money received from annuities, pensions other than Social Security, interest, dividends and rents. Below age 72, your credit is reduced for pay you receive from work. At 72 and older, there is no such restriction.

Beyond that, the retirement income credit rules can get quite complex. It would be wise to seek professional assistance when you reach retirement and are faced with calculating your own credit for the first time.

**Dependency exemptions
— the five
qualifications:**

Most taxpayers also rely heavily on dependency exemptions to help reduce their tax bills. Each exemption is worth $750 (subtracted from adjusted gross income, regardless of whether you itemize deductions or not), but five specific tests must be met for an individual to qualify as your legitimate dependent:

1. Support test

• Support test. You must furnish more than half the dependent's total support during the calendar year. Note: scholarships are not considered in determining total support, but student loans are. (See page 119 for an example.)

2. Gross income test

• Gross income test. The dependent's income must have totaled less than $750 during the year in question. Social Security benefits need not be counted. Children under 19 years of age and full-time students are exempt from this test.

3. Relationship test

• Relationship test. A dependent doesn't actually have to live in your house as long as he or she is related in one of the following ways: child, grandchild or great grandchild, etc.; stepchild, brother, sister, half brother, half sister, stepbrother or stepsister; parent, grandparent, stepparent, etc., but not foster parent; aunt; uncle, nephew or niece but not cousin; father-in-law, mother-in-law, son-in-law, daughter-in-law, brother-in-law or sister-in-law. Any other person must actually live with you to qualify as a dependent.

4. Citizenship test

• Citizenship test. The dependent must live at least part of the year in the U.S., Canada, Mexico, Canal Zone or Republic of Panama or, failing that, must be a U.S. citizen.

5. Joint return test

• Joint return test. Anyone who files a joint tax return is not eligible to be claimed as your dependent. An exception: you may still claim an exemption for a married dependent if neither the dependent nor his or her spouse is required to file a return but they file anyway to claim a refund.

WISEGUIDE

The fact that your child files a tax return and claims his or her own $750 exemption doesn't in anyway deprive you of also claiming that exemption, so long as the five tests are met.

**Which divorced parent
can claim the children
as exemptions?**

Confusion over the claiming of a dependency exemption often arises in the case of couples who are divorced or legally separated. Who is entitled to list any children as dependents?

The rule is that an exemption goes to the parent with custody, except under these circumstances: If the parent who does not have custody contributes $600 or more in support, he or she may claim the exemption if the divorce decree or separation agreement stipulates so. If there is no agreement, the parent with custody gets the exemption. However, if the parent without custody can show receipts for $1,200 or more of support, the parent with custody may have to give up the exemption if he or she cannot prove greater support.

Claiming yourself as an exemption

The rules for other types of exemption claims also can become rather complex. You can claim yourself as an exemption, of course, But what about claiming your spouse? Yes, if the two of you file a joint return.

WISEGUIDE

If your spouse dies at any time during the tax year — even on January 1 — you can claim an exemption for the full year. But if you get divorced at any time — even on December 31 — no exemption is allowed.

Other exemptions: age and blindness

You automatically become entitled to claim a second exemption for yourself the day you reach 65. A quirk in the law is that you are actually considered to become 65 on the day before your 65th birthday. Furthermore, you are entitled to claim a full age exemption for the year even if you don't reach 65 until December 31. One interesting side effect occurs if your birthday happens to fall on January 1; you are considered to have become 65 on December 31 and you pick up a full year's age exemption as a result.

An extra exemption also is available to the blind. Can you claim the age or blindness exemptions on your own return for a dependent who qualifies for them? No. An example: you claim your mother as a dependent. She is 68 years old and legally blind. You are entitled to only one $750 exemption.

Capital gains and losses

Tax treatment of securities profits and losses is an area where proper tax planning can save you considerable money.

WISEGUIDE

All securities transactions are divided for tax purposes into two categories — short term and long term.

Short-term versus long-term transactions

Six months is the dividing point between the two. Short-term capital gains and losses result when you sell a stock or other security *within six months* of purchasing it. Long-term capital gains and losses, on the other hand, result from the result of a security held *six months or more.*

Long-term gains

• Long-term gains are given preferential treatment. The tax rate is half the rate on other types of income, and the tax rate can never exceed 35 per cent.

Short-term gains

• Short-term gains are taxed at the same rate as any other source of income (70 per cent maximum rate).

Long-term losses

• Long-term losses are applied first as an offset against the year's gains, if any. *Half* of any excess may then be deducted directly from your overall taxable income, up to a maximum deduction of $1,000. If there still is an excess, it may be carried over as a deduction against the next year's income and so on until it is completely used up.

Short-term losses ● Short-term losses are likewise first applied as an offset against current-year gains. Any excess is then applied *dollar for dollar* as a deduction against taxable income up to a maximum of $1,000, and any excess beyond that is carried over to subsequent tax years.

An awareness of these rules can help you plan your capital gains and losses to best advantage in minimizing your taxes.

WISEGUIDE

A common technique involves year-end tax planning of investment decisions.

How to do it Here is how to do it: toward the end of the year — by mid-November at latest — sit down and list all stock transactions completed during the year to date. Divide your gains and losses into long-term sales and short-term sales.

Then list your paper gains and losses on stocks you still hold. Again, sort them out as long-term versus short-term.

Third, check your previous year's tax return for any leftover capital losses. Remember that you can apply unused capital losses from previous years just as if you took the losses in the current year.

Three possible approaches: You now have the information to decide your actions (recognizing, of course, that your tax savings must be substantially larger than your costs in brokerage commissions and transfer taxes to justify any moves). These are three possible courses of action:

What if I have capital gains? 1) If you have sold stock during the year for a gain, you may want to sell off other shares on which you have a loss in order to eliminate any taxes from the gain. This may be particularly true if your existing sales have resulted in short-term gains (taxable, as we mentioned, at full income tax rates). Note: you can reduce your short-term gains by taking *either* short or long-term losses. But the rules specify that long-term losses must be used first to offset long-term gains before they can be applied against short-term ones.

What if I have losses? 2) What happens, on the other hand, if you hold stocks with paper losses. Is there any way to take the losses for tax purposes without selling the stocks?

The answer is no. Nor can you sell the shares and repurchase them within 30 days. This is a "wash" sale that bars you from deducting your loss. But there are other ways to achieve your goal:

● Sell out, take your loss and wait 31 days to repurchase.

● Switch into similar securities in the same industry in the hopes that they will perform approximately as well as the shares you sold. (Be cautious, however. This kind of switching is sometimes recommended by brokers who merely want to earn a commission for themselves.)

• Double up on your securities by purchasing a second block of the stock. Then wait 31 days and sell the original shares at a loss. If the price of the shares increases in the interim, you have your tax loss plus a paper profit. If it drops, you have your tax loss plus an investment mistake.

3) Finally, you may have substantial paper profits in a stock that you want to sell now while delaying the profit for tax purposes until next year. The way to do this is to sell an equivalent number of the shares "short" (a short sale involves the sale of shares borrowed from your broker). That way you freeze your sales price at current levels, but won't have to report the profits until you subsequently wipe out the transaction by turning your own shares over to your broker in repayment of the borrowed stock. This is a riskless transaction, but it does increase your costs somewhat since there is an extra charge for borrowing the shares from your broker.

How can I defer my tax on gains?

An even more intriguing approach involves the way you make donations to charity. Give securities instead of cash, and you may come out ahead on taxes.

WISEGUIDE

Your generosity will be rewarded two-fold if you make major charitable contributions this way. To qualify for special tax treatment, however, the securities must be ones in which you have a long-term gain.

Donating securities to charity

Take the case of $2,000 worth of stock, bought a year ago for $1,000. If you were to sell the shares and donate the $2,000 sale proceeds to charity, you would get a full $2,000 tax deduction but also would have to pay taxes on your $1,000 profit from the sale.

By donating these securities directly to charity, on the other hand, you can have your cake and eat it too. In this instance you can take the same $2,000 deduction on your tax return but need not pay any capital gains tax on the $1,000 profit.

An example

What if you prefer to pay by check and keep the shares because you feel that their price will go up even more? Then contribute your shares to the charity and take the $2,000 of cash you would have given, using it instead to buy the same amount of shares. You will thereby raise the cost of your shares from $1,000 to $2,000 (you also will have to pay brokers' commissions, of course), and when you eventually sell these shares your taxable gain will be less than on the original shares.

Should I donate the shares and then buy new ones for myself?

197

Taxation

You cannot get the same tax breaks by donating securities owned for less than six months.

Choosing the right tax table

Once you have calculated your income, exemptions, deductions and the like, you come to the category of "Filing Status" on your tax return. There are four different tax rate tables to choose from: Single, Married Filing Jointly, Married Filing Separately, and Unmarried Head of Household.

Right away we get into a big controversey. While the old adage that two can live as cheaply as one used to apply to income taxes, recent changes in federal tax laws have had some strangely permissive consequences.

It now may be less expensive taxwise for two people to live together out of wedlock than to get married.

How tax rates differ for marrieds and singles

Tax rates for single people are in many cases now less than for marrieds filing separately. John and Mary are in love. Should they get married or just live together? These are the tax consequences:

Taxable income		Total tax liability		
---	---	As single people	As a married couple filing separately	As a married couple filing jointly
John	$4,000			
Mary	$4,000	$1,380	$1,380	$1,380
John	$8,000			
Mary	$6,000	$2,700	$2,760	$2,760
John	$12,000			
Mary	$10,000	$4,720	$5,020	$5,020
John	$16,000			
Mary	$12,000	$6,460	$7,160	$7,100
John	$20,000			
Mary	$16,000	$9,060	$10,400	$10,340

You should not be misled by the fact that there is only a tiny difference in our example between the amount of taxes in filing separately and jointly as a married couple. Big tax savings may actually be available by filing jointly. The reason is that the government assumes that the total income is divided equally between the two partners, no matter who really earned it. The larger half thus falls into a lower tax bracket than would be the case with separate returns. This becomes particularly beneficial when one spouse earns much more than the other.

Filing a joint return

What about the "unmarried head of household" category? This has always been a problem area — one that has led to many legal actions by taxpayers seeking to qualify for the preferential treatment accorded members of this group.

Unmarried heads of households

If you qualify for this category, you have reason to be happy. For example, the taxes on $10,000 of income under the singles tax table is $2,090 versus $1,940 on the head-of-household table. Similar savings are available all the way up and down the income-level line.

Who qualifies? One requirement is that the unmarried taxpayer must furnish more than half the cost of maintaining a household for the entire year for the person who makes it possible for him to claim this status.

Do I qualify?

One of the more interesting wrinkles of this feature is that the taxpayer can qualify as the legal head of a household even if he doesn't live there.

WISEGUIDE

For instance, the taxpayer may maintain an apartment for an elderly parent. It need not be the taxpayer's own apartment, so long as he pays more than half the cost.

Supporting an elderly parent

Finally, there is always the question, once your return has been filed, of whether it will be audited by the IRS. Big income, large deductions or unusual complexities in a return greatly increase its chances for being pulled out of the heap and subjected to an audit.

When your return is audited

If you are called in for an audit and feel that the agent is trying to extract more taxes than you should legally have to pay, you have the right to appeal.

WISEGUIDE

The Tax Reform Act of 1969 set up what are called Small Tax Case Procedures. These allow taxpayers with disputes involving $1,000 or less to take their case to the Tax Court for an informal hearing presided over by a U.S. Commissioner. There is a $10 filing fee.

Small Tax Case Procedures

Administrative appeals

Paralleling this effort, the IRS has been simplifying the procedures for administrative appeal by small taxpayers. First, you have the automatic right to appeal to the IRS district office. And if the dispute involves less than $2,500, no formal filing or written protest is required; you do not have to hire a lawyer or accountant to represent you (although you can if you like).

If you still aren't satisfied, you can go one step further and appeal to the IRS regional office — again through informal procedures that don't require written protest or use of a lawyer.

WISEGUIDE

If you still aren't satisfied, however, you no longer can appeal administratively to the IRS. Further appeals must be made formally in the courts.

Chapter 18

Money and the law

Paper money is "legal tender for all debts, public and private." It says so right on the front of each U.S. dollar bill. What this means is that money has legal standing as a medium of payment and exchange. If you offer cash in payment of a monetary debt, your creditor may not turn it down and insist on some other form of payment — like gold or diamonds or whatever.

But what about the other legal aspects of money? Actually, there is a complex and fascinating set of laws surrounding the use of money and the functioning of everyday trade in this country.

For instance, do you know your rights when you buy merchandise on the installment plan — as millions of Americans do each year? What happens if you stop paying? Under what circumstances can the merchant repossess the goods? What can you do if the merchandise turns out to be defective? (See page 206 to 209.)

Your rights under installment contracts

Or what happens if someone demands payment with threats of "I'll go to your employer"? (Page 215)

Or suppose your teenage son goes to the local department store and, unknown to you, charges a new record player to your account. Do you have to pay? (Page 211)

Money and minors

Or what recourse, if any, do you have if you are denied a loan? (Page 214)

In each case, the law specifies the answer. In fact, every time an individual signs a contract or takes out a loan or even buys a newspaper, the law comes into play.

An intricate web of federal and state laws — some based on common sense, others on tradition, and still others on the whims of congressmen and state legislators — governs just about anything you can imagine involving money.

WISEGUIDE

This chapter reviews some of the basic laws of interest to the consumer. *However, this chapter should not be considered a do-it-yourself guide to the law.* Our objective here is to help you understand your basic rights and help you steer clear of problem areas, not to make you an expert on the legal principles that govern commerce and finance.

At times, your involvement with money will become too important and complex for you to go it alone. Then you will need the help of a competent lawyer.

If you are simply opening a small trust savings account at the bank for your son or daughter or buying a toaster on credit, a lawyer's

When do I need a lawyer?

advice is unnecessary; millions of transactions like this take place every day without the slightest hitch. But professional legal help becomes highly advisable in cases where:

- Complex contracts or large sums of money are involved.

- You are doing business with another individual who is represented by a lawyer.

- You feel that your rights are being violated and you don't know what to do about it.

- Someone sues you in court.

WISEGUIDE

You wouldn't attempt to perform a major operation on yourself; you would go to a qualified surgeon. So why should you try to handle complex legal matters on your own?

Not all lawyers are equally good

There are nearly 250,000 practicing lawyers in this country — some good, some fair, some downright bad. The trick is to pick the right one from the crowd — not always an easy task.

A "family" lawyer

It actually is wise to search around early in your adult life for a "family" lawyer who will be there when you need him. Fortunately, you can take your time when you are looking for a lawyer to advise you about things that haven't yet happened. This is quite different from the mad dash you must make when you suddenly find yourself in a jam and need a lawyer at once.

How to go about your search

Begin by asking your friends for the names of lawyers they know and respect, or ask your company's legal department for names. Or you can consult the Martindale-Hubbell Law Directory, available in most reference libraries.

WISEGUIDE

The Martindale-Hubbell Law Directory is the place to turn for detailed information about lawyers. It lists each lawyer's age, years of experience, nature of practice and other pertinent data.

Finding the right man or woman for the job

What kind of lawyer should you hire? First off, never hire an individual you don't like. This simple rule of thumb will go a long way toward insuring a smooth relationship with your lawyer over the years.

Does the lawyer's background match my needs?

Also look into the lawyer's experience in handling cases similar to yours. If you have need for help in a number of different legal areas — estate planning, real estate and taxes, for instance — make sure that the lawyer himself or a staff aid is competent in these fields or that the lawyer is willing to refer you to someone else who is.

When visiting a lawyer to discuss his services, you must be prepared to pay initial consultation fees — as much as $100 or more for a high-powered, high-priced attorney. What happens, though, if you cannot afford that large a fee? Then you can consult your local Legal Referral Service, sponsored by your county bar association.

Initial consultation fees

There are nearly 300 legal referral services around the nation, and the charge for a half-hour consultation with a lawyer who is familiar with your kind of problem should range somewhere between $5 and $15.

WISEGUIDE

All you have to do is call the bar association and describe your situation. The referral office will arrange the half-hour meeting. A word of warning: in some states panel members are not rated on the basis of experience or competence. You will be forced to take a chance.

How to contact a referral service

If there is no referral service in your area, the bar association president might be willing to help. Consult the bar association listing in the phone book or inquire at the county courthouse. Someone there will know his name and business address. You then can call the president and ask him to refer you to a good lawyer. Be sure, however, to make it clear that you are asking him, in his capacity as president of the local association, for the name of a reliable attorney. And tell him the kind of service you are seeking.

If you cannot afford to pay anything at all for legal advice, your only recourse may be the local Legal Aid Society office. There is one in every major metropolitan area in the country. You can go to the office and tell a lawyer your problem, and he will give you free advice and assistance. If, however, the Legal Aid Society feels that you can pay a moderate fee, it will turn down your case and put you in touch with a bar association referral office.

The Legal Aid Society

Lawyers usually charge by the hour, but don't be surprised if widely different fees are quoted.

WISEGUIDE

The American Bar Association recommends minimum fee schedules of as little as $10 an hour in a few states, but most lawyers charge more than the minimum. ABA surveys have shown that the typical fee for representing a client in court ranges anywhere from $25 to $300 *a day*, depending on the locality, type of case and sometimes the ability of the client to pay. For drawing up documents and handling other legal work in his office, a lawyer might charge anywere from $10 to $50 *per hour*. For certain other types of matters — such as an uncontested divorce or drawing up a will — many lawyers charge a flat fee rather than per-hour or

Basic fees

per-day rate. For a simple will, for instance, the cost might be somewhere between $50 and $100 — perhaps even less. For an uncontested divorce, it might range anywhere from $75 to $1,000.

"Contingency" fees

Also remember that if you file a negligence suit, you may have to pay your lawyer a percentage of the award or settlement. Unlike other legal fees, such "contingency" arrangements are regulated by state law. In New York, for instance, a lawyer is entitled to collect 50 per cent of any settlement or award under $1,000, 40 per cent between $1,000 and $2,000, and 33 $1/3$ per cent over $2,000. In addition, you must reimburse the lawyer for all his expenses — such as witness fees, telephone calls, travel costs, etc.

What to do if a dispute arises over your lawyer's fee

Be blunt about fees. Ask the lawyer directly what he will charge. As an added safeguard, you might ask that the fee agreement be put in writing. If a dispute arises later over the fee, check to see if your county bar association has a conciliation committee that will hear both sides and resolve the matter.

WISEGUIDE

Another possiblity to consider is the purchase of "legal insurance."

Will legal insurance become commonplace?

A variety of plans are emerging, and some experts believe that legal insurance will be commonplace — just like life and health insurance — within 15 or 20 years.

The plans generally work this way: You pay somewhere between $40 and $150 annually to the insurance company, and in return you are entitled to a specific number of half-hour consultations with a lawyer each year on such matters as your will, credit problems and other everyday law situations. Within given limits, the insurance company also will pay your legal expenses in both criminal and civil trials.

A look at one plan

One existing insurance plan pays for legal services within these annual limits:

● Up to $100 for consultations with a lawyer, not to exceed $25 per visit.

● Up to $250 for office work, including conferences, negotiations, title examinations, letters, etc. There is a $10 deductible.

● Up to $325 for trial preparations, briefs and court appearances.

● Up to $40 in court costs and witness fees.

● Up to $150 for out-of-pocket expenses, such as your lawyer's travel and phone calls.

● On top of this, there is a "major legal expense" benefit clause — similar to a major medical health insurance policy — that pays 80 per cent of all costs in excess of the individual limits, up to a

$1,000 maximum major expense payment per year.

Legal insurance, if available, gives you access to competent legal advice if and when you need it for a moderate annual insurance fee.

There are two kinds of lawsuits — civil and criminal. Criminal lawsuits can only be brought by public prosecutors, but you as an individual have the right to file a civil suit when you feel the need for redress in the courts.

Lawsuits

Four types of damages can be sought in a civil suit:

Four types of damages

1)   General or compensatory damages are awarded in compensation for pain, suffering, injury, humiliation, etc.

2)   Special damages are awarded in repayment of actual financial losses, such as medical expenses and lost salary.

3)   Punitive damages are awarded as punishment for an act that was vicious or malicious.

4)   Nominal damages are awarded when the actual damage is slight but the court decides that some sort of award is nonetheless appropriate. An example might involve a case where a group of neighborhood children innocently trespass on your property to play baseball.

Suppose, on the one hand, that you trip over a garden hose that your next-door neighbor has inadvertently left on his front sidewalk, and as a result you end up in the hospital with a badly wrenched back. A court might award you general and special damages for your pain, medical costs and lost wages.

Example 1
You trip over a garden hose

Suppose, on the other hand, that you and your neighbor don't get along and one day, totally unprovoked, he rushes out his front door and slams you in the head with a baseball bat as you walk by. Now, in addition to general and special damages, you might ask the court for punitive damages.

Example 2
You are belted in the head with a bat

Suppose, finally, that the neighbor rushes out the door and takes a mighty swing with that same bat — but, fortunately for you, the bat just brushes your shoulder. In this case, the court might award nominal damages to recognize his responsibility for the incident.

Example 3
The bat just misses

Newspaper headlines about huge court awards usually involve civil suits charging negligence.

In general, however, you must be able to establish three points to win your case if you are suing on the basis of negligence:

Grounds for suing on the basis of negligence

● You must prove that the defendant actually caused you injury or damage.

● You must prove that he didn't exercise proper care.

● You must be able to link points number 1 and 2 together. In other words, you must prove that it was his particular act of negligence that led to your particular damage.

A case in point   The possibilities here become endlessly fascinating. One actual negligence case involved a man carrying a package of explosives under his arm who rushed to board a departing train. The conductor, reaching out to help him on board, accidently jarred loose the package, which fell to the ground and exploded. The shock wave in turn dislodged a weighing scale hanging on a hook in the station, and the scale fell and hit a woman on the head. The woman sued, and the court found both the man with the package and the railroad liable, awarding the woman damages from both.

WISEGUIDE   A more common involvement with the law occurs in our day-to-day credit arrangements, installment purchases, and other dealings with merchants and lenders.

What is a "conditional sales contract"?   Problems frequently arise in this area when merchandise is purchased under a so-called "conditional sales contract." This is merely a fancy name for a common type of installment-payment plan under which the merchant retains actual ownership of the property — a car, refrigerator, TV set, dining room table, clothing, etc. — until you have completed all your payments. Even though you may swear that you have never been involved in such an arrangement, chances are that you have anyway; you just didn't read the fine print.

WISEGUIDE   Conditional sales contracts should be avoided, if at all possible.

The merchant's right of "replevin"   These contracts are a very poor way for you, as a consumer, to do business. But they are nonetheless widespread, and you should therefore at least be aware of your rights — limited as they are — under such arrangements. Essentially, if you fail to keep up on your payments the merchant can arrange for the sheriff to come into your house and repossess the goods ("replevin" is the legal word for this kind of repossession).

WISEGUIDE   A merchant's right of replevin is rooted in 600-year-old common-law doctrine, but recent Supreme Court decisions have broken new ground by restricting this right for the first time ever.

Fuentes vs. Florida: An important "replevin" case

A landmark case — *Fuentes vs. Florida* — involved a Mrs. Fuentes who bought a gas stove and service contract from a local Firestone Tire & Rubber Company store. Later, she went back and bought a stereo set. In both cases she financed her purchases through a conditional sales contract.

Mrs. Fuentes' total cost was about $500, plus about $100 for the financing. For more than a year she paid regularly and owed only $200 when she got into a dispute with Firestone about servicing the stove. She then refused to make further payments.

Firestone's response was to begin an action against her in small claims court for repossession of the stove and stereo. Under Florida law (typical of many states), once such an action is filed seizure of the goods is almost automatic. All that is needed is submission of seizure documents to the court clerk for his signature. Firestone did this, and seizure was carried out by the sheriff that same day.

Once goods have been seized, Florida law specifies that the sheriff must keep them for three days. The defendant has that much time to reclaim them, but in doing so must post a bond equal to double their value — hardly a fair arrangement from the defendant's viewpoint. If bond isn't posted, the property automatically goes to the creditor who sought the writ in the first place, pending the court's final judgment. Final judgment can, of course, take time — and even if the defendant eventually wins he has been without his goods for that whole period.

In a split decision, the Supreme Court took issue with this process, saying that it denied the creditor the due process of law guaranteed by the Fourteenth Amendment. What bothered the court most was that Mrs. Fuentes was given no prior notice of seizure and was allowed "no opportunity whatever to challenge the issuance of the writ of replevin" until after the property was actually seized.

Only time will tell the full impact of this decision, but your rights under a conditional sales contract probably are a bit greater than they were before.

WISEGUIDE

Another important "replevin" case

Don't be fooled into thinking, however, that automatic repossession is no longer possible. The Supreme Court's decision is only binding in Florida. In New Jersey, for instance, the state supreme court recently permitted a car dealer to repossess an automobile without prior notice — the Fuentes case notwithstanding. The New Jersey court pointed out that the dealer had a duplicate key and took the car peacefully. Forced entry, on the other hand, probably would not have been allowed.

A key question — just what am I getting into?

The best answer of all is to avoid conditional sales contracts in the first place. And *always* read the fine print to make sure that you know what you are getting into.

An added reason for avoiding conditional sales contracts is that such a contract actually encumbers you from moving. Since the merchant still holds title until you have completed your payments, the law specifies that you, as the customer, cannot move the merchandise to a new location at any time during the repayment period without first obtaining the seller's permission.

WISEGUIDE

And as if that isn't enough, take careful note of the interest rate in a conditional sales contract before you sign. A good bet is that it is at least 18 per cent a year — and perhaps as much as 36 per cent!

Damaged goods and other problems in dealing with merchants

Let's look at another fairly typical situation. Say that you buy a new dinette set and it arrives in damaged condition. What can you do?

The Uniform Commercial Code

The law is quite specific in the remedies available to you when the merchant fails to deliver as promised, as well as in the remedies available to the merchant if you fail to hold up your end of the bargain. Such situations are covered by the provisions of the Uniform Commercial Code, which is the law in every state except one. (Louisiana, the lone exception, still abides to a large extent by old Napoleonic code.)

WISEGUIDE

As a result of this standardization, the rights and responsibilities of buyers and sellers are similar throughout the nation, although specific laws vary somewhat from state to state.

What can I expect from the seller?

When you buy, the law says you have the right to expect certain basic assurances (or "implied warranties," as they are called) from the seller whether they are actually written into the contract or not:

• You have the right to expect that the seller owns the property and is entitled to sell it to you.

• You have the right to expect comparable merchandise to what you ordered. If you order a certain type of furniture, that is what you should get. The dealer cannot substitute furniture of lesser quality.

• You have the right to expect that the merchandise meets basic standards of marketability. An example: You buy a can of pineapple slices at the corner grocery store. When you get home and open the can, you discover mold. The grocer, in this case, has sold you a product that is not of marketable quality.

When the merchant fails to meet his obligations

What happens, then, if the merchant fails to live up to any of these standards and also refuses to give back your money? You can take one of three possible courses of action, but *only* one of the three. You cannot start off with one approach and then switch to another. You must stick with what you have started.

• You can accept or keep the merchandise and go to court to recover damages from the seller. Or, if you haven't yet paid, you can refuse to do so.

- You can refuse to accept the goods and then, if you want, sue for your money back if you already have paid.

- If the merchandise is already in your possession, you can offer to return it — if the seller will take it back — and then go to court to recover your purchase price.

If you do decide to return goods on the basis that the seller violated the contract, be sure to return them quickly and in the same condition in which they arrived. Failure to do this will jeopardize your case.

WISEGUIDE

As a practical matter, you may decide to avoid all three approaches and take your case to the state attorney general or local consumer protection agency. Generally, these agencies have considerable clout with merchants, and the matter may be resolved quickly and fairly without the need to go to court.

Consumer protection agencies

If you do decide to go to court, however, you will certainly want to retain a lawyer if a substantial amount of money is involved. But don't write off a smaller claim just because you don't think it justifies paying a lawyer's fee. Most states have Small Claims Courts, where you can present your case at an informal hearing without the need for professional legal help. In fact, some Small Claims Courts go to the extreme of actually forbidding either party in a dispute from being represented by a lawyer.

Small Claims Courts

For the most part, Small Claims Courts have jurisdiction over any contractual dispute between a buyer and seller and over negligence claims, such as those arising from automobile accidents. Cases of libel or assault usually are excluded, however.

The maximum size of dispute that can be filed in a Small Claims Court varies from state to state. Typically, though, the maximum is somewhere between $200 and $500. Larger claims must be filed in other courts with more formal procedures.

WISEGUIDE

So far, we have only discussed uncomplicated situations where you buy merchandise and the seller refuses to honor his obligations. Your rights become more complicated when you buy merchandise on credit and the seller then places your installment note with a bank, finance company or other lending institution.

The "holder-in-due course" doctrine

This is a fairly common behind-the-scenes occurrence. Suddenly you find that it is the bank to whom you owe the money, and you wonder what is going on. Well, you may be in for trouble — particularly if the merchandise is in any way defective.

Under a centuries-old doctrine, the bank has become a "holder in due course" of your installment contract and has a legal right to collect from you regardless of whether the merchandise actually

How the bank is protected

works! Since the bank didn't sell you anything directly, it is fully shielded from your complaints unless it somehow knew that the product was faulty — a remote possiblity, at best. You must argue only with the merchant (and meanwhile keep paying the bank, regardless of what happens). And if you don't keep paying, the bank can sue.

Has this doctrine outlived its usefulness?

Although this doctrine originally grew out of the need to facilitate the smooth flow of trade and credit, there is little doubt that it has now outlived its usefulness. Every year, tens of thousands of Americans get stranded along the road of "holder in due course," and each time their story goes something like this: An individual buys a product from a merchant who then sells the buyer's installment contract to a bank or finance company. The product turns out to be defective. But meanwhile the merchant has gone out of business, leaving the buyer holding the bag.

WISEGUIDE

The best way to avoid problems in cases where your installment note is sold to a third party is to deal only with reputable merchants in the first place.

When you fail to keep your side of the bargain

The other side of the coin involves situations where the seller claims that you are the one who has violated the purchase contract. Again, the Uniform Commercial Code comes into play.

What the seller can do

The most common problem arises when the buyer fails to pay fully or on time. What does the UCC say that the seller can do?

• He can hold onto the merchandise if it still is in his possession and then sue for any monetary losses he may have suffered.

• He can sell off the goods and, if the price is below what you agreed to pay sue you for the difference.

• He can simply cancel the deal and take no further action.

• If the property is already in your hands, the merchant's only options are to sue for the purchase price or, if the deal involves a conditional sales contract, seek to repossess.

WISEGUIDE

An interesting sidelight occurs when you buy merchandise that turns out to have been stolen. Where does that leave you as the buyer?

Stolen property

The answer is that you must return the goods to the true owner. Your quarrel is not with him, but with the person from whom you bought the goods. As we mentioned above, you have a legal right to expect that the seller actually is the legitimate owner of the property. If he isn't, he has violated one of the "implied warranties" and you can sue him for damages.

What happens, though, if he bought the property in completely good faith and didn't himself know it was stolen? Your argument is still with him. He is the one who must reimburse you. It then becomes his job to deal with the person from whom he bought the property.

A common misconception is that children have no real legal standing when it comes to money. Actually, their rights and "disabilities" (restrictions) are covered by a complex set of laws and regulations — mostly on the state level.

Children and money

First there is the problem, however, of defining just what a "child" is in the eyes of the law. In many states a child legally becomes an adult — with the full privileges and responsibilities that go with it — when he or she reaches 21. In others, the border line is 18. And in almost all cases, a child will be considered to have come of age when he enters the armed forces — regardless of actual age in years.

When does a child become an adult?

So long as an individual is classified as a minor, he is not permitted to enter into contracts on his own. If he does, they usually are not binding on the child — although they may nonetheless be binding on the other party to the transaction. Thus, the answer to the question posed at the beginning of this chapter — What happens if your teenage son goes to the local department store and, unknown to you, charges a new record player to your account? — is that you do not have to pay. If you don't pay, however, the record player must be returned.

Children and contracts

There are two exceptions to this rule:

• A minor's debts are fully binding if a parent or guardian has acquiesced to them. In our example, you would be liable for paying if you had told your son to go the department store and buy a record player. Similarly, minors can open checking and charge accounts of their own. For instance, American Express Co. estimates that 80,000 teenagers hold American Express credit cards; in each case a parent or guardian has assumed responsibility for repayment, and American Express is thus fully protected.

Two exceptions

• A minor is responsible for any monetary obligation he has incurred to purchase "necessities" — defined in the law as food, clothing and shelter.

If, for example, a teenager buys food in a store, he has in effect entered into a contract to pay for it and must do so.

WISEGUIDE

Money and the law

Paying with cash

Should you send cash by mail? The answer is no. This is a gamble, since if the money is lost you are simply out of luck.

Checking accounts and forgery

Paying with personal checks is a safer method. According to the law, when you sign a check the bank must obey the instructions contained in it. If the check is a forgery, passed in your name, the bank is required to reimburse you the full amount if it mistakenly pays — even though the forger may have been so clever as to have made detection by the bank impossible.

What happens if I was negligent?

However, negligence on your part may relieve the bank of all or part of its responsibility. If, for instance, you are careless about where you leave blank checks and, as a result, a forger has an easy time laying his hands on a book of your checks, the bank may claim that it isn't liable.

WISEGUIDE

Similarly, if a number of your blank checks disappear you must inform the bank at once. Otherwise, if a forgery arises the bank may contend that there was negligence on your part.

Examining your monthly statements from the bank

You also are expected to examine the monthly statements from your bank in order to spot any forgeries, overpayments or other errors that may have slipped through. As a general rule, a bank is always responsible for its mathematical errors but not indefinitely responsible for restitution of forgeries. In many states, if you wait longer than a year to report a forged signature on the front of one of your checks — or more than three years to report a forged endorsement on the back — the bank is no longer responsible for making up any loss.

Usury laws

Usury laws are designed to protect you from paying excessive interest rates on loans. These laws vary widely from state to state and by type of loan. For instance, in some states the maximum permissable interest rate of installment loans ranges between 18 per cent and 36 per cent a year, depending on the size of the loan. On "margin" loans for the purchase of common stocks, on the other hand; the maximum permissable rate is 8 per cent in some states.

Federal lending regulations

The federal government does not get directly involved in regulating maximum interest rates. It leaves this to the states. The main federal efforts in this area are oriented instead toward making sure that borrowers have the information to act wisely.

WISEGUIDE

The two basic federal laws in the field of consumer lending are the 1968 Truth in Lending Law and the 1971 Fair Credit Reporting Act.

212

The Truth in Lending Law specifies that the lender must tell you two things before any credit transaction is finalized:

What is the Truth in Lending Law?

* The dollar amount of finance charges involved in the transaction.

* The true annual interest cost in percentage terms.

This law applies to loans or credit purchases from almost any source — banks, savings & loan associations, department stores, credit card issuers, credit unions, automobile dealers, finance companies, mortgage brokers, doctors, hospitals, plumbers and electricians, to name a few. Exemptions from the law are provided for transactions exceeding $25,000 — except that all real estate transactions are covered, regardless of the amount.

When does this law apply?

Always insist on your right to know the true interest cost *before* you sign any credit agreement.

WISEGUIDE

The Truth in Lending Law specifies that this disclosure must be made by the lender in writing, but the law will fail to do you any good unless you insist on this right.

Disclosure must be in writing

The Fair Credit Reporting Act specifies your rights of access to the information compiled in your credit-rating files.

The Fair Credit Reporting Act

Dozens of private companies, such as credit bureaus and detective agencies, collect and sell personal information about nearly everyone who has ever applied for credit, insurance or a job. Typically, a credit-rating file contains such basic data as your name, address, personal history (former addresses, job record, age, parentage, family size, etc.), reputation, resources and an evaluation of your so-called "creditworthiness."

What information is in my credit files?

Lenders say they need access to this kind of confidential information so they can evaluate your case fairly when you apply for a loan. Problems can arise, however, when inaccurate information makes its way into your file.

The objective of the Fair Credit Reporting Act is to give you recourse when your credit file contains inaccuracies that prevent you from getting a loan or landing a job.

WISEGUIDE

This act says that if your loan application is rejected you have the right to ask the lender in writing for the reasons. If, when the lender responds (as he must), it turns out that there was an inaccuracy in one of your credit-rating files — such as sometimes arises from a misspelling of your name or sloppy work by an investigator — you are supposed to be able to go directly to the credit-rating agency and ask that the erroneous data be corrected.

What to do when your loan application is rejected

But be prepared for the possibility of a run-around! Few credit-rating agencies are anxious to comply with the law; you may have to pressure them into doing so. If you do get into a squabble that seems to be getting you nowhere, it might be wise to retain a lawyer to handle the case.

Am I automatically entitled to a loan?

Note, however, that no law gives you the automatic right to obtain a loan. The lender can always refuse if he feels that you may not be able to repay. His only obligation under the law is to tell you why you were turned down, not to grant you the loan itself.

What to do when a financial crisis strikes

The widespread availability of consumer credit is one of the major factors in the steady rise of financial crises within American families. What should you do if you find that you are simply unable to meet all your financial obligations?

A debt consolidation loan

First, you can seek a "debt consolidation loan" in an attempt to relieve some of the immediate pressure. As mentioned in Chapter 3, this usually is unwise. Interest costs often are much higher than on the loans that the consolidation loan is replacing. Consolidation loans represent more of a marketing gimmick for finance companies than a real benefit for borrowers.

A respite from your creditors

Second, you can go to your creditors and ask for a breathing period to get your financial affairs in order. If they think you really mean business, they may temporarily reduce or suspend payments in an effort to help you get over the hump.

Bankruptcy

If all else fails, however, your only recourse may be to file for bankruptcy.

WISEGUIDE

Two kinds of petitions can be filed by individuals under the federal bankruptcy laws — a Chapter XIII petition or a petition for voluntary bankruptcy.

Chapter XIII

● Chapter XIII, which draws its name from the corresponding chapter in the Federal Bankruptcy Law, does not free you from any of your debts. Instead, it allows you to get together with your creditors, under court supervision, and work out a long-term plan for repayment. The advantage is that the court keeps your creditors off your back while the repayment plan is being drawn up. Chapter XIII is sometimes referred to as the "wage earner plan."

Voluntary bankruptcy

● Voluntary bankruptcy is a more drastic step to take. You are in effect saying to your creditors and the court that you are simply unable to repay all your debts and that there is little chance you will ever be able to meet them. You want a new start in life. If the court agrees and formally declares you bankrupt (as it undoubtedly will), all your assets are then sold off and the proceeds distributed among your creditors. You generally are allowed to retain a limited

amount of your possessions — clothing, pots and pans, your burial plot and such personal effects as your wedding ring and family Bible, to name a few.

WISEGUIDE

Once your case has been fully resolved and you are discharged from all further obligations to your creditors, you are free to start from scratch — except that you will now carry with you the stigma that you were once declared bankrupt.

Garnishment

Short of filing for bankruptcy on your own, your creditors may decide to go to court and ask that your wages be "garnished." This simply means that your employer will be required to withhold a portion of your paycheck each week or month and turn the money over to the creditor or creditors who petitioned the court.

Although such a tactic by your creditors is perfectly legal when you are behind on your payments, take note that creditors are not allowed to harass you in other ways. If a creditor comes to you with threats — veiled or otherwise — that he will go to your employer directly or that he will do physical harm to you, he has violated the law. Similarly, he is not permitted to call you by phone in the middle of the night to demand repayment or to threaten to tell your friends that you are not paying your bills or to threaten you falsely with a lawsuit. You do not have to stand for such tactics. Report them immediately to local law enforcement officials or to the Federal Trade Commission in Washington.

Useful addresses

A variety of organizations, both inside and outside of government, offer valuable assistance and advice to consumers. Here is a partial listing of organizations that operate on the national level.

Where to turn for help

For help in resolving your complaints against merchants, manufacturers, lenders, etc.:

Federal Trade Commission
Washington, D.C. 20580

This agency regulates commerce between states and within the District of Columbia. It is one place to go with complaints about deceptive advertising, deceptive door-to-door sales techniques and unfair credit practices.

Food & Drug Administration
5600 Fishers Lane
Rockville, Md. 20852

The FDA enforces federal laws specifying minimum purity, safety and labeling standards for foods and drugs. Complaints should be filed with the nearest FDA regional office or with FDA headquarters in Maryland.

Interstate Commerce Commission
Washington, D.C. 20423

This federal agency regulates most interstate transportation companies, including railroads, bus companies and household movers.

This is the place to go with complaints about developers or agents selling or leasing land through the mails or through any other means of interstate commerce.

Office of Interstate Land Sales Registration
c/o Department of Housing & Urban Development
Washington, D.C. 20410

This agency supervises the operation of our nation's securities markets. It may help you if you have been defrauded by a broker or other securities salesman. Note, however, that the SEC is not allowed to serve as a "collection agency" or to advise you on whether a particular transaction violates the law.

Securities & Exchange Commission
Washington, D.C. 20549

This White House group is responsible for coordinating all federal activities in the field of consumer protection. Depending on the exact nature of your problem, it will either respond directly to your complaints against merchants, repairmen, lenders, etc. or will refer yo ' to the appropriate organization.

Office of Consumer Affairs
New Executive Office Building
Washington, D.C. 20506

These are industry-sponsored groups that are supposed to watch out for the interests of consumers. Your complaints against merchants can be filed with your local bureau.

Better Business Bureaus
Council of Better Business Bureaus
845 Third Avenue
New York, N.Y. 10022

For help when you are the victim of illegal discrimination:

This is the major federal agency in the area of equal rights enforcement. Its primary focus is on voter registration.

U.S. Commission on Civil Rights
Washington, D.C. 20425

Your complaints about unfair employment practices based on race, sex, religion or national origin should be filed here.

Equal Employment Opportunity Commission
1800 G Street, N.W.
Washington, D.C. 20506

This is the place to go with complaints about job discrimination based on age. Federal protection in this area is limited to individuals 40 to 65 years old working for employers of 25 or more persons. Older workers are not protected against job discrimination based on age.

Workplace Standards Administration
c/o Department of Labor
Washington, D.C. 20201

Complaints about discrimination in housing should be filed here.

Assistant Secretary for Equal Opportunity
Department of Housing & Urban Development
Washington, D.C. 20410

Help for the elderly:

This private organization helps members cope with the financial and emotional problems of adjusting to retirement. It also offers a health insurance plan to supplement Medicare, auto insurance for those who have been denied coverage because of age, low-cost prescription drugs, and consultations on retirement housing.

American Association of Retired Persons
1225 Connecticut Ave., N.W.
Washington, D.C. 20036

This federal agency serves as a clearinghouse of information on services and opportunities available to the elderly. A number of free booklets are available by mail.

Administration on Aging
c/o Department of Health, Education & Welfare
Washington, D.C. 20201

This is the federal agency that administers Medicare and the Social Security retirement, disability and survivors' benefit programs.

Social Security Administration
6401 Security Boulevard
Baltimore, Md. 21235

Other federal organizations:

This organization supervises a joint government/industry program of flood insurance for homeowners.

Federal Insurance Administration
c/o Department of Housing & Urban Development
Washington, D.C. 20410

This agency provides a variety of services for owners of small businesses, including free counseling and low-cost loans.

Small Business Administration
Washington, D.C. 20416

The Manpower Administration, through a system of more than 2,400 employment security offices throughout the country, provides free job counseling services. A number of training programs also are available.

Manpower Administration
c/o Department of Labor
Washington, D.C. 20210

Medical care, educational assistance, home-mortgage guarantees and a variety of other programs are available to qualifying veterans.

Veterans Administration
Washington, D.C. 20420

This is the so-called "anti-poverty agency". It offers low-income consumers free advice on how to avoid being cheated and how to get the most for their money and provides free financial planning services. Legal services also are available to the poor.

Office of Economic Opportunity
1200 19th Street, N.W.
Washington, D.C. 20506

The FHA is the main source of federal mortgage insurance and of insurance for home improvement loans.

Federal Housing Administration
c/o Department of Housing & Urban Development
Washington, D.C. 20410

All federal financial-aid programs (including grants and loans) for college students are administered by this organization.

Division of Student Financial Aid
c/o Department of Health, Education & Welfare
Washington, D.C. 20201

This is the place to obtain all government publications. A large retail bookstore is maintained at 710 North Capitol Street in Washington, plus branches in major cities around the nation. To help you keep abreast of new booklets as they become available, a free biweekly list of selected government publications is yours for the asking. Topics include such areas as child care, tips on home repairs and saving money on food purchases.

Superintendent of Documents
c/o U.S. Government Printing Office
Washington, D.C. 20402

Index